# the birth debrief

# the
# birth
# debrief

reflecting on pregnancy, reframing birth,

redefining post-partum

## ILLIYIN MORRISON

QUERCUS

First published in Great Britain in 2023 by

**QUERCUS**

Quercus Editions Ltd
Carmelite House
50 Victoria Embankment
London EC4Y 0DZ

An Hachette UK company

A CIP catalogue record for this book is available
from the British Library

TPB ISBN 978 1 52941 701 2
Ebook ISBN 978 1 52941 704 3

Some names and identifying details have been changed
to protect the privacy of individuals.

10 9 8 7 6 5 4 3 2 1

Typeset by seagulls.net
Printed and bound in Great Britain by Clays Ltd, Elcograf S.p.A.

I dedicate this labour of love to the woman who took a piece of my heart when she left. I dedicate this book to my mother, Rahimah. You showed me it all. The mother of all mothers. I hope you're proud.

# Author's note

Processing difficult birth experiences can be challenging, and some readers might find parts of the content of this book triggering. I have added an asterisk to the sections that contain potentially sensitive content to allow you the opportunity to pause, if you need to, or to read on with caution.

The case studies and personal stories you will read in this book (including my own) are the experiences and thoughts of real people, many of them my clients, and are used with their permission. To protect their privacy, names and identifying features have been changed.

The information and advice in this book may not be suitable for everyone and is not intended to be a substitute for medical advice. You should consult a midwife or doctor on any matters that may require diagnosis or medical attention.

# Contents

## PART 4: BEING POSTNATAL: THE IMPORTANCE OF MATERNAL WELLBEING BEYOND THE FOURTH TRIMESTER

# preface:
# this book is for you

From the moment we are born, one of our biggest wishes is to be heard. As babies, we cry; as toddlers, we might throw ourselves on the floor in rage; as adults, we might post cryptically on social media. Throughout our lives, this need shows up in different ways, but the desire is always there: as human beings, we need to be listened to, to be validated and to be understood.

Pregnancy, childbirth and early parenthood are some of the most transformational mind and body experiences we can ever undertake. Often, though, we aren't afforded the time and space to reflect on, and reframe, those experiences. The pressure to adjust, to be OK, to ignore any difficult emotions and to 'get on with it' can be stifling.

Perhaps you have picked this book up out of a need to feel seen and understood, to feel validated in your experience and less alone. Whatever you are feeling right now - whether your birthing plan had to be thrown out of the window or your birth was straightforward - I can assure you that you are not alone. If you recognise yourself, or a loved one, in one or more of the scenarios listed overleaf, *The Birth Debrief* is here to help.

**So, if you feel that:**

- your pregnancy and birth experiences were never validated or taken seriously;

- you were not an active participant in your birth experience;

- you weren't listened to in your pregnancy and birth experience;

- your pain or concerns were dismissed by healthcare professionals;

- parenthood has affected your relationship;

**this book is for you.**


**If you are:**

- struggling to make peace with what happened during your birth experience;

- wondering how to have an empowering birth experience;

- worried about having more children following a difficult previous pregnancy or birthing experience;

- wondering if your feelings around your birth are just you 'being silly', 'overreacting' or 'being ungrateful', and that there can't be any more to it than that;

- accustomed to 'getting on with it' and 'don't want to make a fuss';

- grieving the pregnancy or birth you didn't have;

**this book is for you.**

**If you have:**

- ever doubted your ability to give birth;

- ever compared your birthing experience to someone else's;

- ever felt that your birthing experience was taken away from you;

- been left with feelings of guilt following your birthing experience;

- felt unseen since you became a parent;

- felt guilty about not being able to breastfeed;

- ever felt undermined in, or guilty about, your parenting choices;

**this book is for you.**

This book is also for you if you are a partner, friend, family member or 'tribe member' of someone you know, or suspect, has had a difficult birth experience (whether recently or in the distant past). Perhaps you attended a birth and came away from the experience with a host of uncomfortable feelings, which you have not yet processed. I want you to know two things: first, I am glad you are here. And second, this book is for *you*.

# introduction

I never saw myself here. I had planned to welcome my baby in the comfort of my home. Instead I found myself in a sterile labour room, shell-shocked and unable to find even simple words to express myself, let alone get my head around what had just happened. Minutes earlier, via emergency caesarean section, I had delivered a beautiful, healthy baby girl. Yet, despite the jubilant, congratulatory tones of the medical staff, my birthing partner and my husband, the joy and excitement I expected to feel at bringing this life into the world somehow failed to materialise. Instead, an empty void gaped inside me, leaving me bewildered and numb. The whole experience had left me feeling unseen, unheard and unsupported. Here I was, a qualified midwife who – during my own clinical and private practice – had guided countless women through their birthing experiences, yet I had not contemplated the possibility that giving birth to my own, much-wanted, much-loved, child would overwhelm me with feelings of guilt, failure and despair. I had also never anticipated feeling so isolated.

But with the voices of well-wishers ringing in my ears and a new, helpless little one to take care of, I quickly pushed these feelings down and focused my attention on my precious baby. I didn't know it yet, but those feelings had sprung from multiple traumas suffered before and during my daughter's birth. They continued to resurface, almost robbing me of the joy that new parenthood should bring, until I accepted that something was wrong and sought help. That was one of the best decisions I could have made for myself and for my family.

Acknowledging, processing and healing from those traumas would have a huge effect on my professional practice. Ultimately, it would change the trajectory of my life and career.

## Why I wrote this book

Childbirth is amazing and miraculous – and thankfully, for the majority of women in the UK it remains very safe. But it can also leave women feeling a range of emotions that can feel conflicting, especially if things did not go to plan. And let's be real – some women, even if they are happy to be mothers, would still describe their births as traumatic. And they wouldn't be wrong: post-partum birth injuries – both physical and psychological – affect approximately 1 in 20 birthing parents each year in the UK. And those are only the diagnosed cases. Many more do not even report their symptoms, suggesting that the true figure may be much higher. I wrote this book because I want to let you know that if you are one of those who is suffering right now, I see you. You are not alone.

A fundamental aim of this book is to empower women and birthing people of all backgrounds to take control of their experiences, to feel seen and *centred* during their pregnancies and births; to normalise conversations around birth trauma and healing; and to unpack the nuances that are associated with birth. Though the physical recovery from childbirth can take time and is no small matter, time and time again, I have found that it's the lack of advocacy, autonomy, control and consent, rather than the physical aspects of the birth, that contribute to the types of trauma that linger, robbing parents of their enjoyment of parenthood.

The unpredictable nature of pregnancy and birth can make many women feel as though they have lost control of their personhood. Through this book I want to teach you how to take back your autonomy and make the choices – throughout pregnancy, birth and beyond – that are right for you. Part of my work involves providing safety, holding space and listening. I also wrote this book to help you feel seen, and to support you with practical, tried-and-tested tools to help, encourage and empower you on your journey through pregnancy, birth and beyond – and towards healing, if your experience was a difficult one.

As a midwife, a qualified hypnobirthing instructor, a debrief facilitator, a wife, a mother, a blogger and a fierce advocate for positive birth, I have facilitated hundreds of birth debriefs and have a passion for empowering women during pregnancy and childbirth. In supporting women during their birth experiences, as well as processing my own difficult one, I have first-hand knowledge of both sides of the delivery room – the highs and the lows, the good and the bad. I believe that good antenatal education can really make a difference to your pregnancy and birth story, and can help you to have a positive experience, whether or not things go as planned. I realised that if I, with all my expertise and training, had still experienced trauma during my pregnancy and birth, then how many other birthing people needed support to help them process their own birth experiences?

Eventually I left clinical practice and set up my own private practice, Mixing Up Motherhood, offering private birth debriefing and hypnobirthing sessions. I also began blogging as a way to chronicle my own journey, and support and validate the experiences of other women as they acknowledged, processed and healed from their pregnancy, birth and post-partum experiences. As my Instagram following grew, I became inundated with direct messages from women who wanted to share their birthing stories with me. I saw this as confirmation that I was on the right path. I was spurred on by a need to help women and birthing people make sense of their experiences. At the same time, I noticed that they (and their partners) seemed to need permission to let all their 'negative' feelings out in a safe space. They needed a space where they and their parenting would not be judged, but understood. They needed help to sort through the tangle of emotions they were feeling, to reframe those emotions in a way that helped them move forward with their lives, so they could fully enjoy their relationships and parenting. I could see that I was making a profound difference, and my practice became, and continues to be, a calling – a vocation.

## What's in the book

I've divided the book into four parts to help you identify where a birth debrief might be useful to you as you navigate your way through pregnancy, labour and birth and the post-partum period. Part 1 explains the fundamentals of birth debriefing: what it is, how and why you might need one, who else might need one, and how to access one. It also explores the nature of, and treatment for, birth trauma and post-traumatic stress disorder (PTSD), why we don't talk about them enough, and why that needs to change.

Part 2 covers a few of the all-too-prevalent, non-physical issues around interactions with medical staff, as contributors to birth trauma, that routinely crop up in my debriefs, and explores how better, more mindful communication can help lead to a more empowered pregnancy and help prevent birth trauma. Part 3 explores some of the hurdles postnatal recovery might throw in your way, and aims to normalise the non-linear nature of post-partum recovery as well as some of the difficult emotions that you may feel as you heal. Part 4 is all about adjusting to life beyond the fourth trimester: it offers tips on finding and embracing your new identity as a parent, and how to parent in empowering ways that work for you – even if they go against societal norms.

At the end of each chapter, there is a chance to pause and think about what you have just read, and to journal your reactions. Look at these 'debrief deep dives' as an invitation to reflect on your experience, perhaps to see it from a new perspective, one that can empower you to own your experience and move forward. These deep dives include guided exercises, questions to think about, and tips. These are intended to help you think about the things you might put in place to support you during pregnancy, birth and the early post-partum stage. If you are at (or have passed) those stages and are wishing that things had gone differently, the deep dives will inspire you to find a way to reframe your post-partum and parenting experience and to consider how you want things to be from this point forward.

I have also included a number of affirmations in each chapter, which I encourage you to incorporate into your day. Or you can write out some of your own, if you wish. Whether or not you have used them before, I can tell you that affirmations – spoken aloud, with conviction and, most importantly, consistently – do work. As we are using affirmations to reframe our thinking, I find that positive declarations spoken in the present tense work best, as they imprint on your mind the conditions you want to see in the present time, not at some far-off date in the future.

I have also included strategies for coping with some big emotions, such as grief, shame and loss. In some chapters, I have set specific exercises for you to do. You may decide to do all the exercises, none, or the ones you feel are helpful – it's your choice – but you will get the maximum benefit from the book if you approach the exercises with an open mind and actually do them. To assist you, there are blank pages in each chapter where you can write down your thoughts and feelings about what you have read. You may prefer to purchase a separate notebook or journal for this. At the back of the book is a list of helpful resources, should you require additional support.

## A little help from my friends

My husband probably wouldn't agree, but I am keenly aware of the fact that I don't know everything! So I asked some of my most trusted friends and colleagues to share their insights in this book. Their professional contributions are integrated within several chapters. As experts in breastfeeding, physiotherapy, relationships, maternal mental health, PTSD and neonatal intensive care unit (NICU) care, they hold a wealth of knowledge in their respective fields. Their insights bring clarity and invaluable information to some challenging topics covered in this book, and I am honoured that they shared their knowledge and wisdom here.

I also include personal and clinical experiences, and case studies by people who have generously agreed to share their lived experiences and their journeys through many of the scenarios I describe in this book. These all add diverse, unique levels of insight, knowledge and perspectives I could not have provided on my own.

You may find some of the material challenging. When we read something that we find painful or difficult, it's natural to recoil from it, become defensive or angry, to shut down and/or dismiss it. But reframing these feelings not as enemies but as indicators that we need to look at something more deeply might be a better solution. Sometimes just acknowledging, and then sitting with, the discomfort of difficult feelings is exactly what is required to finally face them, voice them, and work through them. I would not expect you to put yourself in a situation that re-traumatises you in any way, however – your emotional and physical safety is paramount. So if there is something you find particularly difficult, stop, breathe deeply, take a break if you need to, reach out for support. Consider working through any strong emotions with a counsellor or therapist – but when you're ready, pick up this book again and keep going. You deserve to be physically and emotionally well, to heal, and to enjoy your life, wherever you are on the childbirth continuum.

I hope this book will help you on that journey. Not everything will apply to you, but there will be many things that will, and I invite you to sit with the full range of your emotions and, in a safe way, express them as they are.

## Self-care is political

Parts of this book are blatantly political. I make no apology for this. Followers of my Instagram page will know that I strongly believe that motherhood and expectations around birthing are political. Twenty-first-century motherhood is wrapped up in patriarchal influence and social media bombardment. Societal expectations suggest that mothering is instinctive – what women were created to do – so harbouring 'non-maternal' feelings or struggling in any way with parenthood feels like a sign of weakness or failure, rather than a normal human response to a high-stress situation. This pressure to be OK and to not respond openly to stress can lead to many mothers feeling silenced and unable to express their honest feelings about birth and motherhood – with far-reaching consequences for their wellbeing, as well as their partner's and children's. I view honest and open self-expression, whatever you're feeling, as a necessary form of self-care, which – to borrow from the famous quote by Audre Lorde – is as political as it gets.

While this book is for all birthing people, whatever your background or experience, as a Black woman directly affected by issues of racism in the medical field, I will always call out racial disparities when I see them. So this book also highlights the additional trauma Black and Brown women are subjected to when pregnant and during labour and birthing. It is extremely important that birth workers, healthcare workers and laypersons are aware of just how pervasive racism is, and how it affects our birthing population.

Though I understand that this might feel uncomfortable for readers who would rather not think about race, I want to make it clear that this book is for all women and birthing people. I am not trying to minimise the experiences of white women; rather, I am amplifying the experiences of Black and Brown women and other women of colour, who have regularly been marginalised in the medical system. I encourage you to engage with the material in these chapters, even if it does not affect you directly. Try to understand the issues at play and empathise with other birthing people who may not share your privilege. You may even find yourself in the position of being able to act as an ally for someone, and become an agent for positive change.

## Note to healthcare professionals

To the many respected and valued maternity healthcare professionals, who do the most amazing work under unfathomable pressures – I salute you. I cover some challenging topics in this book, and have not shied away from highlighting the shortcomings within our profession. I say 'our' because I see you too. I've been you, in your shoes, and I know first-hand what it is to strive day after day to provide a consistently excellent service against the challenges of funding cuts and staff shortages, not to mention the added stresses brought in by the Covid-19 pandemic. I champion every one of you – and in fact, this book is for you too. I want to make it clear that I'm not here to tear you, or anyone, down; this is not an attack on healthcare providers. Rather, my aim is to empower us all to provide the best care possible to the women we look after. I hope that this book will validate the pressures and the constraints of your job, as well as highlight the extent to which the conditions we provide, in and outside the birthing room, can contribute to a safe or unsafe environment – and consequently, a positive or negative experience for the people in our care. The great influence we, as professionals, have over people's birthing experiences gives us a huge opportunity to help to heal and repair what isn't working.

When you have a vocation like ours, the learning is never done. I want to present the parts of this book that may be hard to digest as teaching moments, not criticisms, and leave you with a sense of hope that change, where it is needed, is possible if we all work together. Better standards of care and improved best practices benefit us all. In many ways, we are still learning about the far-reaching impact of emotional distress around pregnancy and birth. We have an opportunity to be at the forefront of change for a better birth experience for all birthing people everywhere. I invite you to take up the mantle with me.

Lastly, I will be using inclusive language throughout this book. I will refer to women, mothers, parents, birthing parents and birthing people, and may use the terms interchangeably. How you identify is your decision: no one term cancels or invalidates another; there is space for all people who birth to exist alongside one another. Whoever you are and however you come to parenthood, you are valuable and you matter. Your pregnancy and birth experience are as unique as you are. And your feelings are valid and you deserve to be heard. I want you to know that I affirm you, and want to let you know that what feels authentic to you is real.

I want you to come away from this book understanding that you are important; you have a voice that you can use; you have agency over your choices; and you can use your knowledge to help you prepare for a positive birth experience and recover from a difficult one. So, I invite you to gift yourself the maternity preparation time, recovery time, the validation and self-compassion you deserve. Let's go on this educational, empowering and healing journey together.

Welcome to *The Birth Debrief*.

# How to use this book

I've created this book as a springboard for the wider conversations you may have been longing to have about your birth experience. This book has not been written as a 'read cover-to-cover' kind of book; rather, it's a resource for you to dip in and out of, a book that you take your time over, read and reread, take a break from and return to again and again as your healing progresses. Work your way steadily through the exercises and deep dive reflections that I have included. The book is meant to be shared and written in, so read it with your partner or a friend, or work through it with a counsellor, a therapist or as part of a parents' book club. Write in the margins; underline anything that resonates with you; practise the affirmations; bookmark the pages.

Healing (of any kind) is a process and usually can't be rushed. I invite you to take your time with each chapter, much as you would when having a coffee (or tea!) and a heart-to-heart with a trusted friend.

I believe we all have an inner wisdom and know what's best for us. Sometimes we just need the space and support to discover it. So consider this book a tool, not a set of rules. It's designed to shine a spotlight on a few of the key challenges around pregnancy, birth and parenting, and to encourage you to reach out for support, should you want to or need to. I hope you will see this book as an accessible resource and a safe space to help you identify, acknowledge and validate your feelings around your maternity, and as a vital part of your toolkit to accompany you through your pregnancy, birth, and post-partum period.

# part 1

## debriefing demystified

# 1
# birth debriefing: the basics

**Debriefing and your postnatal recovery**

## I reflect in order to learn and grow.

Every birth, whether it's your first or a subsequent one, will include a period of recovery. Chances are, if you've picked up this book, you (or a loved one) are discovering a few unexpected twists along the journey. Sure, we all anticipate a few physical adjustments post-birth, but even they can still take us by surprise (I'm talking to you, painful stitches and leaky boobs). You may already have had an informal 'mini-debrief' following the birth of your baby - a conversation or a bedside chat with the midwife or consultant, which may have focused on your physical recovery as a standard part of postnatal care - and this may be more than sufficient if your birth was straightforward. Postnatal healing goes beyond the physical, however, and whether your birth experience was straightforward or complex, you may have been left with a ton of emotions you don't know how to process. Maybe you have niggling questions about what happened during your birth experience and why things happened the way they did, or else you constantly revisit aspects of your pregnancy, labour and delivery, wondering if you could - or should - have done anything differently. Perhaps you're overwhelmed by intrusive thoughts that are affecting your wellbeing and enjoyment of life right now. Or you might be finding the transition to parenthood, your changing body, or your newly expanded family harder to adjust to than you thought. It's natural to feel a range of conflicting emotions after you've had a baby, but if thinking about your birth still leaves you feeling unsettled several weeks, months or even years after the fact, a birth debrief with a trained facilitator can be a helpful step towards healing any issues.

## What is a birth debrief?

A birth debrief (or birth reflection) is an opportunity for you, or anyone involved in the birth, to talk about your birth experience, the good and the bad bits, with a trained professional in a safe, non-judgemental and affirming environment. Think of it as your chance to speak, to tell your story, review your medical notes, ask questions, get clarity and have your unresolved feelings heard, validated and understood.

> *I didn't know what to expect from the session, but the moment Illy introduced herself, I felt safe. I knew I could say what I needed to say without being judged and feeling misunderstood. I came away from the session with a validation I didn't know was possible. I felt able to parent and to live in my truth.*
>
> *— Ellie, ten months post-partum*

Sharing your birth story is a powerful way to anchor your experience in the present, make sense of it and legitimise it. The act of telling also helps provide insight and perspective on what happened and, in the case of a difficult birth, releases the pent-up emotions around it. I see debriefs as new beginnings - the start of discovering and standing in the truth of your birthing experience.

## What debriefing is not

It's important that I manage your expectations here: a birth debrief is *not* counselling or therapy. A debrief cannot guarantee you complete healing, or provide a medical diagnosis or a quick fix. They do, however, work well alongside talking and other types of therapy, if needed. For some of you, a debrief may be sufficient to help you process your experience and continue on by yourselves, while others may need more support on your journey. Often, a debrief becomes a springboard to the exploration of a woman's experience. It then leads them to think, 'Actually, I might need therapy', or to acknowledge for the first time that they need other forms of support. Your GP or midwife will be able to refer you to appropriate sources of help, if that's something you would find beneficial. I have also collated a list of recommended specialists – including in Cognitive Behavioural Therapy (CBT),[1] three-step rewind,[2] Eye Movement Desensitisation and Reprocessing (EMDR)[3] and extended birth trauma counselling – for you to explore further. You can find this list in the Resources at the end of the book.

## When to debrief

Postnatal debriefs are usually booked in three to six months after the birth. Though you may be ready to speak earlier, it can be wiser to wait. First, after a difficult birth, it's not particularly helpful to ask someone if they want to talk about their traumatic birth experience immediately afterwards, without allowing them space for reflection or processing. And second, at least 80 per cent of new mothers heal naturally over time as they begin adjusting to life at home with their babies. In the post-partum recovery period, their feelings often change as their hormone levels balance out and their bodies recover physically. For this reason, in the UK birth debriefs are not usually offered by the National Health Service (NHS) before six weeks post-partum. But if you want to debrief earlier – or later – than this, you can do so privately (see p. 8 for more on this). There is no optimum time to book a birth debrief. Debriefs are there for you to consider when you're ready to share your story. Don't feel pressurised into debriefing before that time. Equally, don't worry about 'too much' time having passed since your birth experience for you to debrief it. I have conducted sessions with women who gave birth two weeks ago and women who gave birth ten years ago: it's never too late to start working through *your* birthing experience.

## Where to debrief

Debriefs are offered via the NHS in the UK, and privately. They are available to all birthing people, though unfortunately, they are not offered routinely (see Chapter 2, p. 11). On the NHS, debriefs are usually given at the hospital you gave birth in, or by a midwife at your home, if you birthed there. You'll usually attend a single session, but not always. If there is a lot to unpack, you might need several sessions. To maintain impartiality, birth debriefs are rarely, if ever, given by the staff who attended to you during your birth. Instead you normally speak with a hospital midwife, obstetric consultant, consultant midwife or sometimes a doula (see p. 121).

Private debriefs are usually run by independent birth workers, mental health professionals or educators. I know of debrief facilitators who will conduct sessions at your home or in a neutral place, but since the Covid-19 pandemic, they are more likely to be run via Zoom. This gives you the advantage of being able to debrief in the comfort of your own home if you choose, and you'll also get to choose your facilitator. The most important thing is that you debrief in a space where you feel safe and able to express yourself freely and openly.

# debrief deep dive

## REFLECT

Grab a pen and your journal or a notebook, or use the space below.
Note five things from your pregnancy/birth/post-partum experience
that stood out for you. Just jot them down as points for reflection; you
don't need to do anything else yet, but allow those thoughts to surface.
You are at the start of your journey of exploration.

1. _____

2. _____

3. _____

4. _____

5. _____

## REFRAME

Affirmations are really helpful for reframing your thoughts. Try
repeating these phrases out loud (remember to take your time and say
them with conviction):

- I am healing a little more every day. I respect the process.

- I'm proud of my progress.

- Healing may take time, but I am kind, patient and gentle with myself
  during the process.

## REDEFINE

As you begin your maternity wellness journey, what small, tangible
action can you take today to support your wellbeing?

# NHS or private?

Should you debrief via the NHS or privately? Thankfully, it's not an either/or decision. You can use both services - plenty of people do.

> I had a debrief with my [NHS] health board today about my birth.
> There was a part of me that was worried about doing it. I felt like
> I was so healed after our [private] debrief and I didn't want to risk
> opening wounds again or putting myself into a space where I
> might not feel supported. But I also had a few specific questions
> I wanted answers to, and I really wanted to give feedback.
>
> Anyway...
>
> I'm glad I went. I got my answers and I felt like my feedback was
> listened to and will hopefully help make changes. I felt listened to
> and ... that was good. But ... I am sooooooo glad I had my [private]
> session first! It was healing and emotionally sensitive in a way that
> [the public health service] never could have been. And because of
> it I was in a much, much better space and could really think about
> what I wanted from this debrief.
>
> – Lottie, twelve months post-partum

I've seen some excellent results from NHS birth reflections. NHS debriefs are free, of course, and you can and should expect a high standard of care, as well as several other advantages:

- If you have questions about clinical interventions and procedures, returning to the hospital where you gave birth (or speaking to staff from that hospital) is often the best place to understand what happened, and why.

- All staff working in the UK NHS (what we call hospital trusts) are required by law to keep detailed medical notes of everything that takes place from the moment you book into the hospital (or are attended to at home, in a home birth) until you're discharged. That means every examination, observation, medication administered and decision taken around your care is documented and will form part of your medical notes, which you can request at any time from the trust you gave birth in.[4] Your records will ensure you get a detailed, chronological, clinical account of the events surrounding the birth from the medical staff's point of view.

- Each trust must also follow a set protocol, which is like an internal/professional code of conduct for all its medical staff. Having these protocols helps to uphold professional standards and creates confidence in the trust's safety practices, as well as increasing transparency and accountability. The protocols alone cannot guarantee that nothing will go wrong, of course, but knowing that there are minimum standards of care and professionalism in place to ensure that mothers and babies are properly looked after is reassuring.

You can discuss everything you'd discuss in a private birth reflection at an NHS debrief. Private debriefs, however, can feel safer for women – and safety is one of the main reasons that women come to see me. My loyalty is exclusively to the person/people in front of me, and my role is to validate their experiences, while giving them the information they require. You might prefer a private debrief for this reason, too – or for one or more of the following reasons:

- You have already had an NHS debrief, but have more to unpack.

- You are planning to have an NHS debrief, but want to speak to someone before your appointment comes up.

- You had your baby years ago, but aspects of the birth still trouble you.

- You want more control over who you debrief with, when and where.

- You feel that a private facilitator (with no ties to the hospital where you birthed) would provide a truly independent perspective.

When considering a birth debrief for yourself, the right choice is what feels best for you. That could be an NHS debrief, a private debrief, an

NHS and a private debrief, or no debrief at all. All are perfectly OK.
The way I see it, anyone who can create and hold a safe space for women
and birthing people and their families in a trauma-informed manner (see
p. 45), whether through the NHS or privately, is providing a much-needed
healing and restorative service for women and families. Their contribution
to the wellbeing of individuals and families is invaluable, and because of
the work they do, they will always have my utmost respect.

# 2
# who should debrief?

**Who debriefs are for, and why you should consider one**

## Sharing my experience is a sign of strength.

The birth debrief is for new mothers, primarily - they are at the centre of the birth experience, after all. But childbirth has an emotional effect on all who witness it - as evidenced by the fact that debriefs are also offered to the medical team who attend births. In fact, anyone who is in the room during any stage of a birth can, and should, have access to a birth debrief if needed, including fathers and/or birth partners.[5] (Though this service is only available privately for birth partners unless they attend the NHS debrief with the mother, it is a worthwhile investment in their wellbeing too. It enables them to feel heard, validates their perspective, and helps them to work through their own experience, which will differ from that of the person who has given birth.)

**'I'm not sure I should debrief ... am I making a fuss?'**

Please don't deny yourself the opportunity to debrief if you feel you would like one. The likelihood is that if you suspect you might need a debrief, you probably do. If you're quick to dismiss your need for one, doing that British thing of not wanting to make a fuss, take up someone's time or thinking that you're 'just being silly' or 'it could have been worse', then you should definitely consider speaking to someone to explore those feelings. And let's not forget the classics: 'I should be over it by now', 'I feel as though I'm being ungrateful' and 'I'm a wreck, but at least my baby is healthy. That's all that matters, right?'

If you have thought, or said, any of these things, or had them said to you, and it bothers you, please give yourself permission to share your feelings at a birth debrief. What you're feeling is valid, and your story is important. Why is it silly to explore all your feelings about one of the most all-consuming experiences of your life? (Answer: it isn't silly at all!)

## The importance of birth debriefing for fathers and partners

I remember the first time someone emailed me and said, 'I know this might be a strange request, but would you mind if my husband attended the session too?' As I read the email I thought how sad it was that, societally, partner trauma has been dismissed to such a degree that it might be seen as a 'weird' request for them to join a session to unpack their feelings about the birth of their own child.

Fathers and partners need to be heard and their feelings affirmed, too. Their experience, perceptions and emotions will be different from yours. They were with you through the birth, but they will have viewed everything through a different lens - as spectator, not active participant. They'll have had a different responsibility and load to bear. But they can be affected by a traumatic birth too, and their feelings are no less valid.

> I saw her on that table, shaking and crying. I felt completely useless. I felt so scared, more than I have in my entire life, and then I felt ashamed. I was supposed to protect her; I was supposed to fight for her, support her and advocate for her, yet there I was, trembling, paralysed by fear, unable to do anything but hold her hand. I can't move past it. I feel so deeply traumatised that I fear I will never be able to bear witness to another birth. I still struggle to look my wife in the eye.
>
> – David, father of one

I invite partners to all my sessions. My aim is to normalise the practice of *both* partners having space to share their stories. When birth partners attend sessions, it helps to create a fuller picture of what happened during the birth. Sometimes there are events that women and birthing people don't recall, or they may recall them differently from how their partners remember them. When partners are present in the session, they are able to clarify and fill in some of the gaps, from their perspective. It's not unusual to discover that many couples haven't spoken to each other about the birth at all - in such cases, the debrief may be the first opportunity they have to do so in an honest, calm and unhurried way.

> *Thank you so much for your support during our debrief.*
> *Our previous birth was highly medicalised and traumatic for*
> *both of us, and the ability to talk it through in a safe space did two*
> *things for us: it helped us recognise the areas of trauma - some we*
> *hadn't even thought of - and it helped us feel empowered in our*
> *decision to have a home birth the second time around.*
>
> **– Samuel and Jess, parents of two**

Sometimes, couples come to sessions having had several conversations about the birth but having reached a sort of stalemate, perhaps even getting frustrated with each other and then shelving the issue, shoving it aside to be dealt with later. This only compounds the problem: like an untidy drawer or messy cupboard, the clutter does not magically vanish just because it has been shut away, and knowing that it is sitting there waiting to torment you whenever you open the door to it only increases your anxiety and irritation and saps your energy. For such couples, a debrief could be the first step towards helping them begin to untangle their emotions. Sometimes these conversations need to be held in a safe space with an impartial professional to facilitate the conversation and ensure *actual* listening is taking place. A time of uncensored sharing and active listening without one or other of the parties shutting down or closing off is hard to achieve alone, particularly when sleep deprivation and the general pressures that come with having a baby are thrown into the mix. If you did not have a moment to check in with yourself after the birth, it's even more likely that you may not have had an opportunity to check in with each other as a couple, either.

## Talking about it as a couple

Some couples don't necessarily need a debrief with a professional, but they do need to create the space to perform the *act* of debriefing. By this, I mean an honest conversation between the two of them, where they each reflect on their individual experiences of the birth and explore their feelings around it. This can bring new insights to the experience, clear the air, and bring a couple closer together (see 'Reflecting with your partner', p. 17).

## Debriefing for non-romantic birth partners

You don't have to have a romantic partner as your birth support; you can choose anyone you like. Many birthing people opt for a close female friend or family member, someone they love and trust to support and look out for them. If you were that birth support person for someone, you'll have witnessed the rollercoaster of emotional highs and lows alongside your loved one. This means that you might also need to debrief your experience as the birth support. The same is true if an unexpected, rapid labour meant you became an unwitting birth partner, to someone close or to a complete stranger. Granted, this is not an everyday experience, but it does happen! My advice to anyone who has witnessed a birth, particularly a difficult, traumatic or unexpected one, is to make time for yourself to speak about your experience and hold space for your own feelings. In a debrief, you can do this in a safe space, respecting the birthing person's dignity and privacy, but speaking openly about *your* experience.

I was with my sister when she gave birth, and it was a life-altering event for me. I spoke to a midwife friend afterwards because the experience was overwhelming and weighed heavily on my mind. Nothing particularly bad had happened, but I couldn't stop replaying the events in my mind. Immediately after my informal 'debrief', I felt better and had a different perspective. Getting the experience out of my head benefited me more than I realised – there truly is something powerful about the act of telling your story.

## Should you debrief?

Here are a few typical scenarios that might lead you to a birth debrief:

- You feel fine and had a straightforward birth, but your relationship with your partner has changed since your baby arrived.

- You had a straightforward birth, but struggled or are struggling with breastfeeding.

- You had a tough pregnancy, with illness such as hyperemesis,[6] followed by a straightforward birth.

- You sailed through pregnancy but had a traumatic birth experience.

- You're going through, have been through, or are about to start IVF.

- You have suffered pregnancy loss – for example, through miscarriage, ectopic pregnancy or stillbirth.

- You're currently in, or about to start, therapy.

- You don't necessarily want therapy, but you do want answers to questions about the clinical outcomes of the birth, as well as to explore the emotional effects the birth has had on you.

- You're dealing with symptoms of PTSD: see Chapter 6.

- You had your baby years ago, but aspects of the birth still trouble you.

- Or you may just want to share your story!

You don't have to have had a negative birth experience to debrief the birth – it's perfectly OK to reflect on and celebrate a good experience in your debriefing session. The session is about you and for you, and your debrief facilitator will be just as happy to celebrate with you and affirm you in your positive experience as they would be compassionate in holding space for you while you recount a challenging or negative one.

# debrief deep dive

## REFLECT

Do you feel you, your partner or birthing partner or someone you know and care about might benefit from a birth debrief? How do you feel about the prospect of it? Relieved? Excited? Fearful? Something else? Don't judge the feelings – just note them down for now.

## REFRAME

Try these affirmations as you prepare for your debrief:

- I deserve a safe space to share my story.

- Every aspect of my story matters.

- As I reach out for support, I gain strength.

## REDEFINE

You are worthy of support and deserve to be well – physically, emotionally and mentally. If you are not there yet, come back to this thought again, several times daily if necessary, until it feels true for you. You could turn it into an affirmation as well, if that helps:

- I deserve to be well – physically, emotionally and mentally.

When you feel ready, take one action towards making that a reality. For example, contact your midwife or GP, or you could research professionals specialising in birth debriefs online.

Remember: your healing journey is yours – you are in charge of the pace.

# Reflecting with your partner

If you'd like to perform a birth debrief with your partner and you're unsure how to facilitate it, you can simply ask them how they're feeling. This may seem obvious, but sometimes even the simplest, most effective acts of communication can become derailed by the 1,001 other concerns you may have as parents to a new baby – especially if you're first-time parents. If it's a conversation you have been avoiding – whatever the reason – then coming back to it can seem daunting. It may feel as if you just don't have the right words. But if this is something you would like to try, I encourage you to go for it. Be aware, however, that conversations like this are usually the most productive when broached at a time when your partner can't walk away or ignore you – so perhaps not when they're about to run out the door to work, are tired or otherwise distracted, like when the football or their favourite TV programme is on. (Trust me – I've tried this, so you don't have to!)

## How to do it

When you decide to raise the subject with your partner, be conscious of how you phrase the question – you want to invite an honest conversation, not shut it down. One way to do this is to ask open-ended questions, which leave space for more of a response than a 'yes' or 'no'. So, instead of: 'Did you think our birth experience was really bad, too?' try: 'How do you feel about our birth experience?'

Open questions leave room for conversation. They allow the other person space to respond in a way that makes them feel comfortable, and to give a response reflective of their true feelings. With closed questions the responses are already implied; open-ended questions create space and safety for the other person. It also shows that you're open to *truly* hearing them, and that is vital when it comes to listening to someone else's experience with the intention to understand. It's a powerful communication tool, which you can use in many situations, not just conversations with your partner!

When asking these questions, have no expectations. Accept that your partner's feelings may be different from yours (and that's OK), acknowledge their experience and validate their feelings. Remember, you were both there during the birth, but that does not mean you experienced it in the same way. If you're a male birth support partner who is struggling with your feelings, know that feeling traumatised by a difficult experience is not a sign of weakness, but of being human. Know that societal and/or self-imposed expectations that you should put your feelings on the back-burner in order to 'be strong' for your family are plain wrong: you do not have to follow that path. It may feel like you should contain your emotions, but you don't have to stay silent or bury your feelings. In fact, you *shouldn't* bury them because they will come out at some point, sometimes in ways you do not want or expect. You *are* powerful – leaning into your feelings is a sign of strength – so trust yourself to let them out without judgement. When you feel comfortable and ready, let the words come out, without censoring yourself and without shame.

**Supporting them to support you...**

The more your partner feels able to express their feelings, have them validated and feel heard and understood (whether or not you attend a formal debrief), the greater the likelihood of them being able to empathise with your feelings and support you better. Working through the debrief together can open an opportunity for you both to check in with each other about how birth and parenthood have impacted your relationship and you as parents. It will also help to find ways in which you can better understand and support each other. I'm not saying it will be an easy conversation, but for the health of both you and your partner as individuals, not to mention your relationship with each other, and as parents, it is a necessary one. It can help you feel understood by your partner, and help you see where they're coming from, too.

# 3
# why debrief?

**Barriers to seeking help, and how to overcome them**

## My story is mine, and I have the courage to share it.

So, we've seen lots of good reasons to reflect on your birth experience. As well as helping to bring you clarity – and hopefully, a sense of closure – there is anecdotal evidence to suggest that birth reflections can also help to prevent and/or reduce post-partum stress disorders, depression and mental ill-health related to the birth.

### Are debriefs always helpful?

A common question I get from women who are considering booking a birth debrief is, 'Will it help *me*?' They can accept that birth reflections can be transformative for some people, but are unsure if it will be right for them, especially if they have had a negative birth experience. Understandably, they are afraid of revisiting their trauma. Some studies seem to back up this concern, suggesting that debriefs make no difference[7] to women's emotional health post-partum in some cases, and in others, that debriefing could do more harm than good.[8] The National Institute for Health and Care Excellence (NICE) does not routinely recommend birth debriefs, precisely because of the risk of creating further trauma by unearthing deep feelings then leaving the recipient to deal with them alone.

So, should you be worried?

In my opinion, you needn't be – but booking a debrief does come with a few caveats. You would be wise to educate yourself about the benefits and limitations of birth debriefs (see Chapter 1, p. 4), do your research, find the right facilitator (this is crucial!) and be prepared to do the emotional work that comes with healing. Opening up to someone and excavating your emotions after a distressing ordeal, even months or years down the line, can be difficult and painful, and it's no exaggeration to say that debriefing takes courage. You may need to work with a therapist or other health support too, and this may have a cost attached.[9] With the right birth debrief facilitator and support, however, you will find yourself on a firm path towards recovery. Many parents who have taken this step, like Zara (below), have found it integral to their healing.

> *I just wanted to message you to say a massive thank you for our conversation yesterday. It was the first time I've ever spoken about my birth and the trauma, and I feel a huge weight lifted off my shoulders. For the first time, I felt listened to, and that my feelings were valid. You cleared a lot of things up for me, allowing me to move forward without any doubts or questions. I felt so empowered and proud of myself. My anxiety for the future and having more children has eased and I can now feel excitement for that, rather than dread.*
>
> *– Zara, eighteen months post-partum*

## Why else might a debrief be unhelpful?

I've spoken with women who felt their initial debrief focused too much on what the facilitator deemed a 'positive outcome' – a version of 'Well, at least you and the baby are OK' – to the detriment of their emotional and psychological wellbeing. Of course it's a relief and a blessing when both mum and baby are physically well post-birth. But if your birth was especially difficult, it can sometimes feel as though what you went through to get that outcome then becomes sidelined, minimised or dismissed entirely. And if the staff or the medical facility contributed to your negative experience, you may feel as though no one is being held accountable for the distress you suffered then, and may still be suffering now.

There can be other barriers to seeking help too:

- You may be unaware that the debriefing service even exists, or that you are entitled to one.

- You may want a private debrief but have limited access, due to lack of finances.

- You may be reluctant to reach out for help for cultural or religious reasons.

- You may be hampered by feelings of shame and guilt, or may feel that delivering a healthy baby means you shouldn't express any disappointment or dissatisfaction with the birthing process.

### Was it traumatic enough?

Some women and birthing people delay seeking help because they feel that their experience is just part of the price you pay for childbirth, and does not warrant being labelled as trauma at all. Others are fully aware that their births were traumatic, and reach out for help straight away, only to find their concerns are not taken seriously, either by medical staff or friends and family. They then try to live with the ordeal as best they can, even though the associated memories and emotions cloud their happiness and wellbeing.

*No one offered me a debrief, or the opportunity to speak about my birth. I think perhaps it didn't seem traumatic enough, but it was. I was deeply traumatised and felt I had nowhere to turn. All I wanted to do was speak. I wanted to feel heard; I wanted to ask the questions, get the answers and understand the whys, while understanding what I could do differently next time. I didn't want to be ridiculed; I couldn't face being told that what happened to me was 'normal'.*

*— Ellie, ten months post-partum*

The 'not traumatic enough' narrative is such a common reason women come to me: they weren't offered an NHS debrief and/or they had convinced themselves that their suffering was not 'traumatic enough' to debrief. This resonates deeply with me because this was my experience, too.

## My story

When giving birth to my daughter, I planned to deliver at home, but during labour I made the decision to move from my home to hospital for the delivery. I was seeking a change in environment – I wanted to feel safe – and hoping to access further support. Unfortunately, the move didn't result in any of those things happening. And although my daughter was born healthy, and physically I recovered well, I couldn't believe how distressed I felt, or how undeserving I felt of the right to that feeling, particularly because both my baby and I were healthy. In the weeks that followed, my thoughts swirled incessantly and I questioned my sanity ('Am I making too big a deal of this?'), my character ('I should be more gracious', 'I'm being ungrateful') and my strength ('Come on, Illy, get it together!'). I convinced myself that calling my experience 'trauma' was somehow wrong – that I should woman up, get over it and be happy with my new family. Essentially, I persuaded myself not to seek support when I should have.

I share this because I'm a midwife, and I have seen plenty of births not go to plan. I have witnessed traumatic births and supported many women and birthing people through their moments of panic, shock and distress. Yet, when it was my turn, none of my professional training prepared me for the avalanche of complex emotions I felt post-birth, or how I could acknowledge, then label, these feelings in a way that made me feel OK about seeking help.

## Who gets to decide what is and is not traumatic?

In my private practice, I always ensure that I create a safe space and give women and birthing people the opportunity to fill it with *their* feelings about their experiences, to let me know what *they* felt was traumatic or difficult, and to express where they felt stifled or invalidated.

> *I had spent the last ten months wondering if my feelings were valid, and within two minutes of starting the session, I knew they were. Illy made me feel sure they were. The first thing she said was, 'If you felt it was traumatic, then it was, but I won't ask you to divulge anything about your trauma that is too hard for you. This is about the events, but more importantly, it's about how you feel about them. Never feel you have an obligation to go to emotional places that aren't safe.' I felt the weight leave my chest immediately and I was able to tell my story.*
>
> *– Ellie, ten months post-partum*

There are many misplaced narratives around what birth trauma looks like – but no one gets to determine your trauma but *you*. Chapter 5 will unpack the clinical aspects of trauma in more detail, but for now, know that whether or not what you feel falls under a medical or clinical definition, you don't have to justify or explain your trauma. If what happened to you felt traumatic to you, then it *was* traumatic, and it is OK to describe it as such.

## Why debrief?

So, in the face of all these barriers, why debrief your birth? Because, quite simply, it works. Yes, there are things you need to consider prior to a birth reflection (it would have been wrong of me to write this book and not tell you this) but now that you have a better awareness of what those things are, you'll be better equipped to make an informed choice about when, where and with whom you debrief your birth. And doing that will bring you a step closer to recovery.

*I don't know what the future holds but I am no longer carrying guilt, a sense of disempowerment, or questioning myself about what I could've done differently. Those moments that Illy shared with me have been truly life-changing. I no longer feel such a heaviness when I think of the moment that our son joined us.*

*– Leila, mother of one*

When it feels impossible to break yourself out of a cycle of self-blame over events you most likely had little to no control over, a birth debrief can help you (as it did Leila), break that cycle, reframe your experience and reduce the harm to your mental wellbeing. For me, being able to shine a light on a different, yet true, perspective and to redefine a potentially destabilising, stressful event as an act of strength, resilience and courage is where the true power of debriefing lies. I hope you will give yourself the opportunity to experience this for yourself.

## One last thing...

In the interests of full transparency, I feel I should mention that research into the effectiveness of birth debriefs in alleviating birth-related trauma has by no means reached a definitive conclusion. With so many variables involved, it's a subject that I expect will continue to be studied. It is also important to acknowledge that an improperly conducted debriefing may exacerbate symptoms of emotional distress or trauma.

However, I don't think we can say conclusively that birth debriefs have zero effect on women who have suffered birth trauma. I know from personal and professional experience that they *are* helpful – provided they are conducted in the right way by compassionate, trauma-informed professionals. All sorts of things impact the success (or otherwise) of a debriefing, including:

- time spent with client(s);

- how soon after birth the debrief was conducted;

- level of trauma-informed training;

- degree of staff impartiality;

- degree of understanding of physical, mental and emotional impact.

I'd certainly like to see more training, in particular across a culturally diverse spectrum of maternity professionals. I want to see medical staff empathising with women's concerns as standard practice, and I'd like to see staff encouraging a more balanced and equal power dynamic, where the women in their care have a sense of agency over their own care, as well as a sense of trust that the medical professional truly has their best interests at heart. And as part of the group of professionals responsible for the care of these injured women, I say we can all review and improve our approach to their care. I hope that maternity professionals, women and birthing people can have an ongoing, open conversation about how this might best be achieved.

# debrief deep dive

### REFLECT

If you know you need to debrief your birth yet still feel reticent about it, ask yourself:

- What if the thing I'm avoiding is the key to my freedom and healing?

- How could I approach that difficult feeling as a bridge to my healing?

- Could I be open to believing that healing is possible for me?

### REFRAME

Try reframing these questions as affirmations as you prepare:

- I walk towards my freedom and healing with courage, a step at a time.

- Difficult feelings are just signals pointing the way to my healing.

- I am open to believing that healing is possible for me.

## REDEFINE

Opening your heart and mind to healing may not feel like a big step, but it is. Without it, it would be easy to allow any of the common barriers to debriefing to stop you from accessing the support you deserve. If you are struggling to believe that healing is possible for you, may I encourage you to share that struggle with one other person? You might be surprised by the new perspective they offer you. No matter who you are or what you've been through, you *do* deserve wellness. Never forget that.

# Difficult emotions around debriefing

During pregnancy and following childbirth, some women are blindsided by emotions that are deemed 'negative' – as if it's somehow wrong to feel them, let alone express them. Often, it helps to know that the feelings you struggle with are probably more common than you think – even the ones you think you 'shouldn't' be feeling (and probably *especially* the ones you think you shouldn't be feeling). Of course, plenty of positive feelings also accompany the arrival of a beloved baby. This isn't about dismissing those wonderful feelings; rather, it's about looking for ways to deal with the difficult feelings, as these make our daily lives that much harder to manage.

**The most common 'difficult' feelings that surface during birth debriefing sessions are (in no particular order):**

- disappointment;

- shock;

- guilt;

- shame;

- anger;

- helplessness/powerlessness;

- grief/sorrow;

- failure;

- exhaustion;

- isolation;

- fear.

**Many of these feelings tend to spring from one or more of the following roots:**

- lack of control;

- not being heard;

- not being supported;

- not understanding why things happened;

- being unprepared;

- expectations not matching reality/the birth not going according to plan;

- difficulties with infant feeding;

- clinical issues such as post-partum haemorrhage[10] or pre-eclampsia[11];

- being dismissed/invalidated by friends/family/society.

**Fathers tend to bring up the following concerns:**

- feeling unseen;

- events spiralling out of control and feeling like a spectator;

- regret over not advocating, or being able to advocate, for their partners;

- feeling scared;

- being excluded from key decisions and communications.

**Non-romantic birthing partners may struggle with:**

- unexpected, overwhelming emotional reactions after witnessing a difficult birth;

- maintaining boundaries with the birthing person and medical staff, and understanding where to step in;

- having nowhere to go to process their own experiences.

Are you surprised by any of the emotions and their causes? The lists are not exhaustive, so don't be put off if your current issue or concern is not listed here. We'll also explore a few of these stronger emotions in Part 3. I hope that reading the list in relation to your own experience will make you feel less alone. Similarly, if you have felt any of these emotions and have put off seeking support because you felt bad about it, let today be the day you change that.

It's so important to practise self-compassion when untangling the mass of emotions you feel as you process your birth experience. If you struggle with self-blame and criticism, you may judge yourself for any feelings you deem negative. This is unhelpful when you are committing to a journey of recovery. I want to challenge you to be open to trying a different approach. Can you find a way to look at your emotions differently – that is, not as indictments of who you are as a person or as a parent, but simply as *feelings*? As a first step to accepting what you feel without judgement, try practising these affirmations for any of the feelings you think are 'negative':

- I accept what I feel without judgement.

- It's OK to feel [*insert feeling*]; it's just a feeling.

- I can process what I'm feeling, and it will pass.

- I am compassionate with myself as I process my feelings.

- I can trust my body.

Remember: Nothing you are feeling right now is silly. Everything you are feeling is valid, and I see you. You are not alone.

# 4

# the practicalities of debriefing

**What to expect**

I allow myself to feel seen and be heard as I explore new ways to heal.

If you weren't offered a hospital debrief through the NHS and you would like one, contact the hospital first. You can do this via your community midwife in the immediate post-partum period (usually within the first ten days after delivery, although bear in mind that the session won't take place until later; see p. 5) or via your health visitor. Otherwise, get in touch with the hospital directly. Be aware that you won't be offered a choice of who conducts your debrief unless they are part of a continuity team (see p.128). Remember too that, on the NHS, a birth partner will often only be invited to debrief with the person who has given birth, not by themselves.

If you've decided to seek a private debrief, ask for recommendations from your hospital trust, GP or midwife. Some reputable organisations like the Birth Trauma Association will also hold a list of recommended private facilitators. You can also have a look on social media – many birth workers and antenatal educators offer some sort of debriefing service. Search using hashtags such as #birthafterthoughts #birthreflections or #birthdebrief, or google the same search terms to find facilitators in your area, if you would prefer to meet them face to face. Websites such as the Birth Trauma Association have made it much easier for women to reach out and talk about any issues in a supportive space. They are a valuable supplementary resource before, during and after a formal debriefing session.

Check with your doula, if you used one – many doulas offer a debriefing service. The advantage of this option is that most doulas write an account of what happened during the birth. They are also a familiar, trusted person who was present at the delivery and who has some degree of impartiality. The disadvantage is that, depending on how much training they have, they may lack a more in-depth knowledge or understanding of clinical events and procedures.

## What to look for in a facilitator

Remember that an NHS birth debrief will not be facilitated by the midwife or doctors who were present at the birth. For some women, this can be disappointing, but in order to avoid defensive practice[12] and to give the participant freedom to say what they feel they need to say, it's important that the debrief is kept as impartial as possible. For staff members working in the same trust, however, it may still be difficult to guarantee full impartiality, as they will be asked to comment on their colleagues' performance at a birth they were not directly involved in or witness to.

When seeking a private debrief facilitator, it may take time before you find a facilitator who you get on with and who is suited to your needs. If you don't find the right person straight away, be patient. In addition to endorsements by reputable organisations (see Resources), there are several key qualities that a good debrief facilitator should have. When making initial contact with a facilitator, look for the following:

- **Recognised professional qualifications** - Your facilitator should be a qualified midwife, registered birth professional (such as an obstetrician), a doula or a mental health professional who has had some trauma-informed[13] education or training.

- **Good communication skills** - Your facilitator should demonstrate a willingness and ability to answer clearly any questions you have and explain any medical terms or procedures you don't understand.

- **Active listening** - Your facilitator should be an engaged, active listener; they should be able to sit quietly and listen to you as you share your story.

- **Empathy, authenticity and impartiality** - Your facilitator should be able to understand how and why you feel the way you do. They should engage with you in a genuine and heartfelt manner while bringing an impartial perspective.

Even a facilitator who has all the qualities listed above might not be right for you. You may have personal preferences about your facilitator's age, sex, gender, religious background, experience and approach. You should not be afraid to ask as many questions as you need to of the facilitator, and their process, before committing to work with them. The good ones won't mind at all – they will want you to feel comfortable with them and safe to be as vulnerable as you need to be.

### How many sessions will I need, and what will it cost?

Every private practitioner is different, so you will need to confirm how they prefer to work and the cost involved. Clients usually see me for one session that lasts one to two hours, but some clients come back for follow-up sessions as needed. I make sure my rates are clearly stated on my website,[14] but it is also important to me to ensure the service I provide is made available to those of limited means. I'm fortunate to have worked with many kind-hearted, generous clients who, after completing a debriefing with me, choose to 'pay it forward' by donating the cost of a second debrief alongside theirs to enable women and birthing people on low incomes to access my service free of charge. This is something I would love to see implemented across all birth debriefing services, so that no woman who needs a debrief will be denied this care, simply because it is beyond their means financially.

## What to expect in the session

Just as every person and every experience is unique, so too is the approach a facilitator takes to a birth reflection. However, the list below gives a good idea of some of the steps you can expect to walk through during a typical birth reflection:

- **Tell your story.** You'll be encouraged to tell your story, and to share – in as much detail as you like, in the language you feel most comfortable using – *your experience* of pregnancy and birth. This is a time to reflect on and verbalise what happened, in a safe environment.

- **Name your trauma.** You'll be encouraged to name what you felt at the time, and what you're feeling now. If you have PTSD symptoms that have left you feeling physically and/or emotionally numb (see Chapter 6), your facilitator will gently guide you towards an awareness of what you're feeling, and help you to name it in a safe space. They will not leave you to cope with any difficult or overwhelming feelings on your own.

- **Have your experience validated.** The facilitator will listen to you without interruption or judgement. Their acknowledgement of your experience and the sense of validation that comes with it may help you feel (perhaps for the first time) as though someone is taking you seriously, that your experience matters, that it was important and that you did the best you could for yourself (or your partner, if you're a birthing partner) and your baby.

- **Explore any feelings** you may be particularly overwhelmed by, such as grief, shame or guilt, and learn new ways to deal with them. This may include the facilitator signposting you towards other sources of help and support, such as therapy or counselling.

- **Reframe your experience.** You'll be given tools to help you reframe your experience, particularly if it was a difficult one, so that you can see it as a high-stress situation in which you did the best you could for yourself and your baby when many factors were outside your control. For example, 'I fell apart during my partner's delivery. I couldn't stand the sight of all that blood' might become 'I had a natural reaction to a shocking experience.'

- **Redefine your experience.** You'll be equipped to look at your experience through an alternative lens, allowing you to move forward. For example, you might redefine 'I wasn't strong enough to cope without an epidural' as 'I opted for the best pain relief available to help me deliver my baby.' Or you might discuss your preferences for an upcoming birth and redefine how you would like this birth to go, compared to a previous one.

Having walked through these steps myself, both as participant and facilitator, I've seen the value of birth reflections first-hand. From a personal perspective, they have been pivotal to my emotional healing following the birth of my daughter Ihsan, and I have no doubt that going through a debriefing made a huge difference to my subsequent birth experience with her brother, Talha. I have also accessed debriefing services after the births I have witnessed and supported in a professional and private capacity, and would do so after any birth that left me with unprocessed feelings.

# debrief deep dive

I cannot overstate the value of being validated by a third party, such as a debrief facilitator. But you can also learn to validate yourself and your experiences. Doing so helps you stand firm in the truth of what you went through. It's also a good reminder to yourself that no matter what you're feeling, that feeling is OK, and that you are doing the best you can. And that's OK too.

## REFLECT

Take your journal and write a list of validating statements or affirmations you might use to encourage a friend or loved one who has shared a difficult experience with you. For example:

- 'I see why that experience would make you feel sad/angry/frustrated/belittled, etc.'

- 'How can I support you?'

- 'I hear your pain and distress – you feel that no one is taking you seriously. Is that right?'

## REFRAME

Using the same statements, rewrite them as though you were encouraging yourself:

- It's understandable that that experience would make me feel sad/angry/frustrated/belittled, etc. It's OK to feel how I'm feeling.

- What could I do to take care of myself right now? (See below.)

- I feel pain and distress, as if no one is taking me seriously. My feelings are valid and it's OK to feel them.

## REDEFINE

The next time a strong feeling bubbles up that you might ordinarily dismiss, pause and validate that feeling using one or more of the 'reframing' statements you have written down.

In answer to the question, 'What could I do to take care of myself right now?', write a list of positive, nurturing things you could do as acts of self-care, such as having a relaxing bath, calling a friend, going for a walk, etc. Plan to take action on at least one of the items on your list.

# the birth debrief

_____

_____

_____

_____

_____

_____

_____

_____

_____

_____

_____

# A glimpse into my process

Clients usually contact me following a difficult birth, or during a subsequent pregnancy, to talk through their experience. Once I have made contact and agreed a time and place to meet with a client or clients, there are a couple of things I normally recommend before the session. It may be helpful for you to think about some of these too:

- You might want to bring your medical notes. Though they are not essential during a session, they help to provide a fuller picture of the decisions that were made during your birth, and why.[15]

- You might want to make a list of things you want to cover, along with a list of any questions. This is not a prerequisite, but it can help you to maintain focus during the session, and ensure you leave feeling like your questions have been answered.

**During the session**

My clients often feel some therapeutic benefit from their sessions, as they are heard and validated, but as I mentioned earlier, I always make it clear that I'm not a qualified counsellor or therapist, and I'm careful to never take on that role during a debriefing session. Although clients sometimes book several sessions with me, they do so with the knowledge that they are there to talk through their experience or ask follow-up questions, not to be counselled. I don't tell people what to do, as that isn't my role, but I might signpost them to other sources of support that might be useful.

**When to go further**

I also guide my clients on what action they can take in cases where, during a pregnancy and birth, medical protocols weren't followed. Your facilitator may be able to do the same. Making this judgement call is always based on the protocol of the hospital where my clients gave birth and/or best practice. Protocols may differ slightly between trusts.

## Resolution

The resolution point of my sessions comes when I give clients ideas for how they can move forward with their lives. These may include tools to help them manage their feelings around their pregnancy, birth or postnatal/parenting experience; practical tips such as journaling, speaking to their partners or seeking further therapeutic support; or a list of people to contact if they have concerns about their experience and the procedures that were followed.

If there has been a loss (through miscarriage, stillbirth, neonatal death or other sudden infant death), I offer ways in which to grieve and commemorate that loss, and move towards a place of acceptance. If required, I also offer ways in which to explore the idea of conception following a loss. This can be quite complex, as it often feels to clients like something unattainable in the immediate aftermath. I never know what will emerge in a session, but I always try to leave my clients with something tangible they can put into action. I find this helps them to feel more empowered and hopeful about their future, even if they have shared sadness, grief, anger and pain in the session.

Professionally speaking, my passion for this work grows deeper with each session I facilitate. I love seeing my clients' faces relax in relief as they feel seen and heard, and I share their joy at the revelations they get when they are truly validated. When the birth has been a difficult one, I have the privilege of holding space for them as they begin their journey of healing. I am always honoured that these extraordinary people have allowed me to bear witness to their courage and vulnerability.

*I didn't know what to expect, but somehow I deeply trusted that my words would be heard and held safely. Not knowing which words would fall, I knew I needed something to shift. I couldn't continue to hold those same thoughts and questions. As soon as I heard Illy's voice, I just took a deep breath, and we had the softest, most natural and nurturing conversation. My birth experience was honoured with integrity and wisdom. There were no moments of bypassing the uncomfortable and raw truths. In those minutes, I was given back my empowerment, I found hope, and I healed my relationship with my birth experience.*

*— Leila, mother of one*

I hope Leila's story and this glimpse into how my process works have answered some of your questions about what to expect in a debriefing. As you consider your options, remember that birth reflection is designed to help you, not cause harm. You have a right to have one, and you're not being a nuisance for asking for what you need.

# 5
# let's talk about birth trauma

**Ending the silence around trauma**

# I am allowed to give voice to what I went through. I am safe now.

It's important to reiterate here that the majority of births *are* safe, and that most women and birthing people have a positive experience and are satisfied with the medical care they receive. And if parts of the delivery were challenging - perhaps they had a difficult labour, a tear that required stitches, an episiotomy or an unexpected medical emergency - most women are able to process these naturally and heal within a few weeks or months. However, when symptoms begin to negatively affect your quality of life, it may be time to seek help.

## What is birth trauma?

The word 'trauma' comes from the Greek for 'wound'. In the Collins dictionary, trauma is defined as: 'any bodily injury or wound ... a severe shock or very upsetting experience, which may cause psychological damage'. In birth trauma, the injury or upsetting experience is related to one or more aspects of a birth. Many people associate birth trauma with a physical event during a birth, such as a major blood loss, an unsuccessful induction or a caesarean section, but birth trauma can be psychological and emotional, and can include anything from poor interactions with healthcare professionals to the fear that you or your baby are going to die.

Not all trauma comes solely from the birth itself. I asked Dr Rebecca Moore, a birth trauma expert, perinatal psychiatrist and co-founder of the Make Birth Better collective,[16] to expand on this further. She told me:

*Trauma can be perinatal - in other words, it can come from something in pregnancy or something postnatal, such as breastfeeding... It includes any experience that you felt was difficult or frightening for you on your journey: from trying to conceive, to pregnancy and beyond - anything that left you feeling intensely afraid, unsafe, out of control or helpless.*

That leaves a lot of scope for potential trauma, doesn't it? And let's not forget, while birth trauma affects approximately 6 per cent of birthing women, it also affects 5 per cent of fathers and birthing partners. I suspect this figure is significantly underestimated, due to factors such as the sensitive nature of witnessing such a vulnerable time; a lack of knowledge around access to a birth debriefing service; a need to keep the focus on the birthing person; and society continuously reinforcing the need for 'machismo', which often prevents men from disclosing feelings of struggle or trauma.

## Why don't we talk about trauma?

Part of my mission with this book was to explore the range of feelings and behaviours that can present themselves after a birth trauma, and to normalise talking about these feelings as a pathway towards healing. Yet I also understand that this is not an easy subject and that, for some, just thinking about the word 'trauma' can feel triggering, never mind talking about it. I get it – I've spoken to so many birthing people and their partners who have been where you are, and I've been there too.

As I've explained, my knowledge of the world of birth trauma began with my own difficult birth experience, so I empathise with the varied and complex ways birth trauma may show up for you. At the same time, we need to find ways to normalise talking about trauma – not in reckless or uncaring ways, but in empowering ones. If you find the word upsetting, it may be a sign that you have some unresolved memories or experiences attached to it, and you may need to pause and work through those experiences with a professional. This is more common than you might think. If this resonates with you in any way, I encourage you to consider reaching out for support from your midwife, GP, doula or a counsellor or therapist.

**Symptoms of birth trauma**

Symptoms are often difficult to spot because so many are easily written off as 'normal, considering you've just given birth'. But awareness of what's *not* normal is vital because, as Dr Rebecca Moore says: 'Trauma can distort how we view ourselves and trust the world around us, and this altered sense of self can ripple out and affect relationships, work, our sexual and/or social life. It can affect women and birthing people bonding with or connecting with their baby.'

So what should you be looking out for?

- Frequent intrusive thoughts. You might keep replaying the distressing events over and over in your head: it feels compulsive, as if you have no control over it.

- Anxiety (beyond the general anxiety that comes with parenting).

- The thought of giving birth again terrifies you.

- You have memory lapses – especially around the events of the birth.

- Feeling numb, spaced out or disconnected from your body, your environment and/or the people around you.

- Difficulty bonding with your baby.

- Difficulty sleeping (even when you're physically tired).

- Flashbacks plague your waking hours and nightmares disrupt your sleep.

- Panic attacks.

- Hypervigilance, and a constant fear that something bad will happen to you or your baby. You just can't relax (see my experience of this on p. 58).

- Distress at, or avoidance of, anything that reminds you of the birth, such as other pregnant women and/or their babies, hospitals, etc.

- Constant feelings of depression, anger, guilt, self-blame or shame.

You may exhibit one or several of these symptoms if you have suffered birth trauma.

### Common causes of birth trauma

There are several well-established causes of birth trauma, and the Birth Trauma Association lists several scenarios that make it more likely to occur:

- induction;

- early labour;

- prolonged labour;

- short, very painful labour;

- inadequate pain relief during labour and/or delivery (and post-partum – afterpains can be brutal!);

- emergency interventions, including forceps or ventouse birth or caesarean section;

- excessive blood loss;

- medical error or malpractice that results in the birth of a baby with a disability;

- baby needing to stay in the special care baby unit or neonatal intensive care unit (NICU);

- fearing for baby's safety;

- suffering a stillbirth;

- poor postnatal care;

- feeling out of control;

- lack of information or explanation about what is happening to you by staff;

- lack of privacy and dignity;

- impersonal treatment, or problems with staff attitudes;

- not being listened to;

- previous trauma (which could include childhood trauma, a previous traumatic birth, or domestic violence).

This list is not exhaustive, but it is notable that medical interventions are associated with birth trauma. That does not mean that medicalised births are 'bad' – far from it. But it does make a case, in my opinion, for more to be done to ensure that antenatal care/birth education adequately addresses women's and birthing parents' physical *and* emotional preparedness for birth, and access to support after delivery. Remember that an individual's perception of trauma affects their emotional, mental and physical states. Ideally, healthcare professionals should find a way to bridge that gap.

**Trauma perception**

Birth trauma is complex, and because the nature of trauma is so person-specific, different people will find different things traumatic. In other words, it's not necessarily about what happened, but about how you felt about what happened that makes an event traumatic. I am labouring the point, but that's because I see in my work all the time that a key reason why trauma sufferers sometimes delay asking for the help they need is because they don't want to be judged or have their experiences invalidated. So it's really, *really* important that you understand that trauma perception is about what is real *for you*, regardless of what anyone else says.

Women have also told me that they feel their trauma was routinely misunderstood and that healthcare workers, friends and family often used themselves as a metric when judging whether the birthing parent's experience was traumatic, rather than trying to understand why the birthing parent found *their* experience traumatic. It's as if people think that trauma, and what causes it, has to involve gore and graphic detail. When you hear about a birth intervention such as forceps or ventouse or significant blood loss, it's easy to say, 'Well, that was traumatic, wasn't it?' There's tangible 'evidence' of trauma - and, I would go as far as to say that there's something societally more 'acceptable' about a visible injury or emergency event. The need for, and offer of, support is usually immediate and palpable: sufferers are quickly listened to and empathised with - as they should be. But what about those whose trauma was caused by something else? Perhaps their trauma came from not being cared for properly or as they expected, or maybe their baby's heart rate dipped during labour or they felt exposed and vulnerable and couldn't do anything about it. Are these people less deserving of empathy and care?

It takes specific training to understand the nature of trauma (i.e. to become 'trauma-informed'). When I was starting out as a midwife in clinical practice, I would offer women the opportunity to have a birth reflection based on what *my* perception of trauma was, rather than letting them know that the option was there and giving them the space to define their own experience. I soon learned to step back and be guided by the woman as to what support she needed and whether she wanted to proceed with a birth reflection.

Childbirth is a phenomenal undertaking. Those who go through it deserve our utmost support and respect. If we are going to make changes in how we treat women and birthing people, we first need to revisit the way in which we, as a society, view trauma.

We also need to normalise asking for help. It's not a sign of weakness - humans are designed to live in communities, to lean on each other for support. Somewhere along the line, we have conditioned ourselves to think that we have to handle everything alone, but that couldn't be further from the truth. There are many pathways to healing from birth trauma, including therapeutic, spiritual and medicinal ones - and with reflection, attention, courage and support, recovery is possible for you.

# debrief deep dive

## REFLECT

We've explored why trauma might feel difficult to talk about for some women and why, despite this, we need to normalise talking about it. Sometimes we need to name our experiences in order to heal. For some women, naming their experience using powerful, truthful language, even when it's difficult, is affirming and fills them with a sense of relief. This is a powerful starting point for healing and moving forward.

## REFRAME

To help you reframe your own experience, Dr Rebecca Moore offers her top tips for coping after birth trauma. Remember:

- Trauma is what has happened to you. It's never your fault.

- Though it can feel difficult to open up to people, it is vital that you do so. Find the people and places that are safe for you.

- Know there are many ways to heal, and you will find your way.

- Know that you're not alone, and you don't have to struggle alone.

- Know that your birth experience may have been the start of your journey to motherhood, but it is not your ending. You and your baby will move forward together.

If you find it helpful, you can personalise these tips as a way of remembering them whenever you are struggling. Take each one in turn and rewrite it as a positive affirmation. I have done the first few for you:

- Trauma is what happened to me. I am not at fault.

- Though it can feel difficult to open up to people, I do so anyway. I find the people and places that are safe for me.

- There are many ways to heal, and I will find my way.

## REDEFINE

Is there anything about your experience that you need to name? And do you need support to name it? If you said yes to either of these questions, make today the day you reach out for support.

# Debriefing fertility issues*

One of the first questions I ask in a birth debrief is about the road to conception. If a couple has had difficulty conceiving, this may add layers to any anxious feelings they may have about the pregnancy and the birth.

## When getting pregnant is a struggle

There's an assumption that when a woman reaches a certain age, a great maternal urge will come over them and they'll decide to have a baby. However, for some, the road to 'we're pregnant!' isn't that simple.

Infertility affects approximately 1 in 7 heterosexual couples. The National Institute for Health and Care Excellence (NICE) lists the main causes as follows:[17]

- ovulatory disorders (25 per cent)

- tubal damage (20 per cent)

- factors causing male infertility (30 per cent)

- uterine or peritoneal conditions (10 per cent).

Around 25 per cent of couples find there is no identifiable cause for their infertility.

When you're having fertility problems, it can feel like the most lonely and isolating time, even if you do know how common it is. It feels like everyone around you is getting pregnant at the drop of a hat. Perhaps you feel additional pressure from family and friends to start a family as well.

*Deciding we were going to become a mum and dad felt like a big, but exciting, decision. Little did we know then that the initial 'fun'* of trying would become an overwhelming and traumatic decade of our lives. I agree this is a particularly long journey compared to some and we are, of course, eternally grateful that we have our daughter Wren, but both before and since our successful pregnancy, the fertility treatment and losses have left deep scars.

January 2016. Four years TTC [trying to conceive]. Three IUIs [intrauterine inseminations]. Six embryos transferred. Two miscarriages. No baby. I was broken.

That was almost halfway through our journey, and the lowest point. I spent that month barely able to get out of bed. I was unemployed (having left work due to the emotional toll of treatment and pregnancy loss). I wasn't a mother. I was overweight due to the medication, plus the binge eating and drinking that often followed a negative test or miscarriage. The strong, confident and capable woman I had once been was lost. I was a shadow of my former self.

Looking back now, I learned a lot from that time. I learned how to rebuild myself one step at a time. I went to art classes to remind myself I was talented. I retrained to remind myself I had a purpose. I explored the world to remind myself there was wonder out there worth living for.

But all that happened has changed me. The not-so-good bits: it's made me less optimistic, less spontaneous, maybe even less fun – all this I'm hoping to get back! The good news is it also made me less judgemental, more open and empathetic.

I also found a new confidence in myself. One that has and continues to serve me well. This confidence has allowed me to take comfort in knowing that whatever life throws at me, I will get through it. It helped me pick myself up again after another unsuccessful round of treatment in 2017 and go again: our 'one for luck' that gave us Wren. And even as I write this, I know that this confidence will get me through my very real and current grief at our fertility journey coming to an end following a negative result for our final ever embryo transfer a couple of weeks ago.

*Motherhood is about nappy changes and feeding. It's about bedtime cuddles and nursery pick-ups. But for me, motherhood started many years before my daughter was born. It has been a long journey that has shaped me into the person I am today - a journey that I believe has made me a better mother than the pretty good one I hope I would have been without all this.*

**– Catherine, mother of Wren, conceived through IVF**

For women and birthing people, trouble conceiving can compound feelings of failure and the idea that their body 'has let them down'. This is never the case, and it's so important that you understand this. There are many factors that are simply outside your control, and you are *allowed* to feel the full range of your feelings as you navigate your journey. Know too that you can work through these feelings, with support, if you need it, and birth debriefs can be a useful part of that.

# 6

# post-traumatic stress disorder

**Identifying and recovering from childbirth-related PTSD**

## I deserve support to heal.

Studies show that of the 30-40 per cent of the women and birthing people who report finding some part of their maternity experience traumatic, around 5-8 per cent go on to develop PTSD. The term 'childbirth-related PTSD' (or postnatal PTSD) is often used synonymously with 'birth trauma', but while the two conditions are closely related, they are not the same. One key difference between the two, says trauma expert Dr Rebecca Moore, is that although a person may experience PTSD as a result of birth trauma, 'not all birth trauma leads to postnatal PTSD'. Many of the symptoms of birth trauma mirror those of PTSD, and the treatment for both conditions is often the same. 'The difference is,' Dr Moore adds, 'that sometimes, but not always, birth trauma may heal on its own and/or with time, whereas PTSD typically needs specialist support.'

The more symptoms you have, and the greater their severity, the higher the chance you could be dealing with PTSD. Dr Moore and I strongly recommend that if you are experiencing *any* of the symptoms we saw in Chapter 5 (see pp. 42–3), you shouldn't try to deal with them on your own – it's vital that you reach out for help. Left untreated, Dr Moore says, 'PTSD can have a huge impact on a woman or birthing person.' In addition to disrupting a woman's quality of life in what should be a happy time of bonding with her baby, her relationships with her partner, friends and family can all be affected. There is also evidence of higher rates of physical health issues[18] (including arthritis, digestive problems and diabetes, to name a few) in people who have untreated PTSD. For this reason, Dr Moore adds: 'It's also really important to screen for, diagnose and treat PTSD quickly.'

### Diagnosing postnatal PTSD

Postnatal PTSD must be formally diagnosed. There are specific, recognised criteria to do this, in the form of the City Birth Trauma Scale. The scale was developed by researchers[19] at City University in London, as a 29-point questionnaire[20] and diagnostic checklist for post-birth PTSD. It is intended to act as a clear, concise measure of postnatal PTSD and to ensure those suffering receive appropriate care and treatment.

'To have PTSD,' Dr Moore told me, 'you need to have *all* the symptoms on the checklist to make this formal diagnosis, [whereas] with birth trauma you may have *some* of the symptoms, but not all.' There are different scales and scores for each symptom, which together help make the right diagnosis. 'It's about looking for these patterns of feelings and experiences to guide us to the right treatment,' Dr Moore says. 'What really matters, though, is that your trauma is heard and seen.'

### Risk factors for postnatal PTSD

One study of PTSD after childbirth[21] found that anxiety about possible birthing problems, unmet expectations of how the birth would go, and the severity of any actual birth problem predicted those who found their birth traumatic. In other words, birth trauma and PTSD aren't always caused by the feared event *actually* happening, but by the *fear* of that thing happening. Of course, trauma can also be caused by what we fear happening *actually* happening. And the way that fear is managed and responded to can also cause birth trauma *and* PTSD.

A recent study[22] also showed that some groups are more vulnerable to experiencing PTSD symptoms, such as those with a history of depression, anxiety or trauma; a history of abuse; a family history of PTSD; a lack of social support; and physical health issues in pregnancy, to name a few. However, Dr Moore notes, 'You could have one or many of these risks and still not develop PTSD.' Although we all have our own unique vulnerabilities, there are many things that can reduce the risk of trauma, such as continuity of care, consent, kindness, respect and feeling safe during labour and birth (see Part 2).

## Pathways to healing: processing trauma

Senses are associated with memories. Perhaps you smell the sea air by the coast or smell the warmth of the grass on a summer's day and you are instantly taken back to when you were a child - to a pleasant memory, a happy place. This is more commonly known as a trigger or flashback. Traumatic memories are no different, except the triggers attached to the senses may take you back to a time when you suffered a trauma, because the trauma hasn't been processed properly. When something triggers that memory, the flashback can feel scary and violent, and you may feel as though you're reliving that moment or that you're 'trapped' in the memory. This is called re-experiencing.

While in trauma, the brain doesn't prioritise the processing and understanding that needs to take place to begin healing. During the traumatic event, the brain overrides the 'processing' part and goes into survival mode, placing you in a state of tension known as the 'fight, flight or freeze' response. And that is exactly what the brain *should* do to keep you alive. But the rush of stress hormones, and the emotions accompanying the event, don't simply leave the body when the threat has subsided; they have to be processed and released. It is important, therefore, that once the traumatic event has passed you give your brain the opportunity to do the processing that leads to healing.

## Pathways to healing: getting help

Suffering from postnatal PTSD can feel frightening. It's the last thing most people expect to have to deal with at the start of their parenting journey – and that in itself takes some processing. But there are professionals you can reach out to for support and guidance if you feel like you cannot manage alone. These include your GP, a specialist birth trauma therapist, or a counsellor specialising in birth trauma.

'If you choose to, you can self-refer for therapy via Improving Access to Psychological Therapies,'[23] says Dr Moore. She recommends trauma-focused CBT and/or EMDR to treat trauma; like me, she is also an advocate of self-care-focused alternative therapies. Several of my clients have sworn by breathing practices, massage and homeopathy, to name a few. Other ways to heal might include exercise, journaling, couples therapy or alternative therapies such as tapping (also known as Emotional Freedom Technique, or EFT), baby massage or craniosacral therapy. Your GP may also prescribe medication if you are struggling with depression and/or anxiety.

'Peer support or online groups such as Make Birth Better or the Birth Trauma Association are other great resources,' Dr Moore suggests, 'and there are some great helplines you can call, such as PANDAS [PND Awareness & Support].[24] Or you can look at lots of stories around healing on the Make Birth Better website.'

Dr Moore and I believe that it's important to have professional and personal support networks around you, too. 'Do your due diligence and ensure that they are fully qualified to advise you,' says Dr Moore. Just as there is no 'one-size-fits-all' approach to an individual's perception of trauma, so the treatments that are helpful for one person may have no effect on another. You may benefit from one or several types of treatment on your journey. Ultimately, Dr Moore says, 'It's about you feeling you have the choices explained to you so you can pick the things that feel right for you.'

Please don't give up if you are struggling. 'Often the hardest step is recognising that something does not feel right,' notes Dr Moore, 'and then it can feel so scary to talk to someone like your GP or health visitor. Please know that they are there to help and not to judge – you're not a bad mother. If the first person you see doesn't listen, or dismisses you, then try to see someone else, take a friend for support, or make notes beforehand and ask questions.' You've already shown so much courage and resilience. You've got this.

# debrief deep dive

## REFLECT

PTSD can feel extremely isolating, and when we're feeling isolated, we can forget how much support we have around us. Visual reminders such as the safe space bubble can help. You can try this 'safe space' exercise in your journal, or better still, on a sheet of paper, which you can tape to your fridge so you'll see it often.

*Safe space bubble*

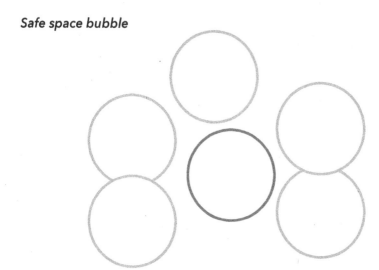

*How to do it*

The image above shows a cluster of five circles or 'bubbles' around a central bubble. Imagine that the centre bubble represents you as you draw the circles on your page. Fill each bubble with the name of a safe place and/or person. This should be someone you feel comfortable enough with to express your feelings freely to them and speak openly about your experiences. The person could be a professional, a friend or family member. The place could be a public place or a familiar home environment, a doctor's surgery or anywhere else that feels safe to you. You can draw more than five surrounding bubbles if you have more than five people/places on your list. Include as many people and places that make you feel safe and supported as you can. You could include contact numbers next to the bubbles if you like – be as creative as you like with this.

The purpose of this exercise is to give you a visual image of your support system. Seeing your 'support bubble' in this way – especially if you are a visual learner – gives you an at-a-glance reminder in times of crisis that you are not alone and that you have somewhere to turn.

## REFRAME

I would not dare to suggest that affirmations on their own will end your PTSD symptoms, but they can be a helpful part of your healing toolkit, acting to remind you that you deserve wellness in the present and in the future. You can try them alongside any other sources of help you access:

- I am more than just my trauma – it does not define me.
- There are so many ways to heal, and I will find one that works for me.
- I'm proud of my strength and resilience.

## REDEFINE

As we gain a deeper understanding of the things that contribute to how we *feel* about our experiences, and understand how far-reaching the impacts of birth trauma and PTSD can be, it becomes easier to find ways to adapt and take charge of our experiences (as much as possible). When I think of my own experience of birth trauma and PTSD, my biggest regret is not reaching out for help sooner.

In the next section, you'll read about how one PTSD symptom – hyperarousal – really did a number on me, and how I came through it with professional help and support from my family. I'm convinced that the education, personal experience and professional help I received (which included a birth debrief, by the way!) made all the difference during the birth of my second child, Talha, as well as in my postnatal recovery period. I know that if I had to do it all again, finding out the risk factors, any preventative measures and actions to take if I were to notice anything amiss would be vital for me. That's what this chapter has sought to provide, so that you can do the same, too.

# The baby is mine, the baby is mine, the baby is mine°

From the moment I was pregnant with my first child, I considered her mine. I would refer to her as 'mine' and would often have to correct myself and affirm that she was also my husband's.

It wasn't deliberate. I was the one growing her and I would be caring for her the majority of the time. Once she was born, I was in tune with her, knew her needs and recognised each and every cry. I could feed her and soothe her from my body. I'm sure the fact that Ihsan was my first baby also played a part, but to me it felt natural that I saw her as mine.

## Hypervigilance

This might have stayed as nothing more than a little quirk, which would have faded in time, but because of the trauma I'd suffered during Ihsan's birth, I developed hypervigilance (or hyperarousal), a symptom of PTSD which causes increased levels of cortisol (the stress hormone) in the body. This means the person suffering hypervigilance is in a constant state of high alert. This can result in panic, trouble sleeping or concentrating, irritability, angry outbursts and/or chronic muscle tension. Hypervigilance mostly affects women and birthing people who have had traumatic birth experiences, but not always. it comes from the heightened sense of responsibility you get when caring for a newborn and you are aware of their dependence on you.

Hypervigilance caused me to feel on edge and hyperaware of Ihsan *all the time*. Although I would let others hold her, and would even leave

---

° If Brandy X Monica will pardon the pun.

her with my mum or sister if I needed to sleep, I never slept deeply.
I would have the darkest thoughts about her coming to harm if I closed
my eyes. Eventually, I had her strapped to me in her sling continuously,
and would rarely relax or allow others to help me. Needless to say, it
was a frightening, depressing and exhausting time for all of us. When
I sought help to address my PTSD, most of my symptoms gradually
subsided, but the sense of Ihsan being mine remained with me for a
long time afterwards. And it's a real thing – I have spoken to many new
mums who report the same feelings, and during debriefs with couples,
the non-gestational parent often describes feeling left out and 'useless'.

Know that if you develop hyperarousal, it has no bearing on the type
of parent you are. We are all individual and have different symptoms
and stress responses. If your hyperarousal has led to insomnia, I
advise you to seek professional help – speak to your GP, health
visitor or midwife. Sleep is essential to our wellbeing. Our minds and
bodies need the opportunity to heal, and that can only be done with
adequate rest. And please keep your partner involved – tell them
about your fears so they can reassure you and share the physical load
as much as possible. Even if you're breastfeeding, partners can take
care of all your baby's other needs, from nappy changing to burping,
bathing them and dressing them, rocking them to sleep and more.
They can watch baby while you sleep too.

## My turning point – accepting help

One day, my dad was offering me parenting advice. Frustrated that he
was trying to tell me what to do, I blurted out, 'But she's *my* child!'

I'm sure that many of you can relate to the defensiveness that comes
with new parenthood – sometimes even advice given in the kindest
way can trigger feelings of judgement. I felt as though someone was
trying to challenge my authority over this little person who I knew like
the back of my hand. This little person who was *mine*. My dad calmly
responded, 'Is she *yours*?' Enraged, I fired back, 'Of course she is!'
But it soon became clear that my dad wasn't questioning my role as
her mother; he was trying to tell me that I was not alone – that the

weight of her being 'mine' was a heavy one to carry when there were so many people willing to help and support me. (You probably have the same – try the safe space bubble exercise on p. 55.) To this day, I don't think my dad realised that he gave me exactly what I needed – he gave me permission. Permission to accept help and support and to parent my child in my way – but not alone. Yes, ultimately, Ihsan *was* mine, and the final decisions about her care were mine to make, but it was important for me to see, and acknowledge, that I could accept help along the way.

You can, too. And what an absolute joy that is.

# part 2

# empowering your pregnancy, labour and birth

# 7
# trauma-proofing your pregnancy and birth

**Upskilling your way to maternity success**

## As I know better, I do better.

We now know that birth trauma is relatively common, and that birth debriefing is one tool that can help in the recovery process. But what about prevention? Is there anything we can do to reduce the likelihood of trauma occurring in the first place? You may already be aware of the physical preparations you can make to maximise your chances of a healthy baby and a straightforward birth: proper antenatal care, learning birthing techniques such as hypnobirthing, healthy eating, taking prenatal vitamins, exercising regularly, managing stress, getting adequate rest and so on. There are a myriad of excellent books and educational resources that cover these important topics in far more depth than I can go into in this book. But in these next few chapters, I want to highlight a few common themes around interactions with medical staff (these crop up regularly in my debriefing sessions) and suggest some useful tips to help you manage these successfully.

When I hear stories told by women who have been through difficult pregnancy and birth experiences and I ask what felt most traumatic to them, it isn't always the physical pain. They often mention feeling powerless, patronised, unsafe, dismissed, belittled or gaslighted in dealings with their healthcare providers. Sometimes this is due to miscommunication and genuine misunderstandings. Your consultants, obstetricians, midwives and other care providers are human, too: they don't always get it right. For the most part, they are doing their best, and are not setting out to cause trauma and distress. But emotional harm does still happen, and it's never acceptable.

## An empowered pregnancy

I wish I could wave a wand to banish all potential trauma triggers from your life and guarantee you a stress-free pregnancy and perfect labour and birth. Unfortunately, no one can guarantee you that, but I can equip you to take charge of your maternity experience, minimise your risk factors for emotional trauma, and empower you in your experience of pregnancy, labour and birth. Empowerment is all about self-determination and autonomy, confidence and self-advocacy. An empowered pregnancy means educating yourself about your pregnancy, labour and birth, and equipping yourself with a few key skills that will help you take ownership of your body and your choices. It's about knowing your rights and having the confidence to make decisions that work for you and your baby, and communicating your wishes clearly to your birth partner.

While much of antenatal care and preparation is – rightly – focused on the physical health and wellbeing of you and your little one, so many women tell me that during pregnancy and birth they felt as though they had lost their autonomy; were not as prepared as they thought they were (despite attending antenatal appointments); agreed to procedures or interventions they now regret; or wish they had spoken up for themselves more. All these factors contributed to the emotional trauma they later experienced. This suggests to me that there should be a greater emphasis on ensuring that birthing parents are equipped with the knowledge and confidence they need to make informed choices that best serve their interests. So how do we go about this? To start with, why not think about the questions below. Can you answer them all?

- Do you know what informed consent is?

- What would you do or how would you react when a well-meaning relative, work colleague or stranger reaches out to touch your baby bump?

- How would you make your dissatisfaction about your treatment by medical staff known in a calm and assertive manner?

- If things did not go so well in your last pregnancy/ birth, do you know what things you can put in place to help you prepare for a better experience next time?

- Do you know what gaslighting is (see pp. 95-9), and would you know how to respond effectively and appropriately if someone attempted to gaslight you?

- Do you know what emotional safety means? Do you know what you need to feel emotionally safe, and how to communicate your needs to those around you?

**Introducing ... your pregnancy superpowers**

The answers to these questions lie in a couple of key elements: being aware of the things that *could* inflict emotional harm on us if we don't recognise them when they are happening, and equipping ourselves with the right knowledge and skills – such as assertive communication, being able to set boundaries, knowing about informed consent – to help us act effectively when they do. I call these skills your pregnancy superpowers. They are essential skills to have – not just in pregnancy, but for all of life. You may know some of these already, and if you are currently practising these skills then that's great! Keep doing what you're doing and remember to use your superpowers at every stage of your pregnancy and birth, whenever you feel it's appropriate.

This might be the first time you have heard of these skills and behaviours, at least in the context of advocating for yourself. If that's the case, I invite you to read on, and think about where these superpowers might apply throughout your pregnancy, particularly in your dealings with medical staff. Doing this will help you pave your way to an empowered, ideal pregnancy and birth.

Notice I used the word 'ideal', not 'perfect'. There is no such thing as perfect. What we are aiming for here is a pregnancy during which you feel in control of the things you can control, and have a plan for how you will cope with things that are outside your control. An empowered pregnancy paves the way for an empowered labour and birth, which in turn has a positive impact on your postnatal recovery, as well as on how you experience parenthood. An empowered pregnancy supports positive, mutually respectful relationships between you and your healthcare providers with clear, two-way communication and appropriate care. In an empowered pregnancy, everybody wins.

## First things first - mind your mindset!

We've all heard the saying 'where the mind goes, the body follows', and this is true for your pregnancy, labour and birth. I want to look at mindset here because it's an essential part of empowerment and taking ownership of your experiences. Minding your mindset is all about being aware of how your thoughts and beliefs impact your actions and reactions in different situations - particularly stressful ones - and focusing on staying positive, present, calm and adaptable in the face of uncertainty. This helps you conserve your energy for maximum wellness instead of allowing external factors to dictate your inner calm. You can see where I'm going with this. Pregnancy and birth, as we've seen, are unpredictable, and if you allow yourself to unravel at every possible scenario, it will make for a very anxious, stressful pregnancy, and that is not good for you or your baby. Cultivating an empowered mindset is about choosing thoughts and behaviours that support your wellbeing, no matter what is happening around you. Having a positive mindset doesn't mean that nothing will ever go wrong in your life (if only!), but it does mean that when things go wrong, you will feel more in control of how you respond.

### How to do it

Preparing your mindset will look different for everyone, but the goal is the same – to stay present, focused and positive and to reduce any stress or apprehension around birthing day. You may opt to practise mindfulness, positive affirmations, visualisations, pregnancy yoga, deep breathing, birth preparation or a regular spiritual practice such as prayer.

Whatever you choose, cultivating a strong mindset will help you to go through your pregnancy with purpose ('I will remember to take my notes to my next midwife's appointment, and ask about birthing options'), and your labour with lots of self-belief ('I've prepared as best I can for this moment and I can do this!'), adaptability ('Our planned water birth is off the table now? OK, so we'll make an informed choice to birth on the labour ward') and calmness ('Staying calm reduces tension and that's good for me and my baby').

What will that look like for you? It may mean arming yourself with as much knowledge as you can so you understand the changes happening to your body and feel more in control. Or you may want to protect your mind against anything that could cause you alarm or distress. You know yourself best and what is or isn't OK for you.

# debrief deep dive

## REFLECT

Maya Angelou gave us the original quote from which this chapter's epigraph is taken. She said: 'Do the best you can until you know better. Then when you know better, do better.' As you reflect on this chapter, what things come to mind as areas you need to upskill? For example, could you be more assertive? Set better boundaries? Could you learn more about these skills? If you are already skilled in these areas, what else could you do to strengthen your mindset or empower yourself for your maternity journey? Journal your answers and refer back to them often as a reminder to learn about, then practise these skills until they become second nature.

## REFRAME

Affirmations are a great way to help you feel more empowered. Try these:

- I act from a place of mindfulness, strength and calm.

- I do the best I can with the information and resources I have available.

- If the unexpected happens, I face it head-on and adapt.

## REDEFINE

In your journal, list five behaviours or thoughts that support your wellbeing and five that take away from it. What small actions can you take to ensure you practise more of the empowering five, and avoid (or do less of) the second five, which don't serve you so well?

# 8
# superpower #1: assertiveness

**Respectfully demanding respect**

# I communicate clearly, calmly and confidently.

You already know that you'll be in contact with a number of care providers during your pregnancy, birth and in the post-partum period. Each time you meet a new care provider, it is important to have any questions ready to ask – don't leave the appointment until you are satisfied with the answers, or have clear guidance as to where you can get the answers or support you are looking for. This is one time when being able to communicate assertively is really important. Being assertive is about clear, direct and effective communication. It involves calmly, yet firmly, stating your needs without rudeness, aggression or other inappropriate behaviour. Assertive people generally have strong boundaries (see Chapter 9). They do not sulk, manipulate, get pushy, intimidate or use bad language to get what they need. In fact, assertive people are often quietly confident. They are honest and direct: they stand firm in the face of aggressive or pushy behaviour directed towards them, and they don't allow the actions of others to derail them from expressing their needs.

## How we communicate

Everyone has a communication style. We all learn how to communicate in childhood, and this is shaped by the communication dynamic in our family, our personalities, and how easy or difficult it was to get our needs met. Growing up, if you felt you had to fight for everything you needed (for example, food, praise, attention or love) or risk going without, you may have developed a core belief that says 'being timid gets me nowhere. Unless I am loud, forceful and aggressive, no one will hear me. I won't get what I need'. If this is not addressed and corrected, this translates into an overbearing, aggressive communication style. You may shout at, humiliate, or attempt to dominate another person to get your way. The irony is that you may not even realise the connection between your unmet childhood needs and your communication style, because it often *does* get you what you want – but people also experience you as intimidating at best, and a bully at worst.

Or you may have been more passive as a child and felt afraid to ask for what you needed. Perhaps, when you grew up, expressing your emotions freely was discouraged, and being loud and aggressive didn't get you anywhere, so you had to use a different approach. You may have used flattery, sarcasm, sulking or avoidance (silent treatment, anyone?) to avoid having to say what you mean or ask directly for what you need. The problem is, if you didn't ask and the other person couldn't guess what you needed (and why should they? No one is a mind reader), you would still go without and your needs went unmet. Though you might have looked calm and unruffled on the outside, make no mistake – on the inside you'd be raging, just as much as the outwardly hostile and aggressive communicator. This passive-aggressive communication style is frustrating for you, as you are never clear about what you need and never say what's on your mind, so you don't get what you need. The other person may find you hard to read, frustrating and/or dishonest.

Both styles are ineffective ways to ask for what you need. If either of them resonates with you, please do not judge yourself harshly. As a child, you were powerless and these were your coping mechanisms. They are learned behaviours, and today you can learn a new, more effective, direct, honest way to communicate. I consider the art of assertive communication a vital life skill for everyone. An in-depth look at assertiveness is outside the scope of this book, but if you have had difficulties with being assertive in the past, or if it is new to you and feels like the scariest thing ever, there are some excellent books and resources to help you develop this skill (see the Resources). I promise you, with practise, you will get the hang of communicating assertively – and once you do, you will never look back.

## Why assertiveness is a superpower

Assertive people are not only more likely to get their needs met, but they also tend to be less anxious, less prone to depression, and have better relationships.[25] They are also better able to cultivate the empowered mindset we saw In Chapter 7. Of course, assertiveness skills apply to all relationships and communications, but when it comes to communicating with your healthcare providers, this is your number-one superpower. Assertive communication helps to minimise trauma as it helps you feel in control and confident about getting your needs met, no matter who you are communicating with. It helps you assert boundaries (see Chapter 9), stand up for yourself against gaslighting (see Chapter 12), and stops you from being treated inappropriately or unjustly.

### *How to do it*

Imagine you have a pregnancy symptom you are concerned about. Perhaps you had a difficult time in your previous pregnancy and want some reassurance this time round that everything is OK. Here are some examples of questions you may want to ask at an antenatal appointment, and how to ask them in an assertive way.

Instead of:

> (Aggressive): 'So you're saying I'm imagining things? No one listens to me!'

Try:

> (Assertive): 'Can you explain to me what you think my symptom means?'

Instead of:

> (Passive-aggressive): 'I see you're busy - no, really, it's nothing. I'm fine [when you are not really fine]. I'll see you at my next appointment.' [You leave, angry that your issue hasn't been dealt with.]

Try:

> (Assertive): 'This symptom has been an issue for X amount of time: can you tell me what my treatment options are?'

Instead of:

> (Aggressive): 'I looked on Google and I know what I'm talking about! I have condition X. So you need to do your job and treat me for that, or there'll be trouble!'

Try:

> (Assertive): 'I have been doing some research of my own about a particular condition. Can you help me understand this better?'

### Where else can I use assertive communication?

Here are a few scenarios that call for assertive communication, and some more tips that will help to improve your experience, especially if you have had poor or unfair treatment in the past:

- If your concerns have been dismissed by a medical professional and you are still worried, request a second opinion. You are completely within your rights to ask to speak to someone else. Calmly and firmly request it.

- Ensure that you know your body, how it responds, what is and isn't normal for you, and trust that knowledge, so you can stand firm in your convictions about what you need.

- Ensure that every encounter with a medical professional is documented in your handheld notes. If you have requested an examination or a test and it has been declined, make sure that this request and its subsequent refusal have been documented clearly.

- If you feel that you are not being listened to or treated correctly, don't give up. Insist that treatment/investigations continue until you are happy with your diagnosis, care management and treatment options. Do not stop applying pressure until you are satisfied.

- If, despite doing all this, you still are not satisfied with the care you are receiving, change care providers. If you are based in the UK, it is easy to change care provider and you should do this if you feel you will receive better care elsewhere.

The effects of communication and their impact on birth and pregnancy trauma cannot be underestimated. When I think about my own birth trauma and what contributed to it, I always come back to the positive and negative interactions with healthcare professionals, as they played a significant part.

## What I should have said...

We all have examples of communications that did not go as well as we'd hoped. Though we can't go back and change what was said or how we responded, we can use these incidents as teaching moments, to review what happened, how it affected us, and how we might respond if something similar happened again. We can also take action after the fact by speaking honestly about our feelings to the people or organisations concerned, if feasible. Being able to state what you did or didn't like about a situation and request it to be rectified is incredibly empowering, and just what assertive communication is all about.

If you are carrying trauma from past experiences of poor communication, where you did not feel able to be assertive, I encourage you to try some of the journal exercises that follow.

- Write down what was said to you that you found upsetting.

- Write down the answer you would have liked to have given in the moment, but didn't. It's OK if it's not perfectly expressed at this point. No one will see it but you.

- Now turn the answer into a firm, direct response that focuses on how you felt and what you would like to see changed. For example: 'When you directed your answer at my partner after I asked you a question about my birthing options, I felt ignored and insignificant. In future, I would like you to address your answers to me.'

- Speak to the person(s) concerned about what bothered you and (if appropriate) where you felt you could have benefited from more support.

- Work on alleviating any blame or shame you may feel for not standing up for yourself. You did the best you could in the moment.

Remember: you are always worthy of good care, and it's always OK to ask for what you need.

# debrief deep dive

## REFLECT

What is your communication style? Would you consider yourself passive, aggressive, passive-aggressive or assertive? It's possible that in some situations you are passive and in others aggressive, for example. We can all learn to communicate more effectively. Remember, you can't change anyone else – but you can change yourself. If you recognise yourself as aggressive or passive-aggressive and want to become assertive, it will take practise and commitment, but change is totally possible.

## REFRAME

If you can see the value of assertive communication but the thought of talking up (or toning down) your communication style seems overwhelming, start by simply *noticing* when you are either not speaking up for yourself, or when you are, but in a belligerent way. From there, begin speaking up every time your natural inclination is to let something go. I'm not talking about nit picking every time something doesn't go your way, but if it's something that matters to you and you're dismissing it because you don't think you're worthy of having it corrected, speak up. And if you are on the more aggressive side of the spectrum, remember that you can still speak up for yourself, but practise pausing before you speak, and truly listening to the other person's response before answering.

These affirmations will help, especially as they involve 'I' statements, which will make you focus on how *you* feel and how you plan to react:

- I'm in charge of my emotions.

- I choose a calm, but firm response.

- I'm direct and firm, but kind.

## REDEFINE

Always use 'I' statements to convey how *you* feel, not 'you' statements (for example, 'You forgot to do this'). This is about taking ownership of *your* feelings and responses. You may want to rehearse what you're going to say, especially if you know there are particular situations in which you back down and overlook your own needs, or that make you emotional. Above all, don't give up – this is a skill you'll be practising for the rest of your life, so begin now and enjoy the journey. Remember: your needs matter.

# 9
# superpower #2: setting boundaries

**What boundaries are and why you need them**

## My yes means yes and my no means no.

One of the most important things we do as parents is set boundaries, and this work should start during pregnancy, if not before. A boundary is, as subject experts Dr Henry Cloud and Dr John Townsend (2017)[26] note: 'Anything that helps to differentiate you from someone else, or shows where you begin and end.' Boundaries keep you and others safe. If you set boundaries, you are communicating your limits – what is and isn't OK with you. This could mean anything from protecting your personal space and who you allow to touch you (and how) to how you spend your time and energy. Healthcare workers are trained to assert professional boundaries with people under their care at all times – and, in the same way, as recipients of that care, the boundaries we set must also be respected. We all need boundaries; they should be a non-negotiable part of the way you do life.

**Why setting boundaries is a superpower**

Being able to set boundaries is an essential part of protecting your mental health as you parent. Clear boundaries might mean making it plain to friends that you won't be providing daily updates on whether you've given birth yet, or advising family that you won't be seeing visitors in the first week after you bring your baby home. This kind of behaviour is empowering because it gives you a sense of responsibility, maturity and independence. That means you take responsibility for your emotions, including your happiness, and allow others to be responsible for theirs. During pregnancy, asserting boundaries early on is key to protecting your health, space and energy. Having poor or non-existent boundaries can have a negative impact on your wellbeing. You don't need to wait until your baby is born to start setting, and enforcing, boundaries, as that may feel overwhelming and stressful. So if you are not already setting healthy boundaries, start today.

*How to do it*

We can set boundaries for anything we like. For example:

- 'I'd love you to come and see the baby, but I won't be receiving visitors until he's x weeks old. Can we set a date then?'

- 'I'd prefer to see a female ob-gyn please.'

- 'I'd prefer not to discuss that right now. I'll let you know if that changes.'

**Boundaries and birth stories**

A clear example of what setting boundaries can look like concerns how and when to share a birth story - or not![27] When I was pregnant, I read and listened to lots of scary birth stories. I witnessed a lot of them too, but because I also had knowledge and clinical experience, it all seemed normal to me. I would even say that they didn't scare me any more. My sister was also pregnant. One day, during a conversation about one of my shifts where we'd had to resuscitate a newborn, she said: 'Do you mind not sharing any more? I am sensitive to this kind of thing because of my pregnancy. Would you mind not talking about it?'

My first reaction was frustration, as I wanted to share my difficult day at work, but I had to recognise that she was setting a boundary for herself and that I had to respect it. That interaction taught me that what felt normal to me, because of my work, didn't feel normal for everyone else. Everyone can decide how much information they wish to consume and digest, and that will be different for different people.

This extends to conversations with healthcare providers, too. Pregnant women and their partners all want different amounts of information about pregnancy and birth, which makes it difficult to teach antenatal classes. Giving too much information might feel overwhelming; too little, and you might feel inadequately prepared for the reality of childbirth and the post-partum period. Through conversations with friends and clients, I have found that inadequate preparation leaves people feeling angry, frustrated and let down by the people who were supposed to be supporting them. If you are attending antenatal classes, let your teacher know how much you want to know, ask the questions you need to, do your own research, and make your boundaries clear, so that your educator can help to prepare you in the way you wish to be prepared.

## Don't touch my bump!

Another good example of boundary-setting concerns whether or not you allow people to touch your pregnant belly. Have you noticed that some people feel that you become public property when you're pregnant, and they feel they have the right to touch you, often without warning and uninvited? I know, I know – they are just showing their excitement about the baby, it's harmless, yada yada yada …
Er, no. It's not OK.

If this is something you, as the expectant mum, are not comfortable with, it is super-important to set this boundary early, firmly and repeatedly, if you have to. I know it's easier said than done (we're back to that British thing of being overly polite again, aren't we?). I know that setting this boundary can feel difficult, especially with friends and family members. My family background champions firm boundaries, and I admit I find this superpower pretty easy to use. But if you don't, here are a few phrases you could practise beforehand, so that the words are ready on your tongue when the moment arises.

If someone touches your bump, you could say:

- 'I do not like to be touched. During my pregnancy, I only want these people [*insert names*] to touch my bump/I don't want anyone to touch my bump.'

- 'I'm not comfortable with you touching my stomach, but I'm more than happy to talk to you about my pregnancy, if you have any questions.'

- 'I'm glad you're pleased for me. I'm excited too, but I'd appreciate it if you did not touch my stomach. Thank you for respecting my space.'

You can reword these examples to something that feels natural to you. Write them down if you have to and practise them until you feel comfortable saying them. And don't be put off if you are met with pained looks or offended relatives. When you start laying down boundaries when you haven't before, you will upset and offend a few people. But here's the thing: you will have to be prepared to sit with some uncomfortable feelings as you flex this superpower. Not everyone will like the fact that you now have boundaries, when before they had access to you whenever they liked. Stick to your guns. Remember, it's your body, and you have the right to assert your boundaries as often as you see fit.

## Enforcing boundaries with loved ones

Firm boundaries will help you to be able to advocate for yourself and your children – for anyone in your care, in fact. And though there are barriers to setting boundaries in some cultures, such as those where the child's grandmother has a dominant matriarchal role, this doesn't mean that setting boundaries is any less necessary. If a loved one, such as a parent, sibling or other family member is crossing your boundaries, it's important that you find a way to speak about it in a productive manner. This could mean sitting down with them and telling them why you have set this boundary, and explaining how it makes you feel when the boundary is crossed. Another option is writing it down for them if you really can't manage a face-to-face conversation, but this is best avoided if there is even the slightest chance of a misunderstanding occurring. Gently, kindly and firmly in a one-to-one conversation is best if possible. Sometimes, however, your wishes won't be received well, no matter how you phrase them. It's not always enough in these cases to simply set the boundary. Sometimes, after you've expressed your wishes, you'll get pushback and resistance, so you'll have to enforce the boundaries you set, using assertive communication and, if you have to, a consequence you'll follow through on if your boundary isn't respected. If necessary, you can create a physical boundary, by not engaging with that person if they are insistent on breaching your boundaries. This might mean only visiting them when you want to, or not inviting them into your safe space unless you truly want them there.

Does that sound harsh? It probably does, if you have had poor or non-existent boundaries in your life so far. But it isn't really. During your pregnancy, birth and postnatal recovery, you should focus on what *you* need for your wellbeing. Doing this is not selfish.

## Picking your battles

When it comes to boundaries and harmonious relationships, 'pick your battles' is great advice. It's up to you to decide which boundaries you want to relax a little and which are non-negotiable. You will be the one having to deal with having your boundaries violated, while those who cross them are none the wiser and will continue to do it. It's important to recognise that how you feel takes precedence. For example, perhaps you can compromise on Grandma dropping round unannounced on weekends when things are more relaxed, but not during the week, when you are trying to establish a routine, or you need your rest. Make sure you also have these conversations with your partner: being on the same page means you can better support each other. When you feel unsupported about the boundaries you are setting, it can make you even more reluctant to assert them. Knowing that you have support will encourage you to stand firm.

Boundary-setting may seem overwhelming but, as you get into the habit, it gradually gets easier to do. Remember, it doesn't matter what your boundaries are; you do not owe anyone an explanation or a justification for why they are what they are. If the boundary matters to you, then that's all that matters.

# debrief deep dive

## REFLECT

Boundary-setting is healthy, and don't allow anyone to convince you otherwise. Just like the assertiveness skills I hope you are actively practising, it takes commitment and consistency, and you will continue to practise boundary-setting throughout your life.

## REFRAME

Affirmations are excellent reminders to honour yourself and others by setting boundaries:

- I am responsible for what I allow into my life.

- I love and respect myself enough to set firm boundaries.

- I respect the boundaries of others.

## REDEFINE

I invite you to use the space below to consider what your boundaries are and how you will begin to assert them if you haven't already.

_____

_____

the birth debrief

# 10

# superpower #3: consent

**Respecting your choices**

# I can say no.

Consent – your legal and ethical right to agree to or decline medical treatment of any kind – is a fundamental principle that should be at the forefront of all care, especially maternity care. Unfortunately, I have encountered a lot of misunderstanding over what consent means. So let's dispel some of the myths around it right away.

**Consent in maternity – as simple as saying yes or no?**

In basic terms, consent is giving explicit permission before anything is done to your person. In healthcare, consent must be gained *before* a procedure is carried out, not during or after the process, unless the context is life-or-death. For example, a care provider is taking a blood sample. While they are taking the sample, they realise that they need to take another sample. When they realise this, they must ask you, the patient, if it is OK to take more blood, and explain what the additional sample is for before continuing. The care provider's explanation of the additional sample feeds into the second part of consent. Consent means more than a simple yes or no: it must be *informed* consent, which means that medical staff must explain the proposed treatment to you, and you must have a clear understanding of what you are consenting to.

## Why consent is a superpower

Like assertiveness and boundaries, consent is about personal autonomy and your right to make your own choices about your body and your person. Without the power of consent, you are at the mercy of other people to make decisions for you – and that is the polar opposite of being, and feeling, empowered. Flexing this superpower protects you from being pressurised or coerced into procedures of any kind, either because you don't have the facts you need to make an informed, free choice, or because you are not comfortable with the procedure being recommended. Your right to consent gives you agency over the medical interventions that are (or are not) carried out on your body.

## What consent isn't

Consent is not consent if you are not actually being given a choice. It's not true consent if you don't have an option to say no. Consent is vital. I'll say that again: Consent. Is. Vital. Pregnancy, birth and the postnatal period may be the first time many people have to interact with medical and healthcare professionals in such close proximity. When you are the layperson amid qualified professionals, it can feel intimidating. Sometimes it can feel that you have no choice but to say yes to what is being offered to you, especially if it is sprung on you at the last minute, or you feel you have to make a snap decision, but that is never the case. Though medical professionals are there to advise you on the best course of action for you and your baby – and, for the most part, are on your side – *you* are the one with the power to make the final decision about your body and your care. No one, however well-meaning, has the right to pressurise, bully or coerce you into agreeing to treatment of any kind. You always have a choice, and if you are not given a choice, then there can be no consent.

Let's check in for a moment. It's a big deal, isn't it? The idea of declining or going against medical advice can seem overwhelming and scary because so much around maternity care feels so emotive and 'risk-associated'. But that is precisely why it's crucial that you know all your options and all the risks that are relevant to your situation so you are able to give informed consent. Yes, medical staff are busy and overworked and they may not always have the capacity to address every one of your concerns over a proposed medical intervention. And in an emergency, there may not always be time to do so. But you still have the right to ask as many questions as you need to in order to make an informed decision about your care.

**Knowing your rights and trusting yourself**

Being well informed is important, but so are assertiveness and having boundaries. If you are not used to questioning authority figures, doing so - perhaps for the first time - will feel uncomfortable. However, stating your wishes calmly and assertively keeps the power where it belongs - with you - and helps you to be an active participant in deciding on the care that is right for you. This takes lots of practise, reminders and reinforcements. It also takes trust - in your care providers, but also in yourself, to make the best decisions you can with the information you have available. Use your antenatal appointments to ask as many questions as you want to. I don't mean that you should scare yourself silly with scenarios that are highly unlikely, but you should talk to your care provider and your birth partner about the interventions you want and those you really don't want unless in an emergency. We'll cover this in more detail in the birth planning chapter (see p. 114). Some people need a lot of information before they make a decision, while others are happy to leave it to the professionals. Inform yourself as much as you need to, surround yourself with people you trust, hear their advice, and know that you will be equipped to say yes or no to the right things at the right times.

**Consent and trauma***

I've already spoken about the importance of an equal relationship between medical staff and expectant mothers. When this relationship

---

* Trigger warning: obstetric violence.

is not equal, it can be a very difficult and sometimes traumatic experience for the birthing person. At the extreme end, it could mean obstetric violence.

Obstetric violence means any act or failure to act by health personnel that results in physical or psychological harm to a woman during pregnancy, birth and the six weeks following birth (puerperium), such as a lack of access to reproductive health services, cruel, inhumane or degrading treatment, or under or over-medication, all of which undermine a woman's ability to make free and informed decisions over her reproductive processes. I know it's shocking, but I have spoken to women who have described their birth experience as an assault. This may seem like an exaggeration to some, but these women were told they couldn't move around in labour, or were ordered to lie down with their legs open, their feet in stirrups, so they could be examined internally, despite their protestations, while being told that this was the only way in which they could have certain treatments or support. There is no place for obstetric violence in modern-day birthing spaces. You have the right to bodily autonomy. Remember:

- You must give consent.

- Consent must be informed.

- You can withdraw consent at any time.

> I wish I'd known about withdrawing consent earlier. I had a bad feeling about the doctor who treated me as soon as he informed me he was going to examine me internally, and then casually mentioned 'Oh, and I've brought along a student doctor - OK?' It didn't feel like a request; it was more of a statement, so it didn't occur to me to say no. I didn't want to be gawped at by a student when I was already feeling vulnerable, and it didn't help that [the doctor] was not gentle at all during the exam and pinched me with the speculum. At the time, I gritted my teeth to get through it, but it bothered me afterwards.

> I always request female doctors now and no students, unless I feel comfortable.
>
> – Helen

As medical professionals, we may feel that we need to be firm and clinical in our approach to get a procedure done efficiently, but we must never forget that the people in our care are individuals who trust us to treat them with respect, dignity, sensitivity and care. And as the person receiving that care, you must remember that you always have a choice when it comes to your maternity care. You can say yes, and you can say no.

## Capacity to consent

In the UK, if you are aged 16[28] or over, you are legally presumed to have the mental capacity to consent, unless it can be proven otherwise. On rare occasions, the capacity to consent might be impaired, and on such occasions (for example, in an emergency, when the person has lost consciousness), healthcare providers may then decide to carry out treatment in the person's best interests without obtaining prior consent. The criteria for assessing capacity are strict, however, and are governed by law.[29]

# debrief deep dive

## REFLECT

It can be difficult to know when coercion or undue pressure is taking place. Often our bodies will send us clues even before our minds realise what is happening. We may feel that something is not right, we may feel uneasy; we might falter or stutter in our answers to the person putting undue pressure on us. Have you ever felt anything like this? What was the situation?

_____

_____

_____

_____

_____

_____

_____

_____

_____

_____

_____

## REFRAME

Affirmations are great ways to remind yourself of your bodily autonomy and help you express this to others. Here are some that will serve as gentle reminders at times when you have to give or not give consent:

- Nothing happens to my body unless I want it to.

- I have the right to be fully informed before I give consent.

- I can withdraw my consent at any time, and ask for more information.

## REDEFINE

In the situation you described in the Reflect section above, did you recognise what was happening and/or give in to the pressure? If you regret this, forgive yourself. You did the best you could at the time, and you are now learning new tools that will give you a different outcome next time.

If a similar situation arises again, what will you do differently? Write about this in your journal or share it with a trusted and supportive person. Remember, you always have choices when it comes to your maternity care. Consent is your superpower: you can say yes and you can say no.

# 11
# bonus superpower: intuition

**The importance of listening to your gut**

# I honour my inner wisdom.

We all like a bonus, don't we? So here's one more superpower, and it's an important one – intuition. I think it's one of the best tools we have. It's like a hidden piece of equipment that sits and waits patiently for us to use it, but the fact that it's hidden means that we often ignore it. There is so much noise around – so many opinions, choices to make and voices competing for our attention, telling us what is right for us – that if we are not careful, these voices will crowd out our own opinions, gradually silence our intuition and bury it. This is particularly common when it comes to pregnancy and childbirth. I hear a version of 'my intuition was telling me...' or 'I should have listened to my intuition' in almost every debrief I conduct, which shows you how vital it is in your 'pregnancy empowerment' toolkit. Intuition, if not used, gets rusty, like an old bicycle left in the shed: when you go to take it out again, it's squeaky, the wheels are stiff, and the bike is difficult to ride. As the saying goes, 'use it or lose it' – but if you are not tuned in to your intuition, relying on it might not feel easy.

## Your gut feeling

So, what is intuition exactly? It's described as a 'gut feeling', an internal guide that is there to warn you that there could be a problem or that something - or someone - could be good or bad for you. It doesn't require logic or explanation, which is why we may be reluctant to listen to it. We like things to be orderly, to have reason, to make sense. It's also much easier to explain ourselves and our decisions to others when we can show logic and reasoning. Intuition can sound a bit mystical and woo-woo, and that can make us feel even more uncomfortable using it.

We have been conditioned not to pay too much attention to our intuition. Instead we're told to listen to advice from professionals, to google things and read books and rely on scientific facts. There's nothing wrong with any of that - but holding space for women as they express their disappointment at having not listened to their intuition, particularly when things have gone wrong, has shown me how we neglect this superpower. These women are often left blaming themselves, and would be the first to say that it's important to pay attention to your gut feeling. I don't think you need to be led solely by intuition or scientific fact. You can (and should) read books, seek professional advice and carry out research - but also pay attention to the clues your intuition is giving you.

## Why intuition is a superpower

Your intuition is like an inner protector - your personal, instinctive, helpful inner guide to the choices that feel right for *you*. Intuitive people are connected to their inner selves and know what will and will not serve them. It doesn't mean they never use their head. Rather, they notice the clues their body is sending them about the right course of action to take in any given moment, and they listen to those clues, as Rochelle did (below):

*I'd been examined and told I was only 4cm dilated and so I should expect to be in labour for several more hours. As my contractions were pretty irregular at that point, the midwife told us to go home and come back when my labour was more established and [the contractions] were more regular and 5 minutes apart. So we left the ward and made our way downstairs to the hospital entrance. When we reached the reception area, something - it was like this inner knowing that if we left the hospital, we wouldn't make it back before the baby came - compelled me to turn around and go back up to the labour ward. I told my husband we needed to go back upstairs, and he said, 'Are you sure?' I insisted I was. Well, thank goodness he listened to me, because as soon as the lift doors opened, my waters broke and my contractions ramped up immediately. I had to be helped to a bed as I couldn't walk - the pain was that intense. My son Troy arrived 40 minutes later.*

*– Rochelle*

### How to do it

So how do we tap into those inner clues? The first thing to do is ask yourself a series of questions around the issue you need guidance on. Let's say you go to your antenatal appointment and the nurse practitioner suggests carrying out a few tests (such as blood tests or further investigations), to check how the baby is developing. Some of the tests might be necessary, while others may feel invasive, and you're unsure if they are worth the risk. If you are attuned to your intuition, you might feel physical sensations such as the hairs at the back of your neck prickling or suddenly feeling your heart race. Some people even report hearing a 'warning voice'. If you are not so attuned, don't worry – you can learn to be, because everyone has intuition. You might just need some time and space to tap into your inner wisdom, and that's where the series of questions comes in. A great way of focusing on these questions is to close your eyes and calm your thoughts. Ideally, you'd do this lying down or sitting in a chair, at a time when you are not distracted. It need not take long, and you can revisit it numerous times, but try to focus as you ask yourself:

- What do I want?

- How does this feel?

- Does this feel like the best thing for me/my child?

- What will happen if I don't do it?

Then listen out for any impressions or sensations you get as a result. What are they saying? Do you feel drawn to a particular course of action? Why, or why not? Use your answers as prompts to ask more questions of the healthcare provider if you need to. You may choose to wait until you have more information before consenting to the procedures on offer, or to go ahead, if you feel comfortable doing so.

This may feel strange at first, but stick with it. You will soon get into the habit of listening to your intuition, and you will wonder how you ever managed without it.

### Does using intuition require planning?

Sometimes your intuition might prompt you to do something that requires a plan - it might tell you to book something in advance or go and see someone at a certain time, for example - but intuition can also be spontaneous. For example, you may have an idea that seems to randomly enter your mind. Pay attention to it and see how your body responds to the idea. Does it feel relaxed? Does it feel safe and positive? If so, go with it.

### *Don't be hasty!*

There are very few decisions in life about which you can't stop and think about them for at least a few minutes. When you have to make a decision, no matter how big or small, pause for a minute. If it is someone else asking you to make a decision, such as a doctor or medical professional, ask them for some time to think. Use that time to lean into your intuition, to check and see what it is telling you, then use it to guide your decision-making. Ask more questions if you feel the need to. Whatever decision you make, you want to feel that you made it because you felt it was the best thing to do, not because you were pressured or forced into doing it.

If you feel you went against your intuition and you are beating yourself up about it, it's not all over. Your intuition hasn't expired; you will have many opportunities to use it.

*Stop and really listen*

There will be many times when you get so caught up in your day that you don't actually hear your intuition. It's not always an internal alarm or a loud horn; it's often more of a whisper. Don't wait for it to shout at you and tell you to stop or go: pay attention. After a while it will become second nature and you will no longer need to focus so much.

# debrief deep dive

## REFLECT

How attuned are you to your intuition? Has it helped you in the past in ways you cannot give a logical explanation for? List some of them in the space below, or in your journal, as reminders that you can trust your intuition. If you don't feel attuned and would like to be, what barriers are stopping you from trusting that 'inner voice'? How might that change if you knew, without a doubt, that your intuition was there to help you? Might you be open to looking into this further?

_____

_____

_____

_____

## REFRAME

Developing your intuition is really about paying attention. When you get that niggly feeling that something isn't right, or that you should or shouldn't do something, it's easy to doubt that voice, or to put too much stock in it and ignore the science and sound advice from professionals. Of course, we need balance, so think of your intuition as a signal that you may need to stop, slow down, speed up, ask for more information, or investigate something further. You can also use the following affirmations to remind yourself of your agency:

- I am open to hearing my inner wisdom.

- I listen to sound advice, including my inner wisdom.

- As I give myself space and quiet, the answers I need come to me.

## REDEFINE

Assertiveness, boundaries, giving and withholding consent and using your intuition are just a few key skills that you can adopt as your pregnancy superpowers. You may be able to think of plenty more that will help you. I have left some space below for you to write them down, and I hope you will go on to journal the ways you will practise them – not just during your pregnancy and birth, but throughout your life. Go, Superwoman!

# 12
# gaslighting in maternity

**When abuse of power isn't 'all in your mind'**

I know who I am
and what I feel.
My feelings are valid.

Gaslighting means 'psychological manipulation of a person ... that causes the victim to question the validity of their own thoughts, perception of reality, or memories'.[30] A victim of gaslighting typically experiences confusion, loss of confidence and self-esteem. They might have difficulty making decisions or expressing their own opinions, and may constantly second-guess themselves. Gaslighting takes its name from the 1944 film *Gaslight*, in which a greedy, manipulative man tries to convince his wife that she is going insane by (among other things) turning down the gas lamps in their home and telling her, when she comments on the flickering lights, that she is imagining things. By manipulating his wife to doubt her reality, he hopes to have her committed to an asylum so he can steal her inheritance. Gaslighting can occur in any relationship where there is an imbalance of power, and unfortunately, this can extend to the relationship between an expectant mother and those entrusted with her medical care.

One US study[31] on the prevalence of gaslighting in obstetric care identified the incidences of this form of abuse - because it *is* abuse - as falling into one or more of four categories. It involved healthcare providers belittling, minimising or denying the mothers' humanity, calling their judgement into question, refusing to validate their knowledge, and dismissing or minimising their feelings. What does this look like in practice? Some examples include:

- Undermining your perception of your symptoms.

- Mocking your perception of events or of medical decisions you have made.

- Dismissing your concerns, or suggesting you are emotionally unstable for raising concerns.

- Preventing or dissuading you from seeking further help.

- Refusing to recommend/prescribe any tests or investigations without a valid reason for refusing.

The doctor-patient relationship is *not* supposed to be authoritarian or dictatorial in nature; it is a *consensual* relationship based on trust, understanding, knowledge, and working together. So how does gaslighting rear its head in maternity care?

## How it happens

When you are pregnant, it can literally feel like you're handing your body over to others. It's as if, suddenly, your ability to reason and speak up for yourself count for nothing. When you are pregnant, you may have many meetings and appointments with healthcare professionals, and it can seem as though a barrage of experts and others are telling you what to do or making decisions for you, leaving you a passive bystander in your own life. One reason this happens is that in the West, we generally view childbirth as a medical event that requires intervention, so we tend to treat pregnant women and birthing people like patients who are unwell. This idea encourages many of us to doubt our own agency and to think we need to be told what to do with our bodies and our babies. This creates fertile ground where gaslighting can thrive.

It is important to note that women have been carrying and birthing babies for millennia. When pregnancy is low-risk and we are successfully carrying our babies, we should be supported to feel empowered by this strength rather than feeling we can *only* birth when we are reliant on a medical system. So why do we shrink away from our inner strength and wisdom at a time when we should feel at our most powerful?

Please understand that I am certainly not anti-medicine or anti-science. It would be wrong and irresponsible of me to ignore the many times when medical intervention and guidance are not only necessary but are lifesaving. There is no doubt that Western medicine has an important role to play in maternity care – when it is used correctly, consensually and in a *necessary* capacity.

But we also need to acknowledge that this medicalised way of managing birth has led to many women feeling like they don't have a say in what happens to them. We take it as gospel, practically from our first doctor's appointment, that we know nothing, the medical professionals know everything, and they, not we, should have the final say on what happens to our bodies. But this couldn't be further from the truth. Doctors are there to help and advise, but they are not the ultimate authority over your and your child's wellbeing – you are (unless there are concerns in regard to capacity to consent, which we covered in Chapter 10). This is why I continue to advocate for all women and birthing people everywhere to feel empowered in pregnancy.

## Gaslighting and defensive practice

Defensive practice may make some people who raise questions about their care in NHS debriefing sessions vulnerable to being gaslighted. Defensive practice is when medical staff deviate from sound practice 'primarily to reduce one's risk of liability rather than to benefit the patient'.[32] In such cases, concerns reported by the person receiving the debrief may be dismissed as 'normal practice' or met with a response such as 'No, I'm sure that's not what actually happened'. Staff may make an attempt to normalise things that they know are not actually normal or commonplace.

All sorts of high- and low-risk variables are at play during a medicalised birth, and sometimes – whether because of negligence, or despite everyone's best efforts – things go wrong and complaints are made. I can definitely empathise with feeling defensive when your practice is called into question – no one likes to be criticised or have their level of care disputed. But if defensive practice is allowed to influence a person's medical care, especially when they were harmed, it may mean that they are denied the space and time to process their experience during the birth debrief, causing them further harm.

## Gaslighting and gender bias

The number of women and birthing people who report being gaslighted when dealing with healthcare professionals is significantly higher than the number of men who report the same issue. This is often because of biases about women's ability to understand their own pain – this is reported anecdotally and backed by research. Women's pain has historically been believed to be influenced by their emotions. Despite advances in medicine, these stereotypes still exist and continue to influence the care that women and birthing people receive. Being gaslighted in maternity makes you question yourself, your sanity and your knowledge of your own body – the opposite of what you should be doing. A victim of gaslighting may find it difficult to reach out for help when they most need it, which can lay the foundation for a traumatic birth.

## My story

I was gaslighted a surprisingly high number of times throughout my first pregnancy, and it contributed to my birth trauma. At the time, I was so angry. Even with all my knowledge and professional experience, I felt undermined and ridiculed. Even though I was a qualified midwife, the gaslighting led me to doubt myself, my knowledge and my abilities –

and in one instance to question the legitimate, informed choice that I'd made to have a home birth, not because I no longer wanted it, but because I suddenly felt silly for having made the choice. It also made me question whether I was putting my child's life at risk.

From many conversations with other women and birthing people, I know that I am not alone in this. We are so conditioned to be submissive when it comes to interactions with healthcare professionals that even during birth – a time when we should be listening to our bodies – we often make choices that are detrimental to us, but which mean we avoid going against 'authority'. Again, this isn't about discounting the expertise of medical professionals, or their advice. It's about ensuring that your concerns and requests are taken seriously and you are treated with the respect and dignity you deserve as a human being. By all means, do all you can to educate yourself about what is happening in your body as your pregnancy advances – and, yes, respect the expertise of your doctor and midwife. But if something is important to you, you are not 'silly' or 'overreacting' if you have questions about it and seek to be heard, respected and understood. Gaslighting is never OK. I've shared my experience in the hope that you will see how easily gaslighting can happen when you are pregnant, how to recognise if it happens to you, and how to prevent it and/or halt it in its tracks.

# debrief deep dive

## REFLECT

Have you ever been gaslighted? Most, if not all, of us have at some point. This chapter is about being aware that gaslighting happens, and recognising it (and believing yourself) when you perceive it is happening. Gaslighting is never your fault; it is always based on abuse of power.

## REFRAME

To strengthen your mindset around this, try these affirmations:

- I know my own mind and I trust myself.

- I am worthy of respect and care.

- I am strong and capable, and can make my own decisions.

## REDEFINE

Recognising when gaslighting is happening is one thing; taking steps to call it out and get your needs met is another. Here are a few suggestions for what to do if you feel like you have been gaslighted over symptoms you have reported, which you don't think are being taken seriously:

- Check in with your body. Are the symptoms persisting? If so, note them down.

- Are you satisfied that everything is OK? If not, speak up, using the assertive communication skills outlined on pp. 71-2.

- Ensure that the conversation and action plan have been documented. If the medical professional has declined to do tests or investigations, ask that their decision be documented, along with their reason for declining them.

- Ask to see another medical professional for a second opinion.

Continue to remind yourself that you have the right to be heard. Your thoughts, feelings and instincts are always valid.

# When you don't feel safe

Modern-day birth is becoming more and more monitored, and this can lead women and birthing people to feel exposed, fearful and emotionally unsafe. As we saw in Chapter 5, a lack of emotional safety can cause trauma. The medical staff assigned to care for you during pregnancy and beyond should do all they can to establish and maintain a trusting relationship with you, but this doesn't always happen. What should you do if you feel emotionally unsafe during labour and delivery?

## What is emotional safety?

Emotional safety means feeling grounded, secure and able to express yourself and be vulnerable without fear of judgement, ridicule or harm. When you feel emotionally safe you feel seen, comfortable and free to be yourself. The environment you are in feels welcoming and/or suitable for your needs and you feel encouraged and supported by the people around you.

Things that can make you feel unsafe emotionally include:

- Having your confidence in your decisions undermined.

- Feeling belittled, judged or ridiculed.

- Feeling invisible – as though you are a 'case' or another number on someone's list rather than a human being with a unique set of needs.

- Having someone intrude in your personal space, either by standing too close, staring at you or using intimidating body language (eye rolling, sighing, turning away from you while you are speaking, etc.).

When you feel unsafe, all your emotional energy is diverted from the task at hand and moves towards protecting yourself. You go into survival mode (everything opposite to your empowered mindset, in fact). You may feel anxious, defensive, irritable and stressed. It doesn't take a rocket scientist to deduce that this state is not good for you during pregnancy or labour and birth. So how can you turn this around?

The good news is that your pregnancy superpowers can work to supercharge you into a place of personal safety. Setting and enforcing healthy boundaries, assertively communicating your needs, consenting only to what you feel comfortable with, and using your intuition to help you tune in to how you're feeling and what's best for you will help you take charge of your experiences and give you a sense of safety. You could also change your environment, or request to do so. And you can also request a change of staff if an individual caring for you is making you feel unsafe.

When I think back to moments when I have felt unsafe, I know that I always had the power to speak up – I just didn't know it then. If the same situations happened today, I would speak up and express how I was feeling straight away, even if the person I felt unsafe around was medical staff. You can do the same – you are worthy of being supported by someone who makes you feel understood, safe and heard. This person is caring for you at one of the most vulnerable times in your life, and you need to feel that they are working with you, not against you. You need to be able to say what you need to, behave in the way that you want, and be respected in the way you deserve.

# 13
# why language matters

**How words hurt or heal in maternity**

I speak to be understood, as I listen to understand.

When I started training as a midwife, the importance of effective communication was instilled into us daily. Regardless of the situation facing us, we were taught that good communication was imperative. It was a tool that could help avoid conflict, support women, birthing people and their families, and create an optimum environment in which to work and/or give birth. I have been on the receiving end of both good and bad communication and have also seen the impact of each on women and birthing people. In my experience, good communication leads to positive birthing experiences and is an essential part of good maternity care.

Assertiveness and boundaries are two key aspects of good communication, of course. Another is language – the words and expressions we use when we communicate with others (and ourselves). But why does language matter? Our words are powerful: they affect our emotions and wellbeing and can impact others, for better or worse, regardless of our intentions. This is especially true during the vulnerable time of pregnancy and birth. Well-chosen words used by professionals – but also by friends, family and others – can be the difference between feeling understood, supported and safe, and (when poorly chosen words are used) feeling judged, confused or isolated. So it's crucial that we use language mindfully, whether verbally or in written form. Poor use of language in this context includes abusive, contentious or inflammatory language, but also careless, judgemental or thoughtless remarks. These should never find their way into any maternity space, but this does happen, unfortunately.

## Shaming language

I'm going to use one personal example to highlight how bad communication can change someone's experience of maternity care. Full disclosure: I am a woman with raised BMI (Body Mass Index).[33] That means my weight falls outside the recommended 'healthy' BMI range of 18.5 to 24.9. I am also a Black woman, meaning that my identity intersects with two groups likely to be discriminated against in pregnancy.

During my first pregnancy I received an automatically generated letter advising me that my 'raised' BMI increased the likelihood of complications for both me and my baby during pregnancy, labour and birth.[34] I remember feeling chastised, as if the letter had said, 'Dear Illy, this is the fat-shaming police and we're here to inform you that you'd better not gain any more weight, or else...' OK, so it didn't *actually* say that, but it may as well have. I felt ashamed. I can laugh about it today, but at the time I didn't find it funny at all. I was mortified. For the first time in my life, I felt self-conscious that my weight might be a problem, and I would be forced to explain myself like a naughty child who'd been caught with her hand in the biscuit tin.

This highlights two important aspects of effective communication: awareness of the other person as an individual, not a 'case number', and awareness of any physical and/or cultural factors that might affect how they present medically.

In my case, I was (and am) healthy and fit, so my raised BMI as a Black woman with a high muscle-to-fat ratio[35] should have been taken into account before the letter was sent out, but it was not. And the cold, impersonal tone of the letter made me feel judged in the way that a face-to-face conversation might not have done. I know that the resources are not always there to enable face-to-face appointments to happen, so I get it – my point is that communication should be individualised, particularly during pregnancy and birth.

**Fat phobia**

As we're on the subject, I'm going to add a little more here about fat phobia in maternity care. First and foremost: weight is not always a true indicator of your overall health (and this is true whether you have a low or a high BMI).

I'm not endorsing unhealthy weight gain in pregnancy, as it does carry risks, but I am here to tell you that you do not have to disclose your weight to anyone, even if you are requested to do so. If you are worried about your nutrition and activity levels and need support while you are pregnant, your GP or midwife should be able to refer you to a nutritionist, dietician or health coach who can advise you.[36]

## So what does 'good' communication involve?

Now we know how important the appropriate mode of delivery (e.g. in-person conversation, phone/Zoom call, letter, email or text, etc.) is to effective communication, what else should we consider? Among other things, effective communication includes:

- Clear, direct and honest delivery of facts and information.

- Being listened to without judgement and feeling heard and validated.

- Listening, with an intention to understand the other person, not just interject an opinion.

- Using empathy and courtesy.

- Awareness of the use and impact of words used, their delivery and tone.

- Awareness and mindful use of body language.

- Awareness of the other person's personal barriers to comprehension – for example, disabilities, language differences and level of medical knowledge (so you can avoid overly technical/ jargonistic terms).

Using language in an empowered way in these areas is a two-way responsibility: your healthcare provider should be mindful about how they use language with you, as you should be with them. This may mean speaking up (or having an advocate speak up on your behalf) and letting them know of any special concessions you may need to minimise misunderstandings. This could be, for example, if there are language disparities and you are struggling to understand what is being said (and/or struggling to be understood), or if the medical professional's use of complex medical terms feels intimidating. Here are some examples of how you (or your advocate) could do this:

- 'I don't know what you mean by [medical term]. Would you mind explaining it in layperson's language, please?'

- 'English isn't my/my partner's first language. Is an interpreter available?'

- 'I consider phrases like "you people" offensive. Please could you avoid generalisations when addressing me?'

- 'I find I difficult to communicate with you when your back is turned. Would you mind facing me when speaking to me, please?'

## Self-talk

I have included self-talk here because the messages we send ourselves are perhaps the most powerful of all. Positive self-talk has a huge effect on our mindset and, as we've seen, a positive mindset goes hand in hand with an empowered pregnancy and helping you feel in charge of your own experience. The affirmations I've included throughout this book (as well as the ones I've encouraged you to create for yourself) are intended to build a positive self-talk habit. I hope you are using at least some of them daily, as they really do make a difference when practised consistently.

## Language in hypnobirthing

In hypnobirthing training (a pain-management method based around visualisation, relaxation and deep-breathing exercises) we talk a lot about changing the words surrounding birth (which are often synonymous with pain, and can be anxiety-inducing) to words that sound more calming, putting you more in control. For example:

- 'Contraction' becomes 'surge'.

- 'Waters breaking' becomes 'waters releasing'.

- 'Pain' becomes 'pressure'.

I encourage the consistent use of these words when you are talking to yourself during pregnancy and labour, and when others are talking to you and about you. The initial reaction to this suggestion is often laughter, but as time goes on people realise that using these new words actually makes a difference. During pregnancy and childbirth many birth professionals will use language that may not feel appropriate for you or that makes you feel uncomfortable. If this happens, you are free to ask them to alter the language they use, to allow you to have a better experience. You could say something like:

- 'In the birthing room, I'd appreciate it if you could use positive language as I'm trying to minimise any anxious thoughts and feelings about my labour. Here is a list of phrases I'd like you to use.'

- 'I'm sensitive to inflammatory language. Please would you mind saying X instead of Y?'

Here are some terms that are routinely applied to birthing parents, and some alternative terms you can ask for them to be replaced with:

'Geriatric pregnancy' → 'pregnancy 35+'.

'Failure to progress' → 'slow progress'.

'Incompetent cervix' → 'premature cervical dilation'.

'Failed induction' → 'ineffective induction'.

'Foetal distress' → 'heart rate changes'.

Midwives can adopt this as best practice and/or ask the women in their care which terms they prefer. The impact that language has is extremely subjective, but you could think about whether you would prefer other terms to be used in your presence. Remember: if the language being used is affecting your experience, then you can change it because you deserve to have an experience that works for you.

On paper, Barbara's birth experience was wonderful, but she was left feeling confused and distressed by the way she was spoken to by doctors and midwives.

*I went into labour naturally and at home. I was happy, because this was exactly what I wanted. I laboured at home until I was established then went into hospital. When I got to the hospital I was told point-blank: 'There's no space on the midwife-led unit.' This threw me as [being on the midwife-led unit] was what I wanted - I knew that my risk of intervention would increase [on the labour ward], and this filled me with dread.*

*I tried to contest it, but was told that I would have to go to the labour ward. The feeling of being out of control started from those words. I spent my labour on a bed because I needed to be monitored as there were concerns over the baby's heart rate. I never wanted this. Externally, I appeared fine but internally, I felt pure chaos.*

*My son came into the world screaming, but I remember, while feeling excited, I also felt sad and shocked. Everyone around me was celebrating; telling me 'well done' and describing the birth as 'perfect', but I didn't feel it. I wouldn't say I was traumatised, but I was so disappointed. I felt I truly didn't have anywhere to put [those feelings]. Who do I tell when everyone says it was perfect?!*

*What should've been the most exciting day of my life turned out to be one of my most isolating experiences, and despite absolutely loving being a mum I can't help but feel that tinge of sadness.*

*– Barbara, 32, mother of one*

Words have so much power – to wound or to heal, to create anxiety or to alleviate it, to discourage or to encourage. We need to communicate with others and ourselves in a way that builds, reassures and empowers. And if we are on the receiving end of hurtful, misplaced or poor communication, we need to use our communication toolkit and pregnancy superpowers to speak up against it.

# debrief deep dive

## REFLECT

Do you feel that language has been used to empower or disempower you in your maternity experience? You can reflect on this in the context of words spoken to you and words you have spoken to yourself and to others.

Below, I have left some space for you to write down language that bothered you or that you found harmful or unhelpful. You can also list terms that you would prefer to be used.

_____

_____

_____

_____

_____

_____

_____

_____

_____

_____

_____

## REFRAME

When we are upset or unsettled by something someone has said, it's often because of the negativity in the words they used. But we aren't always as mindful when it comes to ourselves. I would like you to begin to think and speak more mindfully, paying attention to the language you use and noticing any effects the words you use have on your emotions (positive or negative). Aim to minimise or eliminate negative words. Use these affirmations to help you:

- My words have power - I choose them well and use them wisely.

- I communicate clearly and concisely.

- I speak up when there is an issue to address.

## REDEFINE

How will you use words differently from now on? Journal your answers.

_____

_____

_____

_____

_____

_____

# 14
# to plan or not to plan?

**Disaster-proofing your birth plan**

I plan ahead for the best outcome. I stay calm and go with the flow when plans change.

One of my favourite parts of midwifery is caring for first-time parents. It's a privilege to be able to walk with them through their excitement as well as their nerves. That doesn't mean that those in subsequent pregnancies don't feel nerves or excitement, but there is a real buzz of anticipation with first-time parents. They have no idea of what's going to happen and a cautious sense of optimism, like first-day-of-school nerves. Some have ideas of their perfect birth and some have detailed birth plans, while others have a vision of the parents they will be - and there is something really lovely about supporting them.

## What is a birth plan?

Your birth plan is a written outline of your wishes for your labour and birth. It can be as simple or as detailed as you like, and it usually includes your preferences for things like where you would like to give birth, the type of delivery you'd prefer, pain relief preferences, and your choice of birth partner. Your birth plan is mainly for you, but it also gives your midwife and your birth partner an idea of what your 'ideal birth' looks like, and how best to advocate for you.

You don't have to have a birth plan – it's not for everyone. And if you do have one, you can change it. You're always in control and it's always your choice. But if you do decide to make one, you might find some of these pointers helpful.

## Be yourself

There are so many labour and birthing options, and the kind of plan you make will be as unique as you are. Love peace and tranquillity? Calming music, gentle voices, soft lighting or candles may feature in your plan. Loud and proud metalhead? Well, rock on you if you plan to welcome your newborn to the sounds of Meat Loaf! Your plan will reflect your personality – if you are super-organised and love a to-do list, you'll take to birth planning. If you are a go-with-the-flow type, maybe not so much. No plan is better or worse than another – it's not an exam and there's no pass or fail here. However you choose to approach it, if you have any thoughts about how you'd like your birth to go, it's good to have something written down somewhere that's easy to access on the big day. Then share it – with your spouse, birth partner, midwife or other birth support. And you might want to make several copies of your plan.

## Be specific

Whether it's detailed or simple, printed out and laminated or typed into the notes app on your phone, your plan should be clear and specific. Think about what you want and what you need your birth partner to know before labour, during labour and delivery, and immediately after delivery. Wondering what kind of things to add? I'm glad you asked!

- **Before labour:** Let's say you go to a hospital antenatal appointment and they decide to admit you that day. Who will you ask to pick up your maternity bag for you if your partner heads straight from work to the hospital to be with you? Where will they pick up your spare keys? Where will they find your bag? What about your medical needs? Do you have any health issues, allergies or other pre-existing conditions your birthing support needs to know about? Are your contact details clear and accurate?

- **During labour:** Think about who you'll want with you, how you'll want to labour (both location and position), and how you want to handle medical interventions and pain relief. As well as the things you want, think about things you'd like to avoid (for example, raised voices in the birthing room).

- **During delivery:** How would you prefer to deliver your baby? Talk through your options with your midwife, and write these down. Even if you are planning a vaginal birth, discuss what will happen in the event of a C-section.

- **After delivery:** Do you want immediate skin-to-skin contact with your baby, or skin-to-skin after baby has been cleaned? Do you want your partner to cut the umbilical cord? Do you want to deliver the placenta naturally, or with medical assistance?[37]

### Be realistic

It's rare to find a midwife or birthing facility that will reject your wishes outright, but you must be realistic in terms of what can be reasonably and safely accommodated. Some things to consider:

- Your birthing history and level of risk (a high-risk pregnancy might preclude a home birth).

- Your hospital or birthing facility's policies (these may have changed post-Covid).

## Be flexible

One thing I always advise is flexibility, because the reality is that most first births don't go to 'plan'. We've already seen (p. 96) that the medicalisation of birth tends to increase the rates of intervention, including induction and caesarean section. Aside from that, there are some things you just cannot predict, including exactly when and where you'll go into labour and how long labour will last.

I speak to many women who are battling with feelings of guilt, shame and self-blame because their birth didn't go to plan – as if it was somehow their fault. But this couldn't be further from the truth. You can plan your birth to within an inch of your life, but that doesn't mean it will go the way you planned.

Subsequent births can be difficult too, particularly when the first birth wasn't as expected, because the woman often feels the desire to get it 'right' this time. You can take the lessons you learned from your first birth – they will be useful to inform a subsequent birth. Remember, though, that every pregnancy, labour and birth is different. Doing your best in the moment is good enough. Being flexible is key.

## So is there any point in having a birth plan?

Absolutely, yes – and here are three reasons why:

- Knowing you have the practicalities in place will help you feel calmer and more in control when birthing day arrives.

- Having a plan helps you and your partner be clear about the kind of birth you want. Sometimes, until we are forced to think about it, we don't know what's important to us. Spending time considering our options then writing our wishes down forces us to discover and lean into what matters to us.

- It helps your advocates. Those in the birthing room with you are there to support you and your needs and wishes. Creating and then discussing your birth preferences with your birth partner helps them to know what you want, what is and isn't important to you, and to do everything they can to ensure you get the things you want.

So read widely, learn about your options, ask lots of questions, write down a good birth plan, and make sure you communicate it to all the relevant people. See it as the start of an ongoing conversation between you and your birthing team about what's possible and how they can support you. Disaster-proofing your birth is all about being empowered, informed, communicating openly and regularly with your healthcare providers and birth support, and having one (or several!) back-up plans, just in case.

**Over to you**

On page 118 is a sample birth plan template which you can use and adapt however you wish. Though so many births don't turn out as expected, it doesn't mean that your wishes, hopes and preferences lose validity. In fact, they become even more important. There should always be space to accommodate at least some of your wishes, so don't be afraid to make them known. You have every right to have your preferences heard, whatever they are. Remember, your choices matter. Even the most flexible of plans can get thrown out of the window – the best thing you can do in these cases is to make the best-informed decisions you can about what's right for you and your baby, and be proud of yourself for doing the best you could.

# debrief deep dive

### REFLECT

If you are planning a birth, check in with yourself. How do you feel right now? Perhaps you've created your birth plan, or feel satisfied that you don't want or need a written plan. Wherever you are on this spectrum, it's OK. It's also OK if your feelings change during pregnancy.

### REFRAME

It's part of life that things don't always go the way we want them to, so it makes sense to prepare in advance – not for the worst, but for how you'll cope if something unexpected does happen. What I'm trying to encourage here is a strong mental approach that puts you in control of your responses to any deviations from your plan. Then, if circumstances arise which are beyond your control, you will have already trained yourself to be as calm as you can be, to work *with*, not against, the change, and to make the best decisions you can in the moment. Practise these affirmations to help you reframe your thoughts:

- When plans change, my inner calm remains.

- I am flexible, and adapt to change with grace and courage.

- I make the best choices I can in the moment and show myself grace.

## REDEFINE

Perhaps some of these affirmations have inspired you to write your own. Just like your birth plan, you can adapt them to suit your personality and circumstances. Affirmations are most powerful when they mirror the result you want to experience – either by reaffirming beliefs and behaviours you are already practising, or declaring behaviours you wish to incorporate into your life. In the space below, or in your journal, try writing two or three positive affirmations (or more, if you are inspired to) that will encourage you to redefine how you will approach your labour and birth.

# Birth plan template

Birth preferences

_____

Who's who

_____

_____

What I need

_____

_____

Special touches

_____

_____

_____

WHAT NOT TO DO

_____

_____

_____

Important things to remember

_____

_____

_____

_____

# 15
# you need an advocate

**The importance of advocacy in labour and childbirth**

I stand up for myself, and my allies stand up for me to ensure my voice is heard.

An advocate is someone who works for the interests of a group or person - in this case, for you. Their role is to speak up when you are not being heard, to ensure that the care you receive is appropriate, and to step in when they perceive your care is below par. During pregnancy and childbirth, a woman is extremely vulnerable. Everything can feel so weighted, as if there is so much riding on every decision, and it's up to you to make those choices and get them right. It's a lot to take on and you should not have to do it all alone - this is why advocacy is so important.

Advocates can work in many different ways: sometimes your advocate won't literally speak *for* you, but their presence will be enough to give you the strength to voice your wishes and concerns yourself. They are your cheerleader, your ally and your champion. Having an advocate ensures that you as the birthing parent don't take on any unnecessary stress at a time when you need to be conserving your energy to grow and deliver your baby safely.

## Mikaela's story

My partner walked out when I was three months pregnant, so I knew I was going to face motherhood on my own. I'd geared myself up for the challenge ahead but, aware of the stigma around single parenthood, I felt too ashamed to ask for support. I figured it was my responsibility now, and I'd have to handle whatever came my way alone. When I went into labour, I called my aunt. We weren't especially close, but I had a sudden fear that someone should know I was on my way to hospital, in case something happened to me. As the midwife was checking to see how far dilated I was, in walked my aunt – to say I felt super-awkward is an understatement!

But you know what? Auntie Val stayed by my side as I laboured, and eight hours later I pushed my son into the world. I don't remember her saying much, but I do remember her pushing against and massaging my back as each contraction came, telling me I could do it, and asking a nurse to wait until a contraction had passed before asking me a question. She became the advocate I didn't know I needed.

## Who can be an advocate?

An advocate can be your intimate partner, your parent, your friend or family member. They could also be a doula (a professional provider of non-medical support to women, birthing people and their families during pregnancy, labour and birth). Whoever you feel will do this conscientiously is the person you should have with you. This does not always have to be your partner, or even a relative. Have a conversation with the people closest to you, expressing the type of support you feel you need, get feedback from them about their availability and willingness to help, then choose the right person for you.

In an ideal scenario your advocate will:

- Be your voice when you feel unable to speak up for yourself.

- Understand your wishes and ensure your voice is heard through each and every process.

- Prioritise your needs at all times.

- Ensure that you feel confident.

- Support you physically, mentally and emotionally.

- Bear witness to events that are taking place.

As you can see, it's a weighty role, and it's important that you choose this person wisely.

## Healthcare workers as advocates

Anyone who has anything to do with your care is supposed to be advocating for your wishes to be heard and understood. This includes your doctor, midwife, nurse, or any healthcare support. However, this isn't always clear-cut; sometimes it can feel like those people aren't advocating for you, particularly if your wishes are not aligned with theirs, or there are language, cultural or other barriers which make communications more difficult. Having been on both sides of the consulting room, I get it. You get to choose your personal advocates, but medical staff are assigned to you, and it feels like luck of the draw whether you will click with them or not. That can be anxiety-inducing. And when you don't feel heard or understood, it's natural for those relationships to feel contentious. You may begin to doubt that your care providers have your back.

My policy here is: believe the best, unless there's good reason to believe otherwise. Most healthcare professionals *are* advocating for you to the best of their ability. If you feel that your healthcare provider is not on your side, ask if it is possible to speak to another staff member and ensure that your concerns are documented in your notes, along with your request to speak to someone else. When dealing with healthcare professionals, you should *always* feel that they are advocating for your wishes or giving you alternatives that work for you. Healthcare workers want you to feel comfortable in their care, too – that will enable them to do their best job on your behalf.

## Our partners as advocates

Here in the West, especially in more recent times, we have come to accept that the best person to support us, particularly during childbirth, is our partner. And for many women and birthing people, they are indeed the ideal person. In many other cultures, however, labouring women are always supported by other women. Some may be family, others may be community elders, traditional birth workers or doulas. The benefit of having someone who is not romantically involved as your advocate, or someone who has experience of giving birth themselves, is that they love and care for you, but in a different way to your intimate partner. They don't necessarily have the same fears as your partner may have and may also have different knowledge and experience which might prove invaluable in the birthing room.

When I was pregnant with my daughter Ihsan, very early on I knew I wanted my sister-in-law with me when I went into labour. My husband made an informed choice not to be there, and I was happy to accept this – there is nothing worse than having someone in the birthing space with you who doesn't want to be there.

There was a reason I chose my sister-in-law, even though I have three sisters I'm close to. When choosing my advocate, I thought of who would be there for me, who could stand up for me and encourage me when I needed it, who would be there to cheer me on and who would ensure that all the background noise was drowned out when I needed it to be. I also needed this to be someone who knew me and loved me, but who could approach the events of the birth objectively.

My decision to have a home birth was because I knew I would be better able to advocate for myself in the familiar setting of my home, and I could also have others around who would be able to advocate for me. It would also give my husband room to change his mind – if he wanted to see his child be born, he could. My sisters were with me during labour, as well as my sister-in-law, and my mum and my husband popped in and out regularly. I felt like I had a solid team of people who were there to advocate for me and to encourage me to advocate for myself.

When I transferred to hospital my husband came with us, having made a conscious decision to do so. He sat and watched quietly as my sister-in-law supported me physically. I think her presence was really helpful for us both: she advocated for our family, and that meant the world to us.

Am I saying you should ban your male partner from the birthing room? Absolutely not. He should be as involved as you both want him to be: by your side, pacing the corridor outside or sitting close by – whatever feels right for you. What I am saying is that if, for any reason, you both decide that someone else would make a better advocate for you in the birthing room, then that's OK. You can, of course, elect to speak for yourself at any time. Or you may choose to have your male partner and another advocate, as support for you both.

Remember that this pregnancy is yours, the baby is yours, the birth is yours. You have every right to be advocated for, and you also have the strength it takes to advocate for yourself when you choose to, because at the centre of this life-changing experience, you matter: your wishes, desires, experiences and, most importantly, your voice matter.

## For advocates

If you have agreed to be someone's advocate/birth support, thank you! You are doing an amazing thing and your role is vital. You may feel daunted, and that's natural, but it is the most incredible privilege, and if you feel up to it, you will experience the most incredible event ever – a new life coming into the world. You have been chosen because the birthing woman trusts you and you know them well. You'll need to – perhaps as part of the birth plan – have several conversations with her so you are clear on exactly what she needs. It will be most helpful if you:

- know the signs that the person you are supporting needs your intervention;

- are ready to step in to be their voice when they are not being heard, or cannot speak;

- know how and when to protect their birthing space;

- ensure their needs are met, to the best of your ability.

Here are some examples of how to start that conversation:

- 'What do you want from this birthing experience, and how can I help you to achieve it?'

- 'If there are things you don't want me to do, please tell me, and if there are things you definitely want, the same thing applies.'

- 'I want to support you, but tell me how.'

Keep coming back to the conversation, write things down and ask lots of questions - the more you do this, the more comfortable and confident you will feel when you get that call to say, 'Labour has started!'

# debrief deep dive

## REFLECT

Think about the people you would like advocating for you when you give birth, and why. Then make a plan to ask your chosen advocates if they will be your birth support, and let them know what you will need from them.

## REFRAME

How might you reframe a difficult experience with a care provider? Here is a helpful checklist to consider if you feel that your care provider is not meeting your needs:

- Can you identify which needs are not being met?

- Do you feel you can speak to them about it and improve things?

  » If you can: speak to your care provider, state why you are unhappy and ask that they change the way they provide your care.

  » If you can't: you can request that someone else provides your care, or ask what your options are.

Here's an example of one way to request to change a care provider: 'I feel as if we are not connecting, and I don't feel comfortable. This is not personal, but it's important to me that I connect with the person who's caring for me. For this reason, I would like to change practitioner.'

If this sounds scary, go back and reread the section on assertive communication in Chapter 8 and reclaim your pregnancy superpower. Practise what you want to say beforehand. Consider writing down what you want to say, so you won't lose your train of thought when the time comes to speak up. You can always take an advocate with you if you need moral support.

## REDEFINE

I don't want you to look back at your labour with regret but, given another opportunity, you might do some things differently. This could mean different people being present, or it could mean asserting what you need from those who are present in a different way.

Try these affirmations:

- I made the decisions I made with the knowledge I had.

- In the future, I will be able to give a different level of importance to choosing an advocate.

- If there is something or someone who is not serving me, I am able to use my voice, or that of the person advocating for me, to change my situation.

# 16
# don't break the chain!

**The importance of continuity of care in maternity**

I have the right to be cared for by someone I connect with throughout my pregnancy, labour and birth.

It has long been recognised that continuity of care should be an integral part of midwifery care. The 2017 *Implementing Better Births* report[38] highlighted that the reason for this is to ensure 'safe care based on a relationship of mutual trust and respect in line with a woman's wishes', and recommended a five-year plan to implement continuity models for antenatal, intrapartum-labour care and postnatal care.

Having a known care provider throughout your journey is something I champion because it has been shown to reduce the potential for birth trauma, lessen the risk of interventions such as emergency C-sections, instrumental births and perineal trauma, while increasing birth satisfaction. While researching this book, I spoke to a private midwife who offers complete continuity of care to her clients. She told me that when a woman she is caring for is in labour, there is rarely the need for explanations from either party as there is complete trust on both sides, as well as a mutual understanding and respect. I imagine this to be a completely beautiful space in which to give birth, and something each woman or birthing person is deserving of.

A recent report, *Midwifery 2020*,[39] called for continuity to be provided on the NHS too, so most trusts will have some form of continuity team available – or will at least be working towards providing one. Many NHS hospital trusts have created different forms of continuity of care models, such as buddying, where midwives who work in the community will 'buddy up' with midwives who work in the hospital so that birthing people are seen by someone they have at least met. Many trusts have home birth teams that offer continuity of care and continuity of care models for vulnerable women and families, such as those from refugee families or women with complex mental health or social needs. If you fall into any of these categories and need maternity support, contact your local services to see what they can offer, so you get the proper support as early as possible. If they are not offering this kind of support, ask to be put in touch with any community groups or charities that are offering support and added care in your area.

The move towards specific groups receiving continuity is a brilliant step in the right direction. However, services are stretched, midwifery retention is at an all-time low, and staff burnout is on the rise. This means that even though the intention is there to provide continuity of care, sometimes it just isn't possible. Your first 'booking' appointment is usually lengthier than other appointments, to ensure that you have the chance to discuss and highlight what's important to you in your care, and ensure this is documented. This should prevent you having to repeat the same information at every appointment with a different care provider, and mitigate the risk of getting different advice from each person you see. Seeing a different person at every appointment can be confusing, but unfortunately this may be something you have to deal with, as services are so stretched.

## Doulas

Continuity of care doesn't have to come from midwives. Doulas are a gift to the birthing world. They work alongside midwives to create the most wonderful, supportive environment to birth in. Like midwives, doulas provide emotional and practical support, advocacy and guidance to women and their families during pregnancy, childbirth and post-partum. While doulas are trained and qualified, they don't have the same skill sets, responsibilities or medical qualifications as a midwife, but they can offer continuity and the comforting familiarity of a known care provider.[40]

If this is something you would like, I recommend that you contact your care provider and ask if they offer any continuity services, and also look into doula services in your local area. Your doula is there to support you and make you feel comfortable. You will want to ensure that you're compatible and that you trust your doula, so book one well before your estimated due date (EDD). You may need to interview several candidates before you get the right fit. Doulas are a private service but are not always expensive – many offer reduced rates for those on lower incomes. The Doula UK website has lots of information if you are interested in finding out more. I also recommend the Abuela Doulas – the UK's first doula course owned and led by a Black woman – which has a directory of Black and Brown doulas. Details for these can be found in the Resources section.

## Don't break the chain

Depending on your age and background, the expression 'don't break the chain' could be a superstitious saying, a children's memory game, or a motivational tool to help you build and establish a habit. What these have in common is the idea of continuity and momentum being a good thing – breaking the chain in each scenario leads to having to start again from scratch – or, for the superstitious, bad luck. Now I'm not superstitious at all. As important as it is to have continuity of care, that is not always an option, and I don't believe anything bad will happen if the continuity chain of care providers is broken. In fact, unless you have hired a private midwife, a break in continuity of care is inevitable. But what need not break is the chain of communication (which you keep by ensuring all your interactions are documented), and the trust you have in yourself to be your best ally as you navigate the healthcare system. Trust your intuition (see Chapter 11) when you are interacting with healthcare professionals. What is it saying? Are you getting a good feeling? If not, remember that you have the right to express how you feel.

## Developing a good relationship with the people looking after you

It's always worth the effort to create and build a relationship with the people caring for you, even if you see someone different each time. Though it can be tricky, it's still possible to create a good relationship with multiple care providers if you prepare yourself with the right mindset, have questions ready, and communicate openly, clearly and concisely. Being prepared in this way helps you feel less stressed if you are confronted with yet another new person to speak to. It helps you feel more calm, confident and in control, and helps minimise confusion and misunderstandings. If you know what you want then communicate that, and if you aren't sure yet, ask for advice and ask to have your options laid out clearly. Though the best relationships are built over time, your healthcare providers will still want to do what they can to build trust and make you feel safe. Your goal with each new provider should be mutual respect and understanding, and a shared goal of a positive birth experience for you and your baby. If your healthcare provider is not providing that, you must speak up. And if they are, be sure to let them know!

# debrief deep dive

## REFLECT

If you are preparing to give birth, what does continuity look like for you? Journal the ways in which you would like to see continuity of care throughout your pregnancy and labour. Remember that 'care' goes beyond your hospital appointments, so include all the ways you are caring for yourself too, such as going for regular walks, self-care rituals, etc. This helps you see that even if there is disruption in one part of your life, there are other parts of your wellbeing that you can still keep constant.

If you are reflecting on a previous birth, when you did not experience continuity of care, what impact did this have on your experience? If you had continuity, did that make a positive contribution to your experience?

## REFRAME

If you weren't afforded continuity, I want you to look at how you provided your own continuity: in your choices, in your belief in yourself, and in your convictions.

Use these affirmations as reminders to take charge of your experience where you can:

- I keep my records up to date and ensure everything is documented.

- Meeting a new person is a new opportunity to connect with someone who is here to help me.

- Whatever happens, I take charge of consistency and continuity of care for myself.

## REDEFINE

If you believe that continuity would benefit you, I want you to know that you can assert this need. If you're giving birth through the NHS, continuity cannot be guaranteed, but that doesn't mean your maternity experience should be worse as a result. Take charge of your own continuity where you can - for example, by hiring a midwife or doula. If this is not an option for you, ask a friend, family member or your partner to act as that 'continuity' person instead. Refer to Chapter 15 on advocacy to help you do this.

Remember - you can take charge of your experience. It's OK to do things in different ways. Use the knowledge in this book to find ways to access as much continuity as possible. At every opportunity, refuse to break the chain. Trust that you are worthy of continuity and trust in the ways in which it will serve you.

# 17
# birthing while Black

**Systemic racism and unconscious bias in maternity**

# I am not above anyone, but I am always deserving of respect and good healthcare.

There was no way I could write this book and not speak about the disparities in maternity care between Black and Brown women and their white counterparts. Though overall maternal mortality rates in the UK are low, Black women are still four times more likely to die[41] in pregnancy, childbirth and up to six weeks post-birth compared to their white counterparts. Asian women and women of mixed heritage are twice as likely to face the same outcome.[42] Investigating the causes of these maternal deaths, the 2021 report by Mothers and Babies: Reducing Risk through Audits and Confidential Enquiries across the UK (MBRRACE-UK) found that improvements in care might have made a difference to the outcome in 37 per cent of cases.[43]

These numbers are extremely concerning.

Now, I know that birth trauma, complicated births and medical gaslighting can affect women of *all* ethnicities, and that concerns around care and access inequalities for migrant women[44] and women (including white women) living in deprived areas are well-founded. My speaking up about the trauma and inequalities faced by Black and Brown women in no way diminishes the experiences of white women of all classes, just as it does not silence any other groups who face prejudice of any kind. Often, conversations about race and ethnicity can be overshadowed by a fear that white people's experiences will be relegated simply because the r-word has been used. That isn't what this conversation is about. The reality is that although all women and birthing people are at risk of having traumatic birth experiences, Black and Brown women face a higher risk.

Asking for equity takes away from no one. Look at it this way: if we can have better care and outcomes for Black and Brown women, then we will all receive good treatment. And good treatment for all should be a given.

## The trauma for women of colour – behind the statistics

So what's going on? Why don't all women receive good maternity care? What is putting Black and Brown people more at risk for maternal mortality? There has been no definitive explanation for this worrying statistic, but the MBRRACE-UK report[45] cites the following possible reasons:

- underlying health conditions;

- lack of access to antenatal care;

- poor management of high-risk pregnancies;

- failure to diagnose or treat health conditions;

- co-morbidities (several adverse medical conditions at once);

- language barriers;

- low socioeconomic status;

- inherent racial bias and stereotyping of Black and Brown women.

The last point is telling. And here, we are only talking about increased risk of maternal fatalities during, or shortly after, birth. There is no firm data to prove this, but researchers believe that a similar statistic could also apply to the number of unrecorded close calls or 'near-misses' (for example, when potentially life-threatening symptoms are picked up by chance after having been dismissed, or as a result of the affected person escalating the situation, or other cases of rescue 'just in time', before a catastrophe/fatal consequence). Though these were not documented, I have heard many stories of near-misses through conversations with Black mothers who believe that it was sheer luck that saved their life or their babies' life.

## How could this happen?

How systemic racism and unconscious bias[46] show up in maternity care may vary – but the themes are eerily similar. The pejorative stereotypes resulting in unconscious and unfounded biases that influence the care Black and Brown women and birthing people receive are seen far too frequently in themes such as the 'angry Black woman'; the false belief that Black women have a higher pain threshold than white women; and a lack of understanding about Black and Brown women's response to pain. In Chapter 18 we'll unpack these stereotypes in more detail, discuss where their underlying beliefs come from, and dispel the myths around them.

Some readers may find it shocking to read that something as benign as skin colour could be the factor that makes a difference between a positive birth experience and a negative one. Others will not be surprised at all – you'll either have experienced it first-hand or know someone who has. So much bias is ingrained in contemporary society that some people have a hard time recognising racism when it's right in front of them. (For that reason, I have included some anti-racism resources in the Resources section if you would like to find out more – and I encourage you to do so.) For some readers, reminders that you are 'other', 'less than' or unworthy are a regular, if unwelcome, part of your life in the UK. Though there are small signs of things starting to change, as a society we have a long way to go and a lot of work to do to make racial bias and negative stereotyping a thing of the past. And while we navigate that change, Black and Brown women must understand that safeguarding themselves against racial bias is always OK, and they must be fully supported to do that. They can, and should, always expect the same level of care, safety, dignity and respect as everyone else when accessing maternity and medical care.

## Protecting yourself

I have put together some practical tips about how to protect yourself as a Black or Brown woman receiving maternity care. Though the advice given below is valid for all expectant mothers, these tips are especially important for Black and Brown women. Why? Because what they have been taught about how they are perceived, and the way their behaviour is policed – particularly when accessing maternity services – has in many cases taken away their belief that they can, and should, express themselves freely and safely, and expect the right to live to see their babies grow up.

- **Choose appropriate birth support.** The person you choose to support you is there to advocate for you, to be your voice should you need it, and to protect your experience as much as they can. Whoever you choose, speak to them about the things you fear. Explain to them the things to look out for, such as you not being listened to or what racial stereotyping might look like (see p. 138), so that they are ready to step in, should they have to.

- **Knowledge is power.** Seek antenatal education – education that is appropriate and culturally safe for you. Ensure that it is in your language, if appropriate, and that you ask all the questions you need and want to. The better informed you are, the more empowered you will feel to advocate for yourself. Know procedures, know your rights, know what's normal, and know how to question what you believe isn't normal.

- **Escalate! Escalate! Escalate!** If you feel at any point that you aren't being listened to or heard, or that you are being bullied or coerced, if you don't feel safe or you do not trust the care you are receiving, you can ask to be seen by someone else/someone more senior. You are most definitely within your rights to do this, and you must speak up, to ensure you get the care and experience you deserve.

- **Document.** Ensure that every encounter that relates to your pregnancy and birth is documented. If it isn't done there and then, or if you are given advice that you don't agree with, ensure that the conversation is documented clearly and in full. If you request tests or investigations and they are declined, request that the decision to decline is documented. (NB: This isn't just about poor care being documented; good care should also be documented. *Every* encounter should be documented for the protection and accountability of everyone involved.)

Remember that asserting yourself and requesting appropriate, unbiased care is not asking for too much. It's not being angry or aggressive. It's simply seeking the care and support you need – and are entitled to.

## A call for empathy

I want to make it clear that I see and appreciate the many excellent healthcare workers out there who get it, and who are committed to equitable standards of care for all. But the statistics still make many of us afraid, and no wonder – it's our lived experience. As Nova Reid, author of *The Good Ally*, puts it: 'Since medical practices remain rooted in medical racism, it is no surprise that Black and Brown people continue to bear the brunt of disproportionately negative health outcomes. And it is these outcomes, regardless of intent, that need honesty and interrogation – and fast – to safeguard all of us.'[47]

Put yourselves in the shoes of a Black or Brown woman. Like other women and birthing people, they already have the 'normal' anxieties around pregnancy, but they also have the added worry about the effects of systemic racism. Then consider that only at the time of writing – 2022! – has the UK government set up a task force[48] to investigate maternity disparities in the UK and look into standards of care for Black and Brown women. It's a welcome – if long overdue – step. No one deserves to wonder whether the colour of their skin will be the reason they or their babies die. As a Black woman and midwife who has given birth, I know those feelings: I know those fears, and I give them their validity. I encourage you to do so as well.

# debrief deep dive

## REFLECT

My intention in this chapter has been to arm you with information to support you in your perinatal experience. Having the right knowledge will help you to make the most of your pregnancy. Reflect on the skills in this chapter and how you can use them moving forward.

## REFRAME

In order to reframe your thinking as you navigate this process, use these affirmations as often as you can:

- I am informed and I am capable.

- The colour of my skin is my armour; it is as beautiful and powerful as I am.

- No matter how others treat me, I always treat myself with grace, warmth and kindness.

## REDEFINE

If you are not a person of colour, I want you to look at how you can be an ally to those who might need it.

If you are a person of colour, you have to remain at the centre of your experience. If you feel that medical staff are trying to take control away from you, take it back. I believe in you. You can believe in yourself too – you've got this.

# 18
# the myth of the 'angry Black woman'

**Recognising racial bias, and challenging it when you encounter it**

# I'm not angry because I'm Black; I'm angry because I'm human.

The 'angry Black woman' is the negative stereotyping of Black women as belligerent by nature. Rooted in chattel slavery,[49] this harmful trope found its way into mainstream culture[50] and reinforced in the minds of many people the idea of Black women as 'aggressive, ill-tempered, illogical, overbearing, hostile, and ignorant without provocation'.[51] As a Black woman, this is a stereotype I know only too well. And as a midwife, I am acutely aware of how it affects Black women's maternity experiences. I have done debriefs with women who have been accused of being 'too aggressive' during their births and I have worked with pregnant women who want to use hypnobirthing techniques not to cope with labour pains, but to manage any feelings of anger that may arise during labour.

The 'angry Black woman' label is something you become very conscious of as a Black person when dealing with people in positions of authority, and it crops up in healthcare all too often. Every person of every ethnicity has the right to feel anger and to feel able to express a desire to change the situation that has caused that anger. When it comes to healthcare, however, many Black women fear expressing dissatisfaction with their care, or asking assertively for what they need in case they are seen as overbearing or hostile. As a result, these women may not make legitimate complaints about their care, to avoid being perceived in a negative light by those providing their care. This censorship of expression is hugely problematic. It distracts from the *real* issue of poor treatment and possible racial bias and leads to the normalisation of poor care and experiences. And Black women, manipulated into silence, in turn normalise the suppression of their emotions. Over time, this can lead to a host of other problems, including anxiety, depression and physical illness.

## A closer look at anger

Let's clarify a couple of things around anger. First, there are legitimate reasons why anger may bubble up during pregnancy and/or labour, and we'll look at those below. During the normal course of their working lives, healthcare professionals should expect to observe and deal with expectant and labouring women who are expressing anger and a host of other emotions, including fear, anxiety and sadness as well as excitement, joy and more. Second, despite the UK's culturally diverse society, sometimes righteous anger is provoked by a lack of understanding, leading to Black and Brown women's needs being ignored or dismissed based on things like their language, tone or appearance. This can put these women on the receiving end of racially based microaggressions (microaggressions are 'commonplace verbal, behavioral or environmental indignities, whether intentional or unintentional, that communicate hostile, derogatory or negative racial slights and insults toward people of colour'[52]), such as:

- assumptions about their personal life based on their appearance or stereotypes;

- their assertiveness (or any strong emotion) being interpreted as anger or aggression;

- feeling as though everything they do or say is being judged according to a stereotypical view of their race, rather than accepted as their individual point of view.

**But some Black women are angry!**

If the conversations I have with Black and Brown friends, family, colleagues and people online and offline are anything to go by, *many* Black women are angry. And they have reason to be, if they feel they are constantly having to engage with systems and individuals who do not mean them well, who gaslight them with racist microaggressions, and who tell them, when they call out racist behaviour or speak up about poor treatment, that they have a chip on their shoulder and to 'stop making it all about race'.

> *Dare I express what I'm feeling to anyone who doesn't know me? Hell, no - immediately [in their eyes] I'm the angry Black woman. They won't see [my humanity] at all, let alone hear me. So I keep it in … it's hard, though. It affects me.*
>
> *– Roxy, expectant mum*

Rarely are Black women given the grace of being a human being expressing emotion in a moment in time. So yes, many Black and Brown women are angry about this.[53] And as Black women, we may feel anger about all sorts of things - but guess what? So do white women!

**For every tree, a root**

Angry feelings during pregnancy and labour are more common than you might think. Part of it might be hormonal - oestrogen, progesterone and other hormones change during pregnancy and can affect mood, as can stress, lack of sleep and anxiety (particularly if you have a high-risk pregnancy, or have suffered a previous pregnancy loss). So many pregnant women really do feel extra-sensitive and moody at times, and that is normal.

You may also be facing any number of other challenges, from dealing with your changing body to thoughts about financial security, how you'll cope, physical tiredness and, once active labour begins, pain. (And yes, some people do respond to physical pain with anger!) But if, in addition to these things, you also feel a lack of safety and trust around your medical care, feel belittled or dismissed, or experience substandard or negligent care, regardless of whether it is rooted in racial bias, this can lead to feelings of frustration and anger.

Expecting birthing people of colour not to voice their frustration and anger when they are at their most vulnerable is unfair, especially when they may already feel that all their emotional reactions are policed and interpreted as 'aggression'. And while we may all agree that anger is one of the strong emotions that can make us feel uncomfortable (hence the reason we look to control it in ourselves and others), we also need to accept that women express their anger in different ways. If someone isn't expressing their anger the way you would, but they are not being violent, abusive nor threatening, then they aren't necessarily wrong.

## Dealing with anger

Communication is so important to break down these stereotypes. Normalising anger as a legitimate response to poor or negligent treatment or disrespectful behaviour is vital too. Women's fear of how their anger will be received is valid, so let's look at practical ways to manage this when faced with a situation that triggers feelings of anger.

- Assess the situation: is there a way to deal with it in a productive manner to change or improve things?

- Use 'I' statements: this helps you take ownership of your feelings and communicate them clearly and tactfully. 'I statements' are a key part of assertive communication (see Chapter 8).

- Consider speaking to your care providers to explain how you are feeling. For example, you could say something like: 'I feel angry about the care I have/haven't received. I would like to know how we can rectify this, because I don't want to feel this way.'

- If you have identified your feelings and spoken to your care providers and still had no resolution or improvement, or if you feel your concerns are not being taken seriously and you have suffered further harm as a result, you are within your rights to make a complaint. (See Chapter 20 for how to go about this.)

# debrief deep dive

### REFLECT

This chapter may have brought up some challenging emotions for you. There is a whole community of Black and Brown women who have been through, or are going through, similar emotions. Take a moment to breathe, and remember that you are not alone.

If you are a white woman or birthing person, has anything in this chapter changed how you perceive your place in the medical system? In what ways?

You can write down your responses to what you have read in this chapter in your journal.

Some questions to ponder:

- What has made you angry?

- What has challenged you?

- What has inspired you?

- What would you like to see changed?

- If you are a medical professional, how can you be part of that change?

## REFRAME

Anger can exacerbate feelings of helplessness. Try these positive affirmations to remind you to always stand in your personal power when you feel anger rising in yourself or see it in others:

- I am allowed to feel angry, and to express that anger in healthy ways.

- I set boundaries, and managing my emotions comes easily to me.

- I am both assertive and respectful of others.

- Instead of becoming defensive, I can seek to understand.

## REDEFINE

It's important to focus on the outcomes you want for yourself and your little one, if you're expecting. This isn't about suppressing your feelings, but about managing your responses in a way that allows you to take care of yourself, and communicate your awareness of what is or could be happening in a particular exchange while avoiding self-sabotaging or destructive responses. Allow your emotions to show you the best ways to take care of yourself in the moment. This may include:

- Breathing deeply.

- Verbalising your emotions: for example, 'I feel upset/angry/ frustrated/uncomfortable'.

- If someone has angered you, ask them to repeat or clarify the words you have taken exception to. For example, 'I'm hearing you say ..., which makes me feel unsafe.' Or 'Could you clarify what you mean by ...., please?'

# 19
# do Black women feel pain?

**The origins of systemic racism in maternity care**

I need you to recognise how I express my pain – and that yes, like you, I do feel pain.

One of the major stereotypes Black women face is the belief that Black people don't feel pain in the same way that white people do. This false belief about biological differences between different ethnicities can often lead to a delay in treatment, different pain-management options given to Black women and white women in the maternity room, and even to gaslighting. This kind of thinking is extremely damaging. It means that a Black or Brown person who may desperately need pain relief may not be offered it, and may also be made to feel 'weaker' for asking for it. Why is this? Where did the myth around Black women's 'higher pain threshold' come from?

## Black pain for gynaecological gain

To see how systemic racism has influenced maternity care, we need to begin with the controversial nineteenth-century white American physician James Marion Sims, who is both hailed and reviled as 'the father of gynaecology'. Sims developed tools and techniques that are still used in modern-day reproductive medicine, including the speculum and the Sims position for vaginal examinations.

When developing his techniques Sims used three enslaved Black women – Lucy, Anarcha and Betsey – as well as several unknown others as 'test subjects'. During his 'experiments' he used no analgesia. Though analgesia as we know it today was not widely used at the time,[54] Sims worked primarily under the racist notion that Black women had an unusually high tolerance of pain.[55] The fact that the women were forcibly restrained during procedures they had not consented to, and Sims did not consider providing them with pain relief, shows how little their lives mattered to Sims. He performed thirty procedures on Anarcha alone.

Apologists for Sims argue that we should all be grateful for his work. But appreciating the value of instruments such as the speculum should never overshadow the suffering these Black women endured to facilitate their invention. To do so would be nothing short of inhumane. Even so, the barbaric way in which Sims conducted his research has fed into the idea that Black pain can be overlooked, with the result that this attitude has filtered down through medical professionals for generations. Some people still believe this myth to this day, and it was still being stated as fact in a medical textbook as recently as 2017.[56]

Considering race is a social construct with no biological bearing,[57] it's outrageous that anyone today would buy into the 'Black people don't feel pain' myth. Black pain is real and needs to be treated appropriately, without bias. Withholding analgesia based on racist stereotypes is inhumane, and contributes to maternal dissatisfaction and trauma for Black women.[58]

## The right to be heard

If you feel that your pain is not manageable or it is concerning you, tell the medical professional treating you. You have the right to be heard and have your pain acknowledged appropriately. If you feel that the medical professional is still not listening to you, ask your birth partner or advocate to speak up on your behalf. Ensure that, before the birth, you discuss what you want them to do if you are not being listened to. Some birth partners won't instinctively know what to do and may not feel comfortable being put on the spot, so preparing them for this eventuality is key. (See Chapter 15 for tips on this.)

Let's be the generation to end this faulty, outdated thinking once and for all. I'll say it loud and clear so there is no doubt: Black women and birthing people feel pain just as white people do, and their individual pain thresholds vary, just like those in people of any other ethnicity.

## Responses to pain

Racism has also fed into the way people's expressions of pain are received, and therefore treated. The media has a lot to answer for in the way pain in pregnancy and childbirth is understood and expressed. How many of us have watched films or TV programmes in which a labouring woman is screaming, writhing around in pain, shouting obscenities or crying in agony? These are all valid expressions of pain, and are common. However, they are not the *only* ways to express pain. Through my many conversations with Black women during debriefs, I have realised that this misunderstanding has led to a lack of response from healthcare staff to Black women's expressions of pain.

I don't cry when I'm in pain. I don't scream or shout. I go into myself – and when it's too much, I get really angry. I can see how perhaps this response doesn't help me as a Black woman – we've seen that stereotype already. But does my response make it any less valid or real? Of course not, and if the way you express pain veers from what is 'expected', that's also valid and real.

Black and Brown women should not have to express pain in a way that is palatable or understandable to white people and other ethnicities.

*No one* should be under any obligation to express their pain in a way that is deemed 'acceptable' to another person. However you respond to pain is valid and should be treated appropriately. When doing debrief sessions or antenatal education classes, I ask the person I am working with to document their response to pain in their birth plan. For example, they might write: 'When I'm in pain, I shout and I swear. I can't help it, but I may appreciate being offered pain relief at that time.'

This is a way to help control the care they receive and manage the response of medical professionals to their pain. I would recommend that you do this as part of your birth plan too.

# debrief deep dive

## REFLECT

How do you express pain? Have a good think about this, especially if you are doing so for the first time. If you feel comfortable doing so, share with a trusted person (or write in your journal) the ways you express pain. Have them validate you, or use the affirmations overleaf to validate yourself.

If you are a white care provider who is involved with Black women and birthing people, how have you found yourself responding to anger and/or pain when expressed by people who don't look like you? Be honest – there is no judgement here, simply an invitation to check your biases. If you perceive you do respond differently, recognise that this is a learned behaviour that can be unlearned.

_____

_____

_____

_____

_____

_____

_____

_____

_____

_____

## REFRAME

There is also no standard way to express your pain. Your way is your way and it's OK - as long as you are not harming yourself or others. Do not allow anyone to shame you into expressing pain the way they would. Be yourself, and encourage yourself with the following affirmations:

- If I'm in pain, I allow myself to release the pain.

- I have the right to express my pain, and I do so in healthy ways.

- My pain does not have to mimic anyone else's. I am safe to express my pain and for it to be seen for what it is.

## REDEFINE

As a Black woman, know that if you are in pain, you have the right to analgesia. Know that asking for pain relief does not make you weaker; it makes you human.

Always ask for what you need.

# 20
# speaking up – should I complain?

**When and how to complain**

I can be grateful for your service and still speak up if that service has caused me harm.

The NHS is an excellent service – one we are so fortunate to have in the UK, and one that I am proud to have been a part of. It's important to state here that the majority of interactions and interventions that take place during pregnancy, labour, birth and post-partum are both successful and well received. Sometimes, however, services (both public and private) fail and, whether through human error, ignorance or negligence, people do come to harm when being treated. And as we have seen, when people are harmed during pregnancy, labour or birth, it's complex.

The idea that simply because mother and baby are alive and well following a difficult birth that the outcome was a success can invalidate trauma. Simply being alive is not the benchmark – you should come away from receiving medical care and support feeling well and satisfied. If you don't, then you should feel safe enough to express this. You may be understanding of the things that took place, you may even empathise with the stress the individuals in the system were under, but don't allow that to invalidate your experience. It still matters.

## Barriers to complaining

There is a common misconception that complaining about the care you received is bad practice – that it is ungrateful, especially if you and your baby are physically OK. During my debriefs it's not uncommon to hear phrases like:

- 'Is it worth complaining, especially if we are all well now?'

- 'It was a bad experience, and I just want to forget it ever happened.'

- 'Why should I complain when I'm lucky to have received the care I did?'

I can understand this hesitancy. Most of us find it hard to complain at the best of times. When I talk to my clients to find out more about the reasons for their reluctance to make a complaint, even when there is clear evidence that they have been harmed, we often unearth false beliefs. Either my clients feel somehow unworthy of their voice being heard, or (out of empathy) they feel guilty for not showing more gratitude towards the people who may have harmed them.

Labour and birth are taxing on the mind and body, and the medical staff caring for you are constantly making decisions that they deem to be in the best interests of you and your baby. Of course you are grateful for their evident professionalism and care – but remember that your *whole* experience, not just the good parts, is valid. If an error is never disclosed, then there is no opportunity to learn from it and change. Without feedback, both positive and negative, professionals won't get the opportunity to evolve. If you experience malpractice but don't complain or say anything, those responsible will not be held accountable, and they could go on to do the same – or worse – to someone else. You are worth being heard. Your dissatisfaction matters.

Being grateful for the service and unhappy about the care that you received are not mutually exclusive.

*I have felt, particularly in the last eighteen months, that saying anything negative about the NHS because of all the hard work those working within have done throughout the pandemic is disrespectful and ungrateful, and so I have stayed quiet.*

*– Maxine*

I have heard different versions of this sentiment time and time again, especially in recent months. In my view, it amounts to a type of self-censoring and invalidation of feelings and experiences. While well-intentioned, this can be very harmful. No one wants to disparage the NHS, or indeed anyone who provides medical care, but expecting someone who was harmed by a person or service which forms part of an institution to be quiet and 'grateful' is a form of abuse. If you have found this to be the case when you have expressed dissatisfaction, my advice is to speak up anyway. Understand that one thing does not take away from another. The services may be good, but the specific experiences have caused you personal harm. Tell yourself that: validate your own experiences, even though you might be uncomfortable doing so at first. It's important for your own healing that you do.

You may also decide not to make a complaint because you don't think anything will come of it, or you think you will be dissatisfied with the response. This is also a valid concern. According to regulations, however, every complaint to the NHS must be responded to in some capacity. Many hospital trusts will have a formal complaints system: they will manage grievances through their internal channels, ensuring that complaints reach the right departments and that they are handled efficiently.

Finally, one of the biggest barriers to complaining is time. Having a newborn or small baby can make it difficult to carve out time for yourself, let alone time to sit and rehash a traumatic event. Sometimes the trauma is so deep that you may be unable to face it. You may not even realise that you want to raise a complaint until long after the event, and that is also completely normal and perfectly acceptable. Processing birth takes time, and one of the most overwhelming things about writing a complaint letter can be the idea of creating a full picture of your grievance, the circumstances around it, and its effects on you and your family. So read Chapters 5 and 8 in this book about trauma and communication, take your time and honour your experience.

The bottom line is: no matter the outcome of your maternity experience, if you are not happy about the care you or your baby received, you have the right to complain and to have your concerns investigated and addressed by the appropriate parties. As Birthrights (a UK-based charity on a mission to improve care and practice throughout the maternity system) states: 'It is OK to make a complaint even if you think what happened to you was minor or no serious harm was done.'[59]

## My experience

I once received a complaint. I had unintentionally contributed to someone's negative experience, and my manager came to me to discuss the complaint. I explained my experience of events to her, and she responded through official channels. I never got the opportunity to reply to the complainant directly, but knowing that I had contributed to someone's negative experience has stayed with me to this day. Being held to account meant change – the person who complained might not hear it from me, but through their complaint I was able to acknowledge my own shortcomings and make changes to the way I provided care. Their complaint meant I gave others better care, and if we were ever to meet again, I would want them to know that the way they used their strength to complain had made a difference to the care they would receive in the future too.

> *I really like the midwife that looked after me. She was so kind, and she made us laugh and treated us really kindly. That being said, some of the decisions she made weren't the right ones, and have caused lasting harm. I feel bad complaining about her because I don't want to hurt her feelings.*
>
> *– Sarah*

Nice people can often unintentionally cause harm. It does not mean they are no longer nice. We have to ensure that we recognise these people as human – meaning they can be nice, kind and caring, but they also have the capacity to make mistakes that may leave the recipient damaged emotionally, physically, or both. If the person who cared for you is truly kind, they would want to know that they may have caused you harm, and would want to learn so they don't repeat it. If you choose to complain about something they did or didn't do, you can also mention all the good things they did. Complaint letters can include positive aspects of your care – and in some cases this can strengthen your complaint, as it shows you are looking at the whole picture, not just the negative aspects.

## How to make a complaint

Most NHS trusts have a policy that allows you to complain up to twelve months after either when the incident took place or when you realised there was an issue. It is still possible to complain after twelve months have passed, but you will need to provide a 'good reason' as to why the complaint was delayed[60]. A verbal complaint is often the best place to start, especially if it's a matter that can be resolved fairly easily. Perhaps a member of staff was dismissive or rude and you feel an apology is warranted. You can express that at the time, or anytime afterwards. If you do not get a satisfactory response, then follow up with a letter. If you prefer to document everything, then you may opt to communicate only in writing. This is especially advised when the complaint is more complex in nature.

The mere thought of writing a complaint letter can be off-putting. Many people have no idea what to include or how to structure the letter. My advice is not to overthink it. The Birthrights and Association for Improvements in the Maternity Services (AIMS) websites contain lots of information about complaints procedures (see the Resources), and I have added a complaint letter template (p. 156) to help you to structure your own letter when you are ready to write it. Adapt it so that the content is true to you. Even if you don't send it immediately after writing it, this is an opportunity for you to do all the things we have covered in previous chapters, to get the validation you seek and to hold people accountable in the way you feel they should be. So write from your heart, and hold on to your truth.

# debrief deep dive

## REFLECT

Below, I have left some space for you to record the thoughts that come to mind relating to the care you received. You can write in your journal if you prefer. Jot down some of the things that you remember in those moments - things that bothered or harmed you. You may not be in a good space to write a complaint letter at this very moment, but jotting down a few things will be useful in building a complete story, and will help you to write something relevant and true to your experiences when the time comes.

## REFRAME

Use these affirmations as reminders that you can ask for accountability from those who harmed you, however it happened and whatever they intended:

- I am brave enough to ask for change.

- When I take action, positive change follows.

- I'm proud of myself for speaking up about what harmed me.

## REDEFINE

Did you do something to yourself, or was it done to you? Did you allow something to happen, or were you powerless to change it? Remind yourself: 'I can use my truth in a way that will allow others to speak up against things that may harm them.'

# Complaint letter template

Date

Recipient's name
Title
Company
Address
City. County/Region. Postcode


To whom this may concern

Write the email to named people/heads of departments – this information can be found on the trust website.

I am writing in regards to my experience under your care.

Next, go over what happened. Write chronologically and clearly and include as much information as you have: who was present, names if you have them, dates and times of day. Be clear and to the point.

Here, cover the impact of what happened. This may include the physical, mental and emotional aspects of your experience. You can go into as much detail as you feel comfortable.

Next, outline what you want to come from your complaint. It's really important to write this letter first and foremost for yourself, to hold those who caused harm accountable and to alleviate any feelings of blame or responsibility that you may be carrying.

If you would like a reply, a phone call, an in-person meeting, clarification or explanation, this is the place to request those.

Your name

Your contact details

# part 3

## the fourth trimester:

*postnatal recovery, being a parent, and post-partum mental health*

# 21
# what does 'recovery' look like?

**How to navigate the fourth trimester**

I have been through a major transition. As I parent, I will show myself grace.

Post-partum recovery – the twelve-week period after you welcome your newborn, otherwise known as the fourth trimester – is often the time that catches most new mothers by surprise. Post-partum recovery is lots of things: it's physical recovery from the pregnancy, labour and birth; emotional recovery from the highs and lows of the journey; and psychological recovery from anything that did not go as you'd hoped – particularly (but not always) after a difficult birth. But more than that, it's a transitional time: you've moved from one state (pregnant/ expectant) to another (post-partum; a parent). You may be a first-time parent or a new parent once again. Your baby may have come into the world earlier and more suddenly than expected, or they may have been born with special needs. It's a time of adjustment for both of you.

## Expect a non-linear process

For most new mothers, post-partum recovery is anything but linear. We are all different and will recover differently too. In post-partum recovery, it's so important not to have any expectations about *your* recovery process. I don't mean you should *expect* things to be difficult, but be aware that sometimes even the normal aspects of postnatal recovery, such as fatigue, soreness, and breastfeeding issues, can knock us off balance, no matter how much we have prepared for them. This is true even if you had what you'd deem a 'perfect' birth; it does not mean that the post-partum period will be the same. You have a new little person (or persons!) to look after, on top of any other responsibilities you already have; your hormones may be chaotic, making everything feel overwhelming, and at the centre of it all there's you – and you require healing, love and attention too. With so much happening at once (inside and outside our bodies!), we need to allow ourselves time to take it all in and process it. This is a time to take the pressure off and focus on *your* recovery. Remember that your post-partum recovery (whether or not it's straightforward) has no reflection on the kind of parent you are.

## It's a period of adjustment

Imagine if we gave all new parents the chance to lie in and rest after they've delivered their babies – not just on the day they gave birth, but for a few weeks afterwards. What would life look like for new parents if we lived in a society that accepted that post-partum rest was a necessity, rather than a luxury for the privileged few? Imagine if we didn't have to justify our need to rest after having children, and we could simply be allowed to pause and enjoy being with our new babies while the world carried on, unbothered. Sounds blissful, right? I'm glad you agree – so let's look at how to prioritise rest during the transition into parenthood.

When I had my daughter, I recognised the importance and cultural significance of 'lying-in' – the traditional 'forty days' rest', practised by many in my family and wider community – but I couldn't actually do it. I had no desire to sit still. On reflection, this was partly a trauma response (see p. 22). Although I had buried my feelings around my birth experience deep enough that I could ignore them for a while, it did not mean that they did not exist. Truthfully, I was putting off dealing with them, and no amount of rushing 'back to normal' – aka my constant fidgeting and restlessness – would make them disappear. I had a massive case of FOMO too – fear of missing out on life outside the 'baby bubble' I found myself in. I was fuelled by an obsessive need to seem fine; I feared that if I stopped to rest for too long, everyone I knew would move on with their lives without me.

It would have been better for me if I had rested – and better for my daughter. She was so unsettled – I believe she must have somehow sensed my tension and was reacting to it in the only way she could.

If I had the opportunity again, I would place myself in a safe cocoon and give myself the space to get to know my baby and settle into my new role as a parent – not necessarily for forty days, but I would take time out for just me and my baby, and let the world move on its own.

## Lying-in – and what if you can't?

Sometimes lying-in just isn't possible, especially if you have other children to care for, or are parenting alone. But that does not mean you should abandon self-care during this period. Self-care during this time is about looking after yourself just as much as you did while you were pregnant. What do your mind and body need to feel at their best? What things will make your transition to motherhood easier? Is it nourishing food? A comfortable living space? Big, squishy cushions? Fresh bed linen? Is it having people around you who will ensure you have the space and time to look after yourself?

## A reminder: self-care is not selfish

As a parent, putting yourself last happens so often that it sounds completely normal in our society. Of course, your newborn's needs trump yours, and it's really important to pay attention to their needs and do everything you can to learn who they are in those early days. But notice I said 'trump', not obliterate. Even if you feel fine, you are still recovering. Your needs still matter, and it's important to advocate for yourself in the postnatal period, not just physically but also mentally.

I know the balance can be difficult to strike, especially in the early post-partum period when baby's needs are high and adjusting to parenthood can feel overwhelming. But it is very difficult to care for someone else if you do not care for yourself. It is vital that you prioritise yourself – and that others around you prioritise you too. It might sound counterintuitive, but trust me on this one: prioritising your needs will ensure that you can care for your baby more effectively. I recognise how difficult this can actually be in practice, but if this is something you're finding difficult, I invite you to start small and think of it as an investment in your baby's wellbeing as much as yours.

Not sure what your needs are? Ask yourself the following questions, and journal your answers:

- What do I want? (This could be as simple as a morning to sleep in while your partner or other trusted person looks after your baby, or a long soak in the bath of an evening.)

- What makes me happy? Write it down. Nothing is too big, too small or too silly!

- What will make my life easier right now?

- How do I fill my cup and avoid things that empty it?

Now that you have your list, choose one answer that most appeals to you and resolve to take action on it. If it's a big thing that needs to be broken down into small chunks, what one step can you take towards making it happen?

**Don't forget kindness**

Self-kindness is included here too. By this I mean showing yourself love and grace, empathy, compassion and mega-doses of patience as you adjust to your new routine. At first, it can feel like you're getting it all wrong: the feeds, the changing, bathing the baby, holding the baby, burping the baby. The baby doesn't like anything you do, and you will literally cry over spilt milk – but it's so normal. All of it.

*In those first few days after my baby's birth, there was so much I wasn't prepared for. For example, I was shocked by her first meconium 'poo'. My husband had gone off somewhere and I was on my own in the hospital room when it happened. I'd just changed her into her new babygro and this huge stream of black tar-like goo leaked out of her nappy (which my amateur self had fastened too loosely) and went everywhere! And I mean everywhere! Up her back, down her leg, between her toes, all over her brand-new babygro and all over the hospital bedsheet and blanket. It's funny to think about now, but it was like time just stopped. It felt like a million judgemental eyes were on me; that I was responsible for this explosive mess and I had to get it right as my baby was wholly dependent on me. I had no clue where to start with the clean-up, and didn't feel I could bother the midwives – I just froze. I was so numb I couldn't even cry. Thankfully, one of the midwives came into the room and must have seen I needed help. She helped me bathe and change my baby. I watched the midwife closely so I would know what to do next time, but I'll never forget how overwhelmed and alone I felt in that moment. It took me about six weeks before everything about caring for a new baby clicked and I thought 'OK, yes, I can do this.'*

**– Faith, reflecting on the birth of her first child**

Moments of overwhelm are normal, and they will pass. Things will click into place, no matter how chaotic and overwhelming they seem right now. Perfection isn't the aim here – good enough is good enough.

# debrief deep dive

## REFLECT

If you had the opportunity to be newly post-partum again, what would you do differently? Jot down a few of your thoughts about what you would do differently if you could go back. What would you change? This could be as simple as telling people you won't be in touch as much, or not cooking as many meals in the those early weeks post-partum. How would you prioritise your rest and healing? Once you have made your list, if you decide to have more children you can use it as a plan to make your desires a reality.

If you are expecting your first child, speak to new mums and ask them what they would have done differently. Resolve to incorporate any tips that resonate with you into your post-partum recovery plan.

## REFRAME

If you were supporting a friend or family member who was feeling overwhelmed, I bet you'd have plenty of kind, affirming things to say to them. I would love you to write down some affirmations here that you can repeat to yourself in the post-partum period, that show you the same kindness. Here are a few examples to get you started:

- I am learning on the job. Each day is a new learning curve.

- I am doing brilliantly, taking it a day at a time.

- I let go of unrealistic expectations and go with the flow.

If you find it difficult to put yourself first, try the following affirmations to help put yourself in the right mindset:

- I practise self-care so I can be at my best for my baby.

- It's OK to take some time for myself.

- I move my body regularly to energise myself.

## REDEFINE

You can design your own 'lying-in period' if you want – make it as luxurious or as basic as you like. It can include simply not leaving your home for a period of time (this may require pre-birth planning), or not answering your phone after a certain time in the evening.

# 22
# perineums, patience and perfection

**What 'healing well' looks like**

Healing is ongoing,
one cell at a time,
one moment at a time.

If you had a vaginal delivery, the stretching of your cervix and vagina as you birthed your baby will mean that some soreness in that area is normal, especially if there has been any grazing or tearing of the perineum (the area between the opening of the vagina and the anus), or you had an episiotomy.[61] Perineal tearing affects approximately 75-85 per cent of women.[62] Minor grazes and tears tend to heal on their own, but 60-70 per cent will require suturing. I have spoken to many women whose biggest fear during childbirth was perineal trauma. This topic, unsurprisingly, can cause some concern, so I asked my good friend Clare Bourne to help us explore perineal trauma in more depth, to learn how to prevent, manage, and heal from it. Clare is a women's health physiotherapist who treats many women and birthing people who present with everything from episiotomy and tear repair to issues with continence. She explains:

> *Understandably, any tear that occurs to the vagina or vulva can be traumatic. It is natural to wonder, be concerned and fear how you will heal, whether you will be 'normal down there' again and whether you will have sex again without pain. It is very understandable to just disengage and not think about it, hope for the best and see what happens.*

As difficult as it is to think about the prospect of perineal injury, Clare and I agree that understanding what is happening with your body at each stage (as far as it feels comfortable to do so) helps you stay present and connected to your body, minimising the feeling that labour and birth are something that happens *to* you, rather than you being an active participant in birthing your baby. Know that tearing *isn't* inevitable, but if it does happen, you'll be equipped with the knowledge you need to take care of yourself and find support as you heal. There is lots of support available to you, pre- and post-birth. And as the many women who have experienced tearing during birth will attest, you are far from alone.

Here are Clare's top tips for vaginal recovery post-birth:[63]

1. Keep on top of your pain medication, if you are using any.

2. Allow your vulva to get some air after showering and before dressing.

3. To help soothe swelling, create a 'padsicle': place a maternity or sanitary pad in the freezer overnight. Let it thaw for 5-10 minutes, and wrap it in a flannel or towel before placing it inside your underwear.

4. If you're feeling too much pressure on your perineum when sitting (especially if you're in the same position for a long time), elevate your thighs and bottom with rolled-up towels or blankets. There are also special 'donut'-style cushions available that some women find useful.

## Preventing tearing

We like to talk in terms of reduction of risk rather than prevention because (at the risk of sounding like a broken record) there are no guarantees in childbirth. You will be happy to know, however, that there are ways to minimise the risk of tearing.

In the weeks leading up to your birth, you can try **perineal massage** to help soften the perineal area and prepare it for birth.

### How to do it

- Wash your hands thoroughly and ensure you have removed/ trimmed anything that could potentially scratch the delicate skin in your perineal area, such as jewellery or long nails.

- Ensure your perineal area is also clean – it might be a good idea to practise this massage after a shower or a bath.

- With some lubricating oil (vitamin E oil, almond oil or an unscented lubricant) place your thumb about 3cm inside the vagina onto the back wall, press down with your thumb and sweep to the sides in a U-shaped movement. Think about the area like a clock, with 12 o'clock at the pubic bone and 6 o'clock at the anus. You are aiming to sweep between 3 and 9 o'clock. Then try and stretch and hold for 30 seconds in all directions from 3 to 9 o'clock. You should feel some pressure and a light stretching sensation, but no pain.

- Massage for about 3 minutes each time.

- You can do this once a day. If you feel comfortable about it, this is something you could ask your partner to do for you.

For visual learners, Clare has provided a detailed video demonstrating the technique here (www.youtube.com/watch?v=ceOAGdC5njk).

During the second stage (pushing) of labour, you can also ask your care provider to use a warm, sterile **perineal compress** as a way to keep blood flowing to that area and encouraging elasticity in the perineum. Another thing that can help is for your baby's head to be born slowly. I used to say to anyone I was supporting in labour, 'If you don't listen to my voice at any other time, I need you to listen when I tell you to stop pushing and to pant – don't do anything else!' This helps ease, rather than force, the baby's head out, and it really can make a difference.

If you would like to explore these options, list them in your birth plan.

Above all, remember that none of this is about 'getting it right'. You do the best that you can and accept that some things are out of your control. What you are able to do is good enough.

### Healing and recovering from perineal injury

If you do end up with some perineal tearing, the most important thing is that your tear is assessed and diagnosed correctly, then repaired correctly. This can really improve healing and recovery, so here are a few 'need to knows', in case you find yourself in this situation:

- Perineal injury is measured by grades: first-degree, second-degree, third-degree (further categorised into A, B and C ) and fourth-degree tears. First-degree tears involve only the skin around the vagina; second-degree involve the muscles of the perineum as well, and may require a stitch. Third and fourth-degree are more serious, because they extend to the muscle that controls the anus. These usually require surgery, but are fairly rare, occurring in between 2 to 6 per cent of births. Episiotomies are often classed as second-degree tears, but these are performed in a controlled manner, either by a midwife or an obstetrician, to create more space for the birth of the baby.[64]

- Many people recover from perineal trauma without any problems (this should reassure you!).

- The average healing time from a second-degree tear (which is the most common) is two to six weeks : this means time for the wound to close and for you not to need regular analgesia (pain relief).

- Your body may feel a bit different afterwards. Your vagina may feel tighter or looser than it did before. It may feel uncomfortable, or there may be minimal sensation as the nerves heal. Over time, the scar will heal and feel less noticeable.

- If you are concerned about how your perineum is feeling following a repair, do not hesitate to speak to your healthcare provider.

**Facilitating perineal healing**

Clare says it is important to keep the perineal area clean and dry. Wash regularly, pat the area dry, change your underwear frequently. To help you heal more quickly, don't overdo things and try to get plenty of rest.

Be aware of signs of infection, which include:

- a strong odour;

- increased pain;

- redness/swelling;

- raised temperature/a fever.

If you notice any of these symptoms, contact your healthcare provider straight away. Infections that are left untreated can be life-threatening. I know that it's frustrating to have to return to the doctor when you may have just got home, but you must contact your doctor if you suspect you have an infection. Don't be embarrassed – they are there to help you and will have seen it all before, many times!

**When should I have sex again?**

Although many medics will sign you off for intercourse after six weeks, you may not be ready to have sex yet, and that's fine. Your vagina, your choice. Keep communicating with your partner during this time. If touch is important to you, don't neglect other forms – intimacy goes beyond the physical act of intercourse, and you need not lose that while you recover. Foot rubs, back rubs and hugs are great ways to keep you and your partner physically, as well as emotionally, connected.

**Managing perineal trauma**

This is where patience comes in. Remember what I said in Chapter 21 about recovery being a non-linear process? Here, Clare offers some practical ways to manage perineal injury:

1. Know that healing can take longer than you might imagine. It can be frustrating, demoralising and upsetting at times. The six-week window we talk about is just the general length of soft tissue healing, and not a timescale of the pelvic floor muscles being back to full strength. You are also left with a scar that can feel sensitive, tender and painful, so be patient with your body. Think of the six-week mark as really the beginning of the next stage towards feeling more like yourself.

2. Have a look at your vulva. This is something I really recommend, and isn't something most of us do much before birth. You don't have to do this in the early days when everything is healing, but after the first six weeks or so it can be encouraging and helpful to know how everything looks. Most women are pleasantly surprised. Understanding and knowing your own anatomy is key for reconnecting with your post-partum self.

3. Massaging any new scar tissue can help to reduce any tenderness, tension or sensitivity. It can also help you to reconnect with your body and the process of accepting any changes that occur after birth. You can use the same perineal massage that you might have done during pregnancy to prepare for birth, but this time focusing on stretches around the scar area. It can be hard to know where the scar/s are – often they will feel tighter and more sensitive.

   This massage repeats the steps of the perineal massage on p.168. You should sweep side to side ten times, using the same 3 o'clock to 9 o'clock sweeping motion as in regular perineal massage. This time, however, gently stretch around the scar, holding each position for 30 seconds, or you can stretch in each direction from 3 o'clock to 9 o'clock and hold each stretch for 30 seconds. Remember, you should feel a stretch, but it should not be painful. Aim to do this once or twice a week.

Please only start this when you are at least six weeks post-partum and once your wound has fully healed and vaginal bleeding has finished. Always start gently and see how you get on. If your symptoms don't improve from doing this, then please seek medical attention.

4. Be honest and open about how you feel or about any concerns you have about your physical recovery. Never be embarrassed. It is a journey. It can take longer than you may think, but please don't suffer in silence.

## What about caesarean recovery ?

If you had a C-section, the suggestions around patience and self-care as you recover apply just as much to you, if not more. The average recovery time after a C-section is about six weeks, but you may need longer. Though your stitches will dissolve within two weeks, it might be several months before any soreness at the incision site goes away completely. In the first ten days or so, keep the wound clean and dry and don't lift anything heavier than your baby. It might be several months before you can go back to strenuous exercise, but gentle movement and exercise should be OK to do, as long as you have been cleared to do this by your care providers. When you have been given the OK to do so, you can begin to massage your C-section scar to increase blood flow to the area, promote healing and, over time, flatten it and improve its appearance.

# debrief deep dive

## REFLECT

Here are a few helpful videos to watch:

- How to make a padsicle: https://www.youtube.com/watch?v=myzsA2i6mB0

- A selection of videos by pelvic health physiotherapist Clare Bourne: https://www.youtube.com/watch?v=Y-zat5G9Jss&list=PLKC9h5R2W7qaXzP1jkdNTjSpsCyslhBvV&index=7

## REFRAME

Studies have shown that the mind is a powerful part of your healing toolkit, so try these affirmations as you recover:

- My body is healing every day.

- I'm healing at my pace, and noticing what is going right.

- I am learning more and more about my body, its capabilities and its limits.

## REDEFINE

Healing from birth is different for everyone who goes through it. Take your time. Your body has done something amazing.

# Managing serious injury

Sometimes, perineal damage can be more severe. These injuries can take significantly longer to heal, require more extensive support and care, and can have a significant impact on a woman's overall health and wellbeing and her sense of identity and self-worth.

Few women imagine coming out of what should be an incredibly happy time with a potentially lifelong injury. Any physical trauma has an impact on our emotions, but as Clare Bourne reminds us, 'You are not alone with anything you are struggling to come to terms with.' Know that it is OK to be angry, and to work through your emotions in your own time. Please reach out for support. Opening up about your birth experiences is one way to begin to heal, and to find a way forward in your recovery. My client Laura suffered severe perineal injury during childbirth. She was able to heal thanks to plenty of physical and emotional support, including a birth debrief. She wanted to share her insights on her healing journey to offer hope and encouragement to other women:

> I am not the same as I was before I had a baby, but I imagine not many mothers are. We are all creating new identities for ourselves, some out of choice, some out of necessity, but no one survives motherhood with their previous identity intact. We are all ever-growing; it's how we evolve into the best version of ourselves that we can be, for the tiny people that we love.
>
> – Laura

As mothers, our 'selves' are transitioning in lots of ways – some physical, some emotional. Laura's determination to find new meaning and purpose in her role as a woman, a wife and a mother was a key part of her recovery. If you are dealing with serious injury, you may feel reluctant to reach out for help. I can't emphasise strongly enough, however, that if you are concerned about anything at all relating to your health after birth, you should speak to your midwife, health visitor or GP, as the earlier you seek treatment, the sooner you can be on your path to recovery. You are not being silly, and you have nothing to be embarrassed about.

You can also access help, advice and information through organisations such as the MASIC Foundation (masic.org.uk), an excellent organisation for women who have experienced severe perineal injury.

# 23
# owning your feeding choices

**Doing your best for you and your baby**

## I nourish my baby in a way that works well for both of us.

One of the most frustrating phrases I hear concerning feeding newborns is 'breast is best'. It lacks nuance and flexibility, doesn't leave room for different opinions, and doesn't explore what 'best' means. For many women and birthing people who haven't been able to breastfeed, have chosen not to, or who have adapted their infant feeding methods to suit their unique situations, this phrase can feel harsh and judgemental.

I think the phrase is damaging if you are a midwife or a mother. When I had my daughter Ihsan, I knew I wanted to breastfeed. I'd seen my mother and many other women in my family and wider community do it, so to me it felt familiar and normal. Having supported many new mothers as a midwife, I knew it might be challenging, but I was well informed and knew all the positions, tips and tricks. The one thing I wasn't prepared for was the baby I had birthed. She and I had never practised *together*. All those times I had practised before didn't involve a crying baby struggling to latch on, or feelings of helplessness and inadequacy.

Shall I tell you what else I hadn't factored in? My birth experience, and how that could affect my breastfeeding experience.

Here's my truth: I know that breast milk is great and has so many benefits, but breastfeeding is not for everyone, due both to ability and choice. But I also speak to a lot of women who stopped breastfeeding before they wanted to because of cultural expectations or norms, and other people's opinions. There are advantages and disadvantages to each option, and the 'right' choice is the one that's right for *you*. I believe that 'informed is best' and my aim here is to empower you to make the decision that best suits you and your baby, to give you the confidence to persevere with your choice, and to adapt as circumstances evolve and change.

## Feeding options

Current advice is that babies under six months should only be fed with milk – breast milk, or if that isn't available, infant formula. Breast milk is usually given via direct breastfeeding. It can also be expressed by hand or breast pump and given via bottle. This may be required in the early days if your baby is having problems latching and breastfeeding. If your baby needs milk and you are not able to produce it yourself, depending on your individual circumstances donor breast milk may be an option for you. Most medications are compatible with breastfeeding and for those that aren't, there is often a suitable alternative. An excellent resource is https://www.breastfeedingnetwork.org.uk/detailed-information/drugs-in-breastmilk/. Some parents choose to formula-feed from the outset for personal reasons; while others use formula because of medical issues such as low milk supply, past trauma, surgery or illness.

**Reasons to consider breastfeeding**

Breastfeeding has been proven to:

- save lives in the long and short term, as well as saving the NHS millions in treating preventable illnesses including some cancers, and cardiovascular diseases[65];

- reduce the risk of breast and ovarian cancers;

- reduce the risk of maternal diabetes, obesity, heart disease and post-partum depression;

- encourage your uterus to return to its original size after birth;

- reduce the risk of childhood obesity, gut and ear infections, and asthma;

- contain all the nutrients your baby needs, and these change and adapt with time to account for your growing baby's changing needs.

When it works well, breastfeeding is also a more convenient, cost-effective and less cumbersome option than formula.

**Barriers to breastfeeding**

The UK has lower breastfeeding rates than many other European countries; a recent report found that only 34 per cent of UK babies are receiving some breast milk at six months old, compared with 49 per cent in the US and 71 per cent in Norway.[66] Possible reasons for this include the following:

- **Lack of family support.** Breastfeeding can take a while to get the hang of, so if you are finding it difficult and feel unsupported by your partner or family, it can be hard to stick with it.

- **Lack of professional support.** Access to breastfeeding support varies greatly (and disproportionately) depending on where you live and the resources invested in the public healthcare system to help facilitate breastfeeding - shocking, I know. In 2015 the UK government mandated that pregnant women would receive five visits from a health visitor – a step in the right direction to give women and birthing people the right support – but funding cuts have meant that this has not always played out in practice. The majority of health visitors do not have additional training in breastfeeding support.

- **Being given conflicting advice.** When I speak to women and birthing people about their breastfeeding experiences, one of the most common themes that emerges is that they were given so much conflicting advice from midwives and support staff that it made breastfeeding much more difficult.[67]

- **Discomfort around breastfeeding in public.** This features regularly in my debriefs as a reason not to breastfeed. The Western perception of women's breasts as purely sexual and designed for intimate pleasure rather than for feeding children has led to many women being told off for breastfeeding in public because their 'nudity' is perceived as inappropriate. I speak to women all the time who report being told to either cover up while feeding or to go elsewhere. Some women don't feel comfortable feeding in public, and many public feeding and baby-change rooms are little more than glorified toilet cubicles – hardly inviting! It can be difficult to persist when a culture is not set up in a way that supports breastfeeding in public. It can feel daunting and restricting, especially when your baby is new, when you may be feeding very often – and when you're out in public you can't exactly sit with your breasts out, as many of us do in those early days!

Before I became pregnant, I remember seeing women in cafes, on park benches or even on buses whip a breast out to feed their babies, and I recall it looking so serene and easy. So, once I had established breastfeeding with Ihsan (which took over a month), I thought I would look like that too. When she was about six weeks old, I went on my first solo outing with her. This was an achievement in itself, but I felt ready and armed with everything I needed. I was meeting a friend in a cafe. We sat down and ordered our food. Ihsan was chilling in my arms. Everything was going great and then … she kicked off. You know, in the way babies kick off, going from zero to 60 in a heartbeat. So I rummaged through my bag, pulled out a large muslin cloth to cover my extremely large breasts, and tried to get her under it to feed her. Her cries got even louder, and I became even more flustered. All I kept imagining was all those serene mamas who could feed their babies without all this commotion. Ihsan continued to scream the place down, and people were looking at us. I was still faffing around with the bloody muslin, my friend was asking if I needed a hand, and I was struggling to even find my baby's head underneath the stupid cloth. In the end I ripped the muslin off, took my boob out of my top (I hadn't quite mastered the art of 'lift top and feed' yet) and sat and fed her. To this day I feel embarrassed by the fact that everyone in the cafe saw my boob – a whole size E breast! Being able to confidently breastfeed in public is a skill that takes time to master.

If the idea of feeding in public worries you, take it slowly. Don't put any pressure on yourself. Practise feeding somewhere you are comfortable to feed; wear clothes that are easy to adjust when you're ready to feed; and find places that are breastfeeding-friendly. You could also take your partner or a friend with you for moral support. Keep practising, and it will soon become second nature.

## So, should you persevere?

If, despite your best efforts, breastfeeding just isn't clicking into place, should you stop? Honestly? It depends. Perseverance is admirable, but don't keep going until you're exhausted or jeopardising your mental and physical health. There is no shame in any form of informed decision-making – ever. If you need to make a different feeding choice, do it. It takes courage and strength to make a decision in the face of personal and societal judgement, but prioritising and advocating for yourself is a boss move and it's important you know this.

## Other cultural factors that impact breastfeeding

I find it strange that breastfeeding in public can be seen as problematic in the UK when other cultures don't bat an eye at it.

As Shaheda Yasmeen-Khan, breastfeeding specialist midwife and advocate of breastfeeding within South Asian communities notes, other ethnic groups and cultures have their own beliefs and barriers when it comes to infant feeding too. Some of the following may be familiar to you:

- Some cultures (particularly South Asian) associate breastfeeding with a lower socioeconomic status. They see formula feeding as a sign of affluence, and 'better' for baby.

- Awareness initiatives like Black Breastfeeding Week[68] have found that breastfeeding rates among Black women in the West are lower than in other ethnic groups.[69] These initiatives see representation and emphasising the health benefits of breastfeeding as key to reversing this trend.

- Many people, no matter their ethnicity, believe that breastfeeding is too much hard work, and difficult to juggle with work and sleep.

## Difficult emotions

As we have explored the barriers to breastfeeding, it's important to highlight that 8 out of 10 women stop breastfeeding before they want to.[70] How does this manifest in the feelings women experience? In debriefs, I meet many women who are dealing with layered, complex emotions, including grief, around stopping breastfeeding. Many view the decision to formula feed as a choice, but for others that simply isn't the case. This is nothing against formula; what I witness is the grief for a choice that was stripped away from these women, through no volition of their own.

Navigating these feelings can be complex and conflicting; joy that your baby is fed, alongside sadness that they are not being fed the way you wanted them to be.

These feelings are valid and, in my experience, normal. My advice would be to notice as those feelings arise, often alongside self-critical thoughts. Validate their presence, but redirect the sentiment. Place yourself back in the context of your experience, and remind yourself why you had no choice but to make a certain decision. Keep doing this until it becomes almost automatic, and those thoughts decrease in intensity and frequency.

## Breastfeeding and birth trauma

The 'breast is best' narrative can be especially harmful if you had a traumatic birth experience. It can create pressure, overwhelm, and an overriding need to succeed – perhaps stemming from a need to redeem a birth you felt like you lost control of. A traumatic birth can impact breastfeeding in lots of ways.

Stacey Zimmels is an International Board Certified Lactation Consultant (IBCLC) with over twenty years' experience supporting families with feeding. She shares that women who have suffered some kind of birth trauma may face difficulties breastfeeding their babies. '[These] women start their journey to motherhood with some really big and overwhelming feelings,' she says. 'After a trauma, it is common to feel on edge, restless, anxious or irritable. When this has been our birth experience, feeding can then also understandably seem hard and one more thing to have to do. Mothers may feel so emotionally exhausted because of the birth that feeding feels too much. Birth trauma can sometimes affect milk supply or trauma at birth causes mum to feel detached from baby, so the closeness and physicality of feeding then feels overwhelming.'[71]

But don't worry – a traumatic birth doesn't always mean that establishing breastfeeding will be a problem. For many mothers breastfeeding can be healing, and can feel like a way of regaining control, something they are able to actively manage, and that can feel like a real win. As one lactation consultant notes, 'although trauma can make breastfeeding more difficult, breastfeeding itself offers trauma survivors some amazing gifts. It's as if nature knows that bad things happen and provides a way to reset the clock … While trauma survivors may face barriers to breastfeeding, breastfeeding has the power to heal'.[72]

**Informed is best**

Let's revisit the initial question – is breast really best? Sometimes it is and sometimes it's not. 'Informed' is actually best: you being informed, empowered and supported to make the right choice for you and your family. Trust me, whatever that choice is, it is the best one. It's time to make our conversations around infant feeding more nuanced and understanding of everyone's choices. Our babies deserve to be fed and content. We agree on that, so the way we feed our children should never be something that divides us.

# debrief deep dive

## REFLECT

What was your experience of breastfeeding initiation and continuation like? What do you think affected it, either positively or negatively? If you like, you can write this in your journal as a point of reflection.

_____

_____

_____

## REFRAME

If you have felt guilt, shame, inadequacy or any other negative emotions around feeding, begin to reframe those thoughts. Try rephrasing your feeding experience with the following affirmations when any harsh thoughts creep in. Feel free to add some of your own affirmations as well:

- I am not defined by how I feed my child.

- I have adapted the way I feed my child to suit us both.

- I made the right feeding choices for my child and for me.

## REDEFINE

If you are reflecting on your feeding journey and wondering why you made a particular choice, or questioning whether you could have done more, remember to contextualise your memories. Remember the situation you were in when you made that choice, and remember that hindsight is always 20/20. You did, and are doing, the best you can in the moment. That's good enough.

# 24
# when baby is not born healthy

**Coping with the unexpected**

## This is hard, but I will get through it.

Having an unwell baby is something that no parent wants to contemplate. Unfortunately, some parents will find that their newborn needs extra support and specialist care. Suddenly, the anticipated skin-to-skin contact, celebration and sighs of relief are replaced with fear and worry as baby is whisked off to NICU. I know that worst-case scenarios are the last thing parents want to think about, especially during a vulnerable time such as pregnancy. And it can be scary to think of the events that could result in your baby being taken to a NICU. At the same time, we are so fortunate in the UK to have access to well-equipped NICUs and specialist staff who are trained to give your little one the best chance of a positive outcome if they are born needing that extra support.

I believe that talking about coping strategies for when things do not go as expected should be part of all antenatal education. This is not to cause alarm – there is a positive side to this. Sometimes knowing about something in advance helps us to cope with it if it happens. It's not about dwelling on 'what ifs'; rather, it's about having information that will help you decide how you and your partner will approach any setbacks or unexpected outcomes *if* they appear. This could be by attending a debriefing session, speaking to a therapist or other professional, or simply writing down a list of people or places you could use for support. As always, if you are concerned about anything, don't keep it to yourself. Your healthcare providers are there to support and reassure you, so let them know what's on your mind.

## What to expect if your baby starts life in NICU

Some parents-to-be might know in advance that their babies will need extra support when they are born. They may even be offered a tour of the neonatal unit where their baby will be cared for, to prepare them. With or without advance planning, however, the reality of seeing your baby attached to machines and being given medications will still be challenging, especially if you are not able to hold your baby straight away. It's important to acknowledge how complex those feelings can be. There is a particular helplessness that comes with being a parent of a baby in NICU. Whether their stay is long or short, there is so much that can feel out of your control. You'll almost certainly have mixed feelings: gratitude that your baby is in good hands, and sadness and fear because they are in NICU.

Families who have been in this situation have told me they felt a strange sense of limbo when their baby was in NICU, especially since things can change drastically and rapidly. There is no time to process what's happening, and the focus is often on the 'end goal', which is for baby to be well enough to go home. Being 'well enough' to be discharged from NICU is a milestone to celebrate. However, while they are out of the high-dependency danger zone, your baby may still have complex care requirements, and discharge will simply mean that you can look after your baby at home.

## Supporting parents with a baby in NICU

Sam Harrison supports parents of babies in NICU and is the founder of The NICU Mummy, a social media platform she started after her experience with her son, who spent thirty-one days in NICU. She shares some of her invaluable insights on Instagram (@the_nicu_mummy), and you may find this helpful if you are a parent facing a similar journey with your baby, or if you are supporting someone who is going through a stay in NICU.

*I know from experience that my friends and family all wanted to do whatever they could to support us during that time, and I've talked a lot to people within the NICU community about ways in which parents could have felt better supported by loved ones.*

*For those who haven't experienced it personally, it's impossible to comprehend what parents go through while their baby is in NICU (and afterwards). This is partly because it's an area of parenthood that isn't often discussed, but also because there are some things that parents experience that are unimaginable. It doesn't matter if their little one is in hospital for a few days, weeks or even months, that time can affect parents' mental health, regardless of their baby's circumstances or outcome.*

*– Sam, NICU parent*

### Sam's tips

#### 1. Listen

I cannot stress how important this is. I felt so overwhelmed and experienced such a vast range of feelings very quickly at the beginning - and to an extent, I probably didn't know what I wanted or needed. Listening to what the parents need at that time, and not making assumptions of your own, will go a long way. Some people want to talk. Others don't. Some will find comfort in receiving calls and messages, whereas others can find that overwhelming and stressful. Bear in mind that all parents will handle things differently. Just because one parent you know felt one way about NICU, it doesn't mean another will feel the same way.

#### 2. Meals

We had no desire to cook a meal once we got home from a long day in the hospital with our son. Something as simple as delivering groceries or sending a delivery round to parents will be greatly appreciated. I have heard of some friends and families creating a rota so that the parents never have to think about lunches or dinners!

### 3. Words

This is linked to my first point about listening. Words can be well meant – people want to be able to say something to comfort parents – but sometimes words are not taken in the way you may have intended them, and can do more harm than good. For example, questions like 'When will baby be coming home?' can frustrate parents, as they simply don't have the answer. Plus, it's an answer they desperately want, too. Making parents feel understood will go much further than trying to provide them with words of comfort.

### 4. Financial support

Parents can find that having a NICU baby comes with unforeseen costs. Hospital car parking charges, the cost of food in the hospital, accommodation and even petrol, particularly for those who have to travel to their local hospital each day to visit their little one(s). I have heard from other parents that their loved ones have had a whip-round to help cover these costs during that time, which was very much appreciated. I know that when there is a new baby, it's easy to spend money on gifts for the baby, but a contribution to such extra costs would be just as helpful, if not more so.

### 5. When baby goes home

This is the day that the parents have been desperately waiting for. And while it is a momentous day, it can also be a day full of anxiety and worry. For your baby's entire life so far, you have had a full medical team around you, and being allowed to go home is daunting. It can be a time of very mixed emotions. There seems to be a misconception that once baby is allowed home, parents automatically forget all they have been through, but I can assure you this isn't the case. Having a baby on NICU can be a traumatic experience for parents – one that can take time and professional support to come to terms with. So, even after baby is home, keep checking in on the parents – they may be struggling more than you realise.

Of course, Sam and I hope you won't need to draw on this information, but it is here for you if you do. As Sam says, 'How are people supposed to understand the realities of NICU, or how to help families in NICU, if we don't talk about it?'

## Processing takes time

I believe all parents should be supported well into the post-partum period, but the families of NICU babies may need specific support with processing and acknowledging their experiences. If I could give you one piece of advice for if your baby needs care in NICU, it's to accept for now that processing the birth and early post-partum period might need to take a back seat – there really isn't time or space for it during such a stressful time. And that's OK.

This was true for Emily, who experienced mental health difficulties after the traumatic birth of her first child. She sought help and support and delayed trying for another child, then when she got pregnant again she experienced a second traumatic birth. Her first son, Arthur, was induced at 42 weeks and delivered by emergency C-section. His little brother Henry spent his first three weeks in NICU after being born prematurely (also by C-section) and diagnosed with a rare genetic skin condition. Unsurprisingly, two years on from Henry's birth, Emily was still processing and recovering emotionally from both birth experiences. Debriefing her experiences (alongside several other forms of therapy) was a pivotal part of her recovery:

*Henry and his birth have changed my life – I believe I was given to Henry and Henry was given to me. We are a little team. Along with his big brother and my supportive husband, we really have gone through the mill and come out the other side.*

*My experiences of motherhood have led me to being a holistic gentle sleep coach, helping families with their children's sleep and supporting mothers with their mental health.*

*– Emily, mother to Arthur and Henry*

Contemplating a long journey to recover from your birth experience may seem daunting, but Emily's story shows that, with support, you can recover.

# debrief deep dive

## REFLECT

If your baby is, or was, in NICU, it can be helpful to debrief your feelings around your experience. I would love you to share your feelings here, along with the ways in which you feel you either would have liked to be supported, or how you were supported.

Though you might want to save a formal debrief for a time when you feel emotionally stronger, you need not censor yourself now. Just free-write your feelings – write down whatever comes to you. When you have written them down, consider sharing your feelings with a trusted friend or other safe person who will ensure you feel heard.

## REFRAME

It can be hard to focus on anything but your unwell baby when you are in the thick of it. I hope these affirmations will encourage and strengthen you through this challenging time:

- My baby is getting the very best care. So many people are rooting for us.

- It might get tough and I might cry, but I will trust that everything will be OK.

- I recognise that nothing lasts forever – the hard times or the easier times. Nothing lasts forever.

## REDEFINE

It can be easy to lose sight of the excellent job you are doing if you are a NICU parent. Remember that your baby is in a safe environment and you are doing the best you can from moment to moment.

# 25
# is it baby blues – or something else?

**Postnatal mental health: how to recognise and manage post-partum depression**

My mental health
is as important as
my physical health;
I prioritise care of both.

There's a time, around day three or four after your baby is born, when you may feel like the sky has come crashing down. The 'high' that can come from giving birth and the warm embrace of oxytocin (the 'feel-good' hormone) has faded, your hormone levels are changing, your breasts are filling with milk to feed your newborn, and overwhelm creeps in – otherwise known as the baby blues. Baby blues affect nearly every birthing parent: approximately 80 per cent of them, in fact.[73] The primary cause of baby blues is, as with most things postnatal: hormones, primarily oestrogen. During pregnancy, your body produces more of it in order to sustain the pregnancy, but in the three days after giving birth, your oestrogen level will drop dramatically. This leads to a clutch of symptoms you may already be familiar with:

- crying (seemingly for no reason!);

- irritability and frustration;

- impatience;

- mood swings;

- anxiety.

Baby blues tend to last a maximum of fourteen days, and unfortunately, there is not really a way to avoid them.[74] If you have any of the symptoms listed above, you can make them a bit easier to manage by ensuring you have adequate support around you, resting as much as you can, and making sure you eat well and drink plenty of fluids. If you feel comfortable doing so, cocoon your baby in a baby wrap or sling, get outside and go for a gentle walk – even a short walk will help boost your mood and alter your perspective.

In the midst of these feelings, it's common to feel as though you will never feel like your old self again. I always remind my clients that the baby blues are normal, that your hormones *will* stabilise, and these feelings usually pass on their own. If you are prepared for them, understand what is happening to your body and prioritise self-care, I promise you will get through it. Above all, don't hide what you're feeling. Women are often conditioned to respond that we're fine even when we're feeling lousy. We might feel as though we *should* be feeling loved-up and happy now that our long-awaited little one is here. Be honest if that *isn't* what you're feeling. Open up to your partner, a friend, family member, doula or midwife. It's OK to say, 'Actually, I'm struggling right now and feeling sad/irritable/anxious. Would you mind *[fill in the blank with whatever you need in the moment]*?'

### When sadness doesn't pass

Sometimes, the baby blues linger. For about 10–15 per cent of women, the baby blues may actually be something more serious: postnatal depression (PND)[75]. It's important not to self-diagnose PND. You should let your midwife or GP know if you are struggling or begin to struggle after starting out fine – they will be able to point you to the best sources of support and treatment.

Postnatal depression does not discriminate; it affects people of all ages and all ethnicities. However, the NHS lists the following risk factors that link to a higher risk of developing postnatal depression:

- antenatal depression or depression before being pregnant;

- limited or non-existent support networks;

- high levels of life stress;

- current or previous domestic abuse;

- relationship problems.

There's a lot of confusion between the symptoms of postnatal depression and the baby blues, so let's see if we can clarify this. The biggest differences between postnatal depression and baby blues are timing and duration. Postnatal depression can develop at any time after birth, and is not predominantly caused by hormonal changes. Symptoms of postnatal depression can also last for significantly longer than baby blues – months or even years, in some cases. Another difference is that the mood changes that happen with baby blues are quite extreme, swinging rapidly from happiness, excitement or joy to sadness, frustration or irritability, whereas postnatal depression is more commonly described as a constant state of sadness.

In my experience, there is still a stigma around PND, which prevents women who are affected from saying anything; some prefer to stay quiet out of shame or fear. I believe that postnatal depression is under-reported because of this.

My good friend and colleague Tessa van der Vord is an NHS maternal mental health specialist midwife, and you can find her at @mentalhealth_midwife on Instagram. Tessa is passionate about raising awareness of maternal mental health and ensuring that women and birthing people speak up and access the right support when it's needed, whether during pregnancy or the postnatal period. She and I strongly believe that we need to let go of the belief that asking for help is a sign of weakness. In fact, it is the exact opposite. 'We have learned to be almost hypervigilant in checking our moles for changes, our breasts for lumps, our blood for unusual markers, our eyes for distortions and so on,' says Tessa. 'If we have an acute pain or an injury, we don't ignore it - we tell someone about it and ask for help. We need to start doing this for our emotional health and making it a priority.'

I couldn't agree more. I find it astounding that this stigma should exist in this day and age, and this is another reason why I wrote this book. We have to get rid of the stigma surrounding depression once and for all. If you suffer from PND, it's not your fault, and you are not a bad parent. If you feel you are suffering from postnatal depression, please do get help. There are online groups and in-person groups, and you can also seek help from your GP, health visitor, midwife or health provider. It may take a while, but you will recover. Be patient with yourself through the process.

I recognise that when you're suffering with low mood, seeking help and support may feel too difficult. If you don't feel ready to seek professional help, please consider confiding in your partner, a friend or a family member. PND is not something you should try to treat alone. As a second step, perhaps you could find out where help is available (see the Resources) and save the contact details for when you do feel ready.

### Lara's story

During a debrief with Lara, a woman who had recently been diagnosed with postnatal depression, we discussed how best to deal with feelings of failure and self-loathing. Lara didn't understand why she was suffering from postnatal depression. She'd desperately wanted her baby, and had a great relationship with her husband. She had been diagnosed with depression when she was younger, but felt that she had overcome it with the support of her family and medication.

*I had a complicated birth, and as I progressed through the immediate postnatal period, I felt myself becoming increasingly sad. I just couldn't shake off this overwhelming feeling of despair, like I'd lost something important that I'd never get back. I had the odd good day here and there but over time my mood was low more often than not, I had a low appetite, and I was finding it hard to care for my baby's needs.*

*My husband gently asked me one day if I might be suffering from depression. I could see it took a lot for him to ask. He didn't want to upset me, but I was upset – I loved my daughter and thought I must be a bad mum for feeling this way. Deep down, though, I knew I needed help, and shortly afterwards I confided in my health visitor and told her how I was feeling. That led to starting CBT – and after a few sessions, I also contacted Illy for a birth debrief. By then things were improving in regard to my mental health, but I was still battling feelings of failure and had a deep sense of having let my daughter down. Illy helped me to gain a new perspective on my feelings: she explained that I'd had a normal reaction to a difficult birth and I hadn't given myself the time or space to process it. This gave me the chink of light I needed to push forward towards recovery, and I am doing so much better today.*

*– Lara*

Tessa van der Vord has first-hand knowledge of what your care under the NHS will look like. 'In the UK, your GP, health visitor or midwife is fully trained to have these conversations [around mental health] with new parents, and it is their duty to ensure the right help is arranged,' Tessa notes. There are many treatment options. Below are a few of Tessa's recommendations for women with PND:

- Self-help techniques such as mindfulness and meditation can help as a maintenance or temporary measure.

- Psychological (talking) therapy can provide a collaborative, safe and confidential space in which to explore your feelings.

- Medication can also be helpful, either alone or in conjunction with a talking therapy.

'What may work for one parent may not work for another,' Tessa concludes, 'but by working with a health professional, you will, in time, be able to feel better and recover.'

# debrief deep dive

## REFLECT

If you're one of the many who do find themselves experiencing symptoms of poor mental health in the post-partum period, please don't suffer in silence. Remember, there will be countless other new mums feeling the same. You are not alone.

## REFRAME

As you recover, daily affirmations may help. Below are a few you can use if you are going through postnatal depression:

- Depression is part of my experience, not my whole experience.

- The way I'm feeling does not define the parent I am, or the love I have for my child.

- I am overcoming this day by day – it is a process and there is no rush.

## REDEFINE

Every phase of parenthood comes with its own challenges. Keep in mind that what you're feeling in the moment, no matter how difficult, is temporary. It will pass.

# When mental health is an emergency: post-partum psychosis

Post-partum psychosis, also known as puerperal psychosis, is a serious mental health condition that requires emergency treatment. It affects approximately 1 in 500 women. As the chance of experiencing it is quite low, many people may not be aware the condition exists. Similarly to baby blues, its onset is normally hours to a few days post-birth, but it can develop a few weeks post-birth, too.

The symptoms of psychosis include:

- hallucinations;

- manic moods, or rapidly cycling manic and low moods;

- difficulty sleeping, low energy;

- anxiety and agitation;

- feeling scared and fearful;

- feeling fearless and 'unstoppable';

- delusions;

- acting 'out of character'.

Because post-partum psychosis can occur very rapidly, the person suffering may not self-report. The condition is often noticed and reported by a partner, relative or healthcare professional. Due to the risk it poses to both mother and baby, it is vital that if you are concerned that someone you know has this condition, you must seek help immediately by calling the emergency services or taking the person to A&E. Women are more likely to suffer from this psychosis if they have an underlying condition such as bipolar disorder or schizophrenia. If they do, they should receive additional monitoring and support in the perinatal period.

## Treatment

The treatment options for post-partum psychosis vary, but it usually requires specialist hospital treatment, usually in a mother and baby unit where the mother and baby can stay together.

Symptoms can last from two to twelve weeks, and recovery can take six to twelve months. With the correct treatment, there is every reason to expect a full recovery. One of the most important things to aid recovery is support: from family, peers or professionals.

If you have suffered from psychosis, be aware that your recovery may not be linear. Following a psychotic episode, it is common to have a period of depression, anxiety or continued feelings of sadness. You might also feel grief over the time you have missed with your baby or due to not having a 'normal' post-partum experience, due to this condition. All of these feelings can take time to navigate.

If you are supporting someone who has suffered from psychosis, let them know you are there for them if you have the capacity to support them. Have no expectations of them; allow them to come to you when they need to. If you are wondering what you can do to help, you can research local or online support groups or services for them. You can also ask them what they need and how you can best support them. They may not have a ready answer, but simply knowing that you are there for them will be helpful.

# 26
# debriefing shock

**Coping with post-partum feelings linked to trauma**

I can be calm,
even when life is
unpredictable.

In Part 1, we looked at some of the more challenging feelings that
sometimes emerge after childbirth. Women tell me all the time about
feeling shock, guilt, shame, grief, regret and remorse as part of their
birth experience. But did you know that emotions linked to trauma are
usually also closely linked to each other? For example, psychological
shock can lead to difficulty bonding with your baby, which can lead
to guilt and shame. This does not mean that if you felt any of these
emotions you were definitely traumatised, but they can be indicators.
So if any of the feelings outlined in these next few chapters resonate
with you, you may have some emotions to investigate further (perhaps
with a debrief facilitator, therapist or counsellor).

## Psychological shock

Psychological or emotional shock[76] means the rush of emotions you feel
after a stressful, highly charged or traumatic event. As your brain tries to
process what's happened, you become unable to respond as you would
in normal circumstances - this is the 'freeze' part of the 'fight, flight

or freeze' response discussed in Chapter 6. Your brain does this as a survival mechanism, to keep you safe. You might experience symptoms such as shortness of breath, going numb, feeling lightheaded, sick or dizzy, or you might disengage and feel unable to speak.

Disengaging was how I experienced psychological shock after Ihsan was born. I remember the midwives showing me my baby wrapped in towels. I could just about see her little face, this tiny, adorable little girl, but all I felt was an urgent need to close my eyes and take a minute. The sense of overwhelm was so intense – I couldn't believe she was actually here – that I simply disengaged. It must have looked like there was something wrong with me, that I wasn't the nurturing earth mother I 'should' have been, but when I think about it now, it makes complete sense. Yes, I had just welcomed a wonderful little human into the world, and I was happy and thankful, yet I was also a person who had gone through a life-altering and traumatic experience.

Labour can look different from person to person. For some, it is long and exhausting; for others, quick and intense, with a wide spectrum in between. Whatever kind of labour you had, there will probably be at least one aspect of it that takes you by surprise. And sometimes, it's surprise at seeing the baby – a baby who is part of you, yet essentially a stranger. Your initial feelings towards your little one may be all-consuming, or you may feel numb. The effect of shock on our feelings is something we really don't give much thought to; we expect to be swept up by feelings of love and connection immediately. When we hear about birth in a conversation or see a birth on television or read about one in a magazine, there's so much talk of 'bursts of love that make us forget the pain'. I don't agree with this expectation, which may make birthing people feel that we have failed somehow if we don't 'follow the script'. If we expect to feel a particular way, it can surprise us when we feel a different way. We might wonder whether anyone cares how we really feel, whether it matters, whether we still matter.

Emotional shock can also result from how the birth happened – for example, if you had a birth where everything felt out of control or overwhelming or went totally differently to how you planned or imagined. The sense of loss of control or autonomy during childbirth can impact how we parent, particularly in the early days. I often hear women and birthing people berating themselves. They say things like 'I don't know why I expected to feel in control' or 'I don't understand why I'm shocked - I felt so overwhelmed!'

My response to this is always the same: 'It's one thing to know it, but another thing to experience it.' It's very easy to have expectations of yourself before you have experienced a situation that are impossible to live up to when you are actually in that situation. This goes for subsequent babies as much as the first. Hindsight is wonderful, but if you are stuck in a pattern of harsh self-judgement over how you felt or reacted to an overwhelming situation, it doesn't leave much room for kindness and self-love.

## Coping with shock

In the moment, the overwhelm may mean that you are not even aware you are in shock. But if you or those around you notice you're not acting like yourself after you've given birth, shock could be the reason. Here are a few things that could help:

- Breathe deeply. You may not be able to speak or respond, so you will need to find a way to communicate non-verbally to people around you. Placing your hand on your chest, closing your eyes and breathing deeply may give you the space you need to rebalance yourself.

- Give yourself a moment. Remind yourself, as you breathe, that the symptoms will pass. You've just been through a major event, and your mind and body need a moment or two to process it. And that's OK.

- Have your partner, birth partner or doula hold you, advocate for you, or speak to you in a calming manner, reminding you that you are safe and your symptoms will pass.

- If the symptoms linger long after the event, don't ignore them - reach out to your health provider for more support.

- When the symptoms have subsided, you may question the way you reacted in the moment – and this is when it's easy for other emotions, like guilt, shame and regret, to sneak in. It's really important that you are kind to yourself in these moments. You were in shock, and we all behave differently when we are in shock. You did – and are still doing – the best you can.

## Shock and bonding difficulties

About 30 per cent of women have difficulty bonding with their newborns,[77] and shock can be a factor in this. But bonding is an ongoing, ever-evolving experience. It doesn't happen overnight, despite our expectations for it to happen quickly, so you need not feel anxious if you don't instantly feel an overwhelming love for your baby. You should also be aware that difficulty bonding with your first child doesn't necessarily mean this will be the same with subsequent children. When you find it easier to bond with a subsequent child, you may feel guilty, and you may grieve over the way you felt about your first child. I want to remind you – and urge you to continuously remind yourself – that they are different situations. You did the best you could in both situations and that's OK.

For most women and birthing people, the shock will ease in time, and as it does, this will leave a space where your love for your baby will bloom. If the shock takes longer to ease and you find yourself experiencing ongoing difficulties, speak to your GP or health visitor and see what support they can offer you.

# debrief deep dive

## REFLECT

Educating yourself and your birth partner about signs of shock to look out for can be helpful. Using the following prompts, agree a list of actions you, your partner and your birth partner could take if you or they notice any symptoms of shock. You know yourself best, so think about the things that make you feel safe, calm and balanced, and include those.

If you notice that my breathing is shallow, I need a moment to collect my thoughts. You can help me by

_____

_____

If I don't respond to questions straight away, it means

_____

so I need

_____

If I raise my hand it means

_____

_____

If I close my eyes, it means

_____

_____

If I seem distressed, I need you to

_____

_____

## REFRAME

If you experienced shock and are berating yourself for the way you reacted, let's reframe the situation. What would happen if you thought something like 'Wow, the things that happened were so unexpected. I did what I could with the information provided to me and worked with the feelings I had.' Reframing your self-judgement as compassionate statements makes you calmer.

You can also use these affirmations as tools to help you rebalance yourself if you experience emotional shock and to help you be kind to yourself afterwards:

- I make the best choices I can in the moment.

- No matter what is happening, I always show myself compassion.

- I do the best that I can, and that's good enough.

## REDEFINE

Now let's begin to look at exactly what you felt was out of control. Did you feel that you lost the ability to make decisions? Did you feel unsupported? Did you have to have an intervention you didn't want? Was communication poor, or was it a mix of everything? Try to pinpoint exactly what felt out of your control. Once you have done this, you can look more closely at what you really could have controlled – and you may find that, actually, there were lots of things you *couldn't* have changed. Continue to use your affirmations to remind yourself that you did the best you could then, and you are safe now.

# 27

# debriefing guilt and shame

**How to deal with emotional wellbeing saboteurs**

# I let go of guilt and shame and embrace my humanity.

Guilt and shame are sneaky thieves of our peace, joy and wellbeing. Guilt is the nagging feeling that we have either done something wrong or failed to do something right. As we've seen, it can creep in when aspects of our birth experience did not go to plan, and at other times too. Almost all mothers report feeling guilty about one thing or another. Even before our children are born, we feel guilt. It's such a common emotion among mothers that it might as well be rebranded as a ticket to the 'mum club'. Societally, we have been conditioned to be conscientious, so whenever we feel we have somehow not been a 'good parent' – whether or not this is actually true – the result is a flood of guilt.

## Healthy vs unhealthy guilt

Guilt can be healthy: it's appropriate to feel guilty if we've *actually* done something morally wrong – deliberately harmed someone, for example, or not done something we should have done. Generally, we feel healthy guilt over tangible things we have control over. But when guilt comes from something we merely *think* we've done or not done, from negative self-talk or judgement – whether our own or that of others – with no basis in truth, it's destructive and has no place in our lives. This unhealthy 'false' guilt is rooted in feelings of inadequacy and the fear of making mistakes. No one wants to feel inadequate, or as if we're not good enough for our children or our families. This thinking comes from expectations placed on us not only by ourselves but also from wider society. And no one wants to make mistakes, even though the sensible, compassionate part of us knows that everyone makes mistakes; they are part of being human. We have to challenge and reject false guilt at every turn.

A prime example of unhealthy guilt is when women return to work following parental leave – so many women struggle with this and feel guilty for leaving their baby. I did too when I went back to work after Ihsan was born. But do you know what? I also desperately *wanted* to return to work. I needed some time for myself, some adult company, to see if the old me was still there – and much of that identity lay in my work. Interestingly, a lot of people asked me if I felt guilty for leaving Ihsan. Even though I knew my daughter was in safe hands, I still felt like I had to say yes, even though deep down I was overjoyed to be back at work (yes, I said it: O-V-E-R-J-O-Y-E-D!). But at the time, that was difficult to express, so out of fear of not fitting in I said what I thought people wanted to hear. And then I felt guilty for not staying true to myself!

When feeling guilty overwhelms you and consumes you until it is preventing you from doing anything that brings you joy and fulfilment, it's time to rethink things. A lot of the things we feel guilty about are out of our control, anyway, and we can't change them. In the end, these feelings of guilt do nothing but make us more upset and insecure.

## Shame

Most of the time, similarly to guilt, feelings of shame are wrapped up in a sense of inadequacy. We put ourselves under pressure to reach goals and targets that are unrealistic – and sometimes they don't even reflect what we actually want.

Shame can be more insidious than guilt, because while guilt torments us with 'I did a bad thing', shame tries to convince us that 'I am a bad person'. Carrying the weight of that can be unbearable. You are not a bad person – and it's time to release the shame that tells you otherwise once and for all.

A lot of our feelings of shame are driven by societal expectations that we unconsciously agree with or aspire to, coupled with the fear of outside judgement when we don't match up to them. Feelings of shame can start when you conceive, especially if you have fertility issues, or during pregnancy – if, for example, the pregnancy was unplanned. Or shame may arrive later in your parenting journey, perhaps if you feel you haven't lost the pregnancy weight fast enough, or you get impatient when you're trying to get your baby to sleep. Shame may sound like anything from a mild whisper to a critical, nagging voice in your head. You may feel like you always have something to feel ashamed of, but where does that come from? Are we naturally inclined to feel shame? Or is shame many other feelings all grouped together?

**Shame in early post-partum**

One of the most common causes of shame in the early post-partum period, along with feeding choices and difficulty bonding with your baby, is how you gave birth. As I shared earlier, my daughter was born via caesarean section, but it was documented as a 'failed home birth'. Even writing that today makes me wince. You see, I had told everyone I was having a home birth. I was aware that things might not go to plan but I was committed, and had dealt with positive and negative responses to it from family, friends and professionals. I never expected to feel shame at not delivering my baby at home, as I had wanted, and it took me a while to reconcile my feelings of shame around how I ultimately gave birth. In the end I was able to process these feelings and see that I was not a failure because I transferred to hospital. Far from it. I made the right decision in the moment for my baby and me.

**Parental shaming**

Another area that is worth exploring is where others shame you. Parental shaming has to be one of the most toxic aspects of parenting, stealing any joy you may feel as a parent and putting pressure on you. This pressure can manifest in many ways, from rage and anxiety to obsessive behaviour and depression.

When anyone attempts to shame you for any of your choices, whether around birth, feeding or parenting, it is often because they have unresolved issues themselves. The issue is theirs, not yours. If you view something, perhaps on social media, that makes you feel ashamed or makes you question your self-worth, as hard as it may be, don't suppress these feelings. Instead, lean into them and check their validity. More often than not, you'll discover that they are *not* valid – and once you realise that the 'accusing voices' are not the truth, that they are irrelevant to you, then let them go. If you find that those feelings do have some validity, then explore them further. Remember I said earlier that feelings are signals, inviting you to investigate deeper? Sometimes when we do this we aren't always happy with what we find, but we can use the information to help us improve or change things, and this is a positive step too.

# debrief deep dive

**REFLECT**

An effective way to handle feelings of guilt and shame is to use the 'stop, check, reflect, change/continue' technique. When a feeling of guilt or shame arises, pause (stop), check in with it (check), then challenge it (reflect). Then you change what you can, forgive yourself (or others) for what cannot be changed, and move forward with your life. This is a way of halting the feelings in their tracks, checking in with them, honouring what you're feeling and ensuring that your response is appropriate. You can then change something (if the guilt is healthy guilt), or let it go and continue with your life.

I think this routine is helpful to do, as parents: a quick stop, check, reflect, change/continue.

Ask yourself:

- What am I feeling guilty/ashamed about?
- Can I change the thing that is making me feel guilty/ashamed?
- Is the guilt/shame a consequence of something I have done that I can control?
- Is anyone, including me, being negatively affected by the things I'm feeling guilty/ashamed about?
- Do I *actually* feel guilty, or do I simply feel pressure to feel guilty, so I sound like everyone else?

## REFRAME

Ask yourself this question: can I let myself accept that I'm doing the best I can and let the guilt/shame go? If you find yourself answering 'no' to that last question, then you may be being too hard on yourself. I invite you to try reframing the question as an affirmation and saying it out loud every time you feel guilty about something:

- I accept that I'm doing the best that I can. I release the guilt/shame.

## REDEFINE

The most important piece of advice I can give you in regard to guilt and shame is to stand firm in your own values. Examine your ideals and see if they are actually your own. You create your ideals, what you want, what matters to *you* as a mother. Let go of standards that don't align with your values. Own your true feelings and become comfortable with them. This can be difficult to start with, but the more you do it, the more natural it will feel and the more confident you will feel doing it. Finally, remember self-kindness and compassion as you go.

# 28
# grief, regret and remorse

**When you have a healthy baby, but you still feel sad**

# I allow myself to let go of suffering.

You may have imagined pregnancy, birth and the post-partum period a particular way: how you would feel, how the birth would be, the first feeding experience, how you would connect with your baby, and how you would be treated and looked after, only to find that not all these things happened. You didn't enjoy pregnancy; you had a traumatic birth; you weren't able to breastfeed; you didn't feel an overwhelming sense of love for your baby when they were born. These things feel like a loss – the death of a cherished dream – and an intense sorrow hits you. Sometimes, parents do not even realise that the emotions they are feeling could be grief. Sadness, disappointment, numbness and fear can all be masks for grief.

## Dare I call it 'grief'?

Giving birth to a healthy baby after a traumatic labour or birth can sometimes make parents feel that they don't have the 'right' to grieve – as if their feelings are self-indulgent or misplaced, especially when they know they are lucky compared to parents who have lost children. When I see clients who are grieving (whatever their reason), I remind them – as I remind you – that grief, however you experience it, is valid, and you are not wrong or selfish for feeling what you feel. Mourning the loss of aspects of your birthing experience you hoped for and missed out on is a completely normal way of coming to terms with what happened.

For about six weeks after Ihsan's birth, I struggled to see any joy, even in moments with her, such as the little sounds she'd make when she slept, or precious changes that were taking place as she became accustomed to life outside the womb. My head was too foggy, and I was simply trying to survive. I still grieve those lost moments and have felt angry, sad, remorseful and everything in between. To me, it makes complete sense to call it grief.

I understand that it might feel challenging to label your feelings as 'grief'. If that's true for you, you don't have to do so. What's important is that you allow yourself to acknowledge the emotion, feel it fully, and don't try to go through it alone.

### Nia's story

Nia had high hopes for her baby's birth – she had planned everything meticulously. When the time came for her to give birth, however, nothing went the way she had hoped. Nia described this as feeling like her world had come 'crashing down'. She felt that she had gone through a loss rather than having gained her child. She felt she had lost control; she had been robbed of the birth experience she had hoped for; ultimately, Nia felt that she had lost belief in herself.

Nia spent the first four months of her child's life in what she described as a 'cycle of grief with many moments spent either angry or very sad'. She had birthed her daughter via emergency C-section under general anaesthetic and felt that she had missed her baby's first few hours, as well as the birth she envisioned. She couldn't figure out how to come back from it.

During the debrief, we spent a long time unpicking those feelings of grief and holding space for them - something Nia didn't feel like she had done before. She had never really considered herself to be in a state of grief until we began to unpack her experience. It was only then that she was able to give herself the permission to validate her experience and her emotions around it, and to start to heal.

You may be familiar with psychiatrist Elisabeth Kübler-Ross's model of the five stages of grief (denial, anger, depression, bargaining and acceptance). It's a useful model, but not a universal one. Like any form of healing, the stages are not linear and you may not experience all of them, but it's helpful to know that grief is a healthy reaction to loss and that there is a way through it. Your path may differ from others', and that's OK. If you are grieving, there is no right or wrong way to do it.[78] The aim is to reach acceptance of the loss, not to 'get over it' or 'move on'.

## Regret and remorse

Something that comes up often in debriefs is people wishing they had done things differently. Some wish they had used their voice more, while others wish they had made different choices in regard to certain aspects of their pregnancy or birth. It is *normal* to look at things that have happened and to feel remorse when you realise something could have been different.

Hindsight is a marvellous thing, but we don't have the benefit of this when we're in the middle of a situation. All we can do is the best we can in the moment, and the likelihood is that there was nothing you could have done - or not done - to change the outcome.

During debriefs I ask clients for a specific example of a decision they made and how they might change it. They might say: 'I was given the option of labour being induced. I didn't know what this meant, but the doctor told me that if I didn't have it, I would be risking my baby's life, and that they believed it would be the safest thing. I agreed to have one, but the induction turned out to be the worst thing I could have done, and I wish I hadn't done it.'

In response, I would encourage my client to reframe their experience whenever they had thoughts of regret and remorse, by practising an affirmation like this: 'The decisions I made at the time were made with all the information I had at the time.'

People often forget the important fact that the choice they made was the one that they felt was best at the time, made with the information they had then, not the information they have now.

If this resonates with you, remember that you were not alone in any decision-making process. You may have had your partner, a midwife, doctor, consultant, doula, your mother or friend with you. It may help to ask your birth partner questions about what happened at the time, or medical professionals during a debrief. This may also help you to paint a realistic picture of what happened, rather than one where you were 'to blame' for everything. It will help if you share accountability around so that it doesn't all fall on your shoulders. You can also channel regret into a positive thing, and use it to help you to create change.

### How to do it

Write down what you felt went wrong, whether that involved people, places, interventions, behaviours or anything else. This will probably feel challenging and you may want to do this with support – for example, with your partner, a friend or in a debrief. You can also use what you have written to give you an idea of how you would like things to go for subsequent pregnancies, or simply for your own peace of mind.

Here's an example. 'I agreed to a 38-week induction when I didn't want one' could become 'I made the decision to have an induction at 38 weeks with the information I had at the time. If I was presented with that option again, I would ask more questions and see if the pregnancy could be left to progress naturally to 41 weeks.'

It's your turn. No more regrets: choose peace of mind.

# debrief deep dive

## REFLECT

Grief, regret and remorse are closely linked because they are all rooted in past events that you wish you could change. We've seen that healing is rarely, if ever, linear, so mourning loss and forgiving yourself for the things you regret are not one-off steps. You may have to repeat them regularly, and I encourage you to do so with support. Therapy, support groups, community and family can all help. I've listed some additional resources at the back of the book to help you if you are struggling with loss (whether through bereavement or otherwise).

## REFRAME

Allow these affirmations to comfort you as you work through your grief:

- My grief matters; it's OK to mourn what I've lost.

- I seek out healthy ways to grieve.

- I will reach out for support – I do not have to walk this path alone.

If you're struggling with regret and remorse, remind yourself each day that you are a different person now with a different frame of reference and different experiences. If the same situation were to arise again, you may not make the same choice you made before. These affirmations will remind you that this is a positive thing, even if it may not feel like it:

- I was not alone in my decision-making; I do not need to carry the consequences alone.

- I place the accountability where it belongs.

- I did the best I could in a high-stress situation. I forgive myself.

## REDEFINE

Redefining grief, regret and remorse is about finding your way to hope and new purpose. It's recognising that your reaction to the pain of loss, or decisions you made or didn't make, is normal, while also knowing that these emotions need not define everything you are, or everything you will be. You can honour and accept your loss – and, in time, let go of your suffering around it. You can forgive yourself for the things you regret, change what you need to, and move forward in peace.

# 29
# it's OK not to be OK

**Overcoming the stigmas associated
with mental health problems**

## Today this is the best I can do, and that's good enough.

A lot of women face huge pressure to take everything in their stride
and press on. We feel discouraged from complaining or making a
fuss, even about things that do not feel right to us. How have we been
conditioned into suffering in silence?

Worse still, we may be accused of being 'emotional' when we pluck
up the courage to speak up and seek help. Guess what happens next?
Because we fear judgement and ridicule, many of us don't seek help
when we are not OK. From feeling shame when we don't meet societal
expectations of how we 'should' be coping, to thinking we have failed
as parents or somehow don't deserve support or shouldn't bother
other people with our issues – we convince ourselves that we should
cope on our own with everything we're feeling (or not feeling, if our
distress means we've numbed out).

The good news is that we're moving in the right direction when it comes to support that is offered to women and birthing people, both in terms of resources and messaging. To combat the stigmas around women's physical and mental health concerns, the issues we face are being highlighted more frequently in mainstream and on social media, and that's great to see. However, we still have some way to go. The societal expectation that we will soldier on, no matter what, is a cross-generational, cross-cultural issue that we still haven't fully overcome. Of course, this doesn't mean that it will never change: I'm encouraged to see more open discussions about mental health than ever before, but the more we normalise admitting that we are not OK when we are struggling, the easier it will be to reach out for help earlier. And the earlier we ask for support, the quicker we can start to heal.

Dropping the pretence of being OK when you're not is a real process of 'unlearning', but over time you'll come to see several new perspectives:

- If you are struggling with any aspect of your mental health, it's not your fault. You are not a failure.

- By honouring how you really feel you are revealing your truest, best and most authentic self (this is a good thing!).

- Making your mental health a priority is good self-care. We all should be doing it. If you are, you're ahead of the curve (also a good thing!).

- There is support out there. It may be hard to find, but persevere until you find what you need.

- You may have to work through some really uncomfortable feelings, but it will be worth it.

- You don't have to suffer in silence or alone if you are struggling. It really is OK to not be OK.

### Recognising when you need help

When I had Ihsan, I moved back in with my mum. It wasn't something I ever saw myself doing beforehand. It wasn't the thing to do, because

Western society encourages distance and independence rather than dependence and familial support. But I was sure that in order to thrive I would need support; for me, the decision was a no-brainer. I never told my mum this but she knew, and that was enough.

A few months before my son was born (and while writing this book), I had the devastating news that my beautiful mum had passed away. I knew I would need to reach out for support again in my early post-partum days. Fortunately, I have a strong and vibrant village around me – sisters, friends and a wonderful sister-in-law – who made themselves available to me. Mum will always be irreplaceable, but the support of my loyal tribe was, and continues to be, invaluable. If you don't have your village at the moment, you need to find one – it is essential! And if you don't know where to start – perhaps you are shy or introverted, find it difficult to ask for help or are unable to call on family members – do not fear. I will show you how you can find and build your own village in Chapter 36.

Only you know what you might need help with, but nothing is too big or too small. My advice is, when you feel overwhelmed, pause. Instead of barrelling through, either because that's what you've always done or because that's what you think you have to do, ask yourself: 'Could I do with some help?' Be honest with yourself. If your answer is 'yes', then decide who you'd like to ask – then ask them.

Here are some examples of things you may need help with:

- **Mental health support.** This is a big one. As I said above, many women are reluctant to ask for help. This is especially true of Black and Brown women, who may also fear that any treatment they do access may lack cultural sensitivity.[79] But it is essential that you do ask for it, and there are some excellent organisations out there that will support you, such as the Black, African and Asian Therapy Network (see Resources).

- **Community support.** Many women find motherhood isolating and inaccessible. A strong community support network is a great resource for new mothers, and this is one resource that I encourage you to persevere with if you truly want to thrive. Community support is essential. This could mean having accessible breastfeeding clinics, baby weighing centres, coffee mornings for new parents, and so on. Don't force yourself to go to endless mother-and-baby clubs if that's not your thing, but befriending even one other mother will help you to feel less alone. Have a look in your local area, see what is available, and test the waters to see if it's the support you are looking for.

- **Family support.** I'm not going to glamorise living with family, because of course it comes with its challenges, but if you have a good relationship with your extended family and you can lean on them, don't be afraid to ask them to help you. It may mean them popping over to hold the baby so you can shower and wash your hair, or them taking the baby out so you can get some sleep. It may even mean them letting you pop over regularly to see them and be with adult company. Sometimes family don't want to overstep, so this may be a conversation you'll need to initiate. But now that you are (hopefully!) practising your assertiveness skills, you can use these to ask for what you need. And if you don't or can't ask (I know not every family can or will offer support), it's even more important that you find your own tribe and build your village. Pop over to Chapter 36 to see how and why you should do this.

- **Medical support.** If you are still not feeling like yourself physically after having your baby, you should seek support from your GP, a physiotherapist, or any other medical professional that you feel can support your needs. If you believe something is wrong and does not feel normal to you, see your GP. This applies equally to issues relating to mental and physical health (incontinence, wound/ perineal healing, breast changes, etc.). Don't fear seeking support to feel better; it is your right. Looking after your physical health will help you to better be able to care for yourself and your family.

# debrief deep dive

## REFLECT

How are you feeling? How are you *really* feeling? Have you been carrying the burden of feeling like you always have to be OK? Now that you know that it's OK to not be OK, how will that change how you approach reaching out for support? Write your answers in your journal using the following prompts:

* Right now, I am feeling

---

* When I'm not OK, I tend to pretend I am by

---

* If I were to drop that pretence, the first thing I would say is

---

* I would say it to

---

## REFRAME

If you are struggling with feelings of unworthiness, inadequacy or failure, nip those in the bud with these affirmations:

* I deserve to be cared for by others.
* I'm learning as I go, and that is good enough.
* I can learn to ask for help, and to keep asking.

## REDEFINE

How do you react when others ask you for support? If you find it easier to give than to receive support, can you reflect on why this might be? What would happen if you offered yourself the support you can give more freely to other people?

# part 4

## being postnatal:

*the importance of maternal wellbeing beyond the fourth trimester*

# 30
# forever
# post-partum

**A gentler approach to continued healing after childbirth**

## This is my post-partum journey. I am free to travel at my own pace.

There's a myth that the post-partum period is only the first six weeks of parenthood, but I'd like to point out that the fourth trimester actually lasts approximately twelve weeks, not six. Hormonal changes, physical and emotional changes, and getting used to the 24/7 responsibility of caring for a new human all take their toll. The post-partum period continues to be an intensely challenging time for almost all new mums way beyond week twelve. And yet many of us can't help feeling as though we're doing something wrong if we are still not fully healed, ready to exercise, have sex or even go on holiday when Day 43 post-partum rolls around. Here's the thing (spoiler alert): you don't stop being postnatal after your six-week check-up, or even after the fourth trimester is officially over. You don't even go back to being who you were before children – **from the moment you have a baby you are forever postnatal.**

You mean forever? For ever-ever?

Yes – forever! Let's pause for a second. What feelings come up for you when you read the words 'forever postnatal'? Whenever I ask parents this question, their mixed reactions amaze me. For some mothers, it's as if a light goes on, and they fully embrace their new state. I can almost see them mentally giving themselves permission to take care of their changing needs post-partum, and that's amazing. For others, it can feel depressing, particularly if they are dealing with some of the more challenging consequences of pregnancy and childbirth, such as significant perineal trauma or mental health struggles. If that's you, I understand that the idea that you might be in this postnatal state forever may feel daunting, and as though there's no light at the end of the tunnel – but hear me out. That is not what I'm saying at all.

What I am trying to get across is that our needs just don't stop at six weeks. We aren't suddenly healed from the previous months of growing, birthing and nurturing a baby. In some ways, you may need *more* support than before – maybe not medically, but you'll definitely need ongoing practical, emotional and holistic support. So I want you to think of 'forever postnatal' in the context of your wellbeing as a woman and a mum: your new routine, your changing needs for support, and your plan for how you will have your needs met.

**Under pressure to recover quickly?**

The main flaw in the Western idea of the arbitrary six-week cut-off point for postnatal care is that it pressurises women and birthing people into thinking that they should feel well and healed much sooner than is realistic. And because this is also the point at which input from healthcare professionals ends, the assumption is that (apart from exceptional cases) medical or midwifery support is no longer needed. We should all float off into the sunset – post-partum period supposedly over – and get on with it. We should be accustomed to the sleeplessness, we should have mastered the relentless juggling act, and we should be able to take care of our homes, relationship and family, as well as slotting in going for a run or to a yoga class. Of course, this is unrealistic – and for many women, unachievable. Post-partum healing is different for everyone, and everyone's needs will be different. No one should feel under this kind of pressure for *any* reason.

Your baby's needs don't suddenly evaporate at six weeks – just the opposite, actually. By six weeks babies are awake for longer, may need more stimulation, may be experiencing colic or digestion issues, and may also be less settled at night. What might also happen at this time is that the 'new baby' novelty is wearing off: you have fewer visitors, people may no longer be dropping meals off for you, your partner may have returned to work, and the true impact of birth, feeding and interrupted sleep may be taking its toll. It is then that extra support may be even more vital – and often where it is least available. This is why I advocate for all mothers to be closely supported throughout this time and beyond. I also encourage all mothers-to-be to include a wellness plan for their post-partum period. If you're looking for some ideas on how this could look, keep reading. Like a birth plan, a wellness plan can be flexible and you can add to it or take away from it as your circumstances dictate.

## How will I know that I'm healed?

As a mother or parent, ensuring your health and wellbeing is a lifelong priority – at least, it should be. As we saw in previous chapters, it is very easy to ignore your own needs and to neglect your own health to ensure your children are well – but your wellbeing as you parent is essential. If you have travelled anywhere by plane, you'll have heard the advice that is given by cabin crew prior to take-off: if the air pressure in the cabin drops and oxygen masks are automatically deployed, parents should secure their own masks before securing their children's. The thinking behind this is that if you attend to your children first, you could be incapacitated before you are able to secure your own mask. From today, if you haven't done this already, please commit to prioritising your wellbeing. Embrace your 'forever post-partum'! Think of it as giving yourself the care you need to equip yourself to be the best, most present and nurturing parent for your child. Maternal wellness is more likely to promote and facilitate infant health and wellbeing in the long term.

## How do I fit in time for wellbeing?

Ways to improve your wellbeing include:

- Take regular breaks.

- Ensure you eat well.

- Socialise with friends (preferably in person).

- Exercise (should you want to).

- Check in with your mental and physical health. If you are concerned about anything at all, no matter how small, trust your gut and see a health professional.

## Your new normal

Even though pregnancy lasts about 40 weeks, it can sometimes feel like the baby you have just given birth has come out of nowhere and you are just expected to know what to do. This is reinforced by societal messaging such as:

- Motherhood is 'natural'.

- You should enjoy every moment.

- Everything feels worth it.

- She's a yummy mummy/she's a supermum.

- An angry mother is a bad parent.

- So many other women have done it – why can't you? It's easy!

These narratives create difficulties when you're adjusting to parenting and establishing the practices and routines that work best for your family. These expectations rear their heads and fill our heads with pressures and ideas that aren't even our own.

I have been a parent for four years, and there are so many phases and stages when insecurity – about how I am not achieving society's expectations of what I should be doing, how I should be feeling or responding to my child – still creep in. I am gradually getting better at quietening these voices, but no one is immune to them. Periodically, I reflect on these societal expectations, jotting down the ones I think affect me and reflecting on how they affect me. I also think of the expectations that I feel come from my own desires and the things I think will benefit me and my family.

I want to invite you to do the same in the space below. You may find that external, societal expectations are the same as the ones that you feel yourself. That's fine, but writing it out will help you to see it clearly.

_____

_____

_____

_____

_____

The best thing to do is find a way of managing and creating norms and expectations that actually apply to you, that are achievable for you, and that suit you and your family. Ask yourself these questions:

- What kind of parent do I want to be?

- Am I rushing myself?

- How can I achieve the goals and expectations I have for myself?

- What is the best way I can drown out the noise of societal expectations?

- Do I need any support in order to be the parent I want to be, and for us to be the family we want to be?

This exercise is just the start of identifying *your* priorities, and placing expectations on yourself that you are happy with. Like everything, it'll take practise, but it will liberate you from those narratives that are holding you back.

## Celebrate your milestones

There are so many more milestones when you are a parent that warrant celebration and excitement. There are many moments of change and self-reflection, particularly in the first year, and it's important that we don't lose sight of these when looking after post-partum women and birthing people.

I remember celebrating the first time I stayed somewhere overnight with Ihsan. It might not sound like anything to write home about, but it was for me. It took organisation and being well outside my comfort zone in someone else's home without all our familiar things and people. To tell the truth, I celebrated most things. Sometimes I'd simply celebrate getting to the end of a week without either of us having a major breakdown. I'm sharing this to show you that *you* should decide the milestones and the things that are important and worth celebrating. Yes, getting to six weeks is worth celebrating, but there is so much more beyond that.

# debrief deep dive

## REFLECT

What are some of the milestones you are most proud of achieving? Write them down in the space below. There is something powerful in the act of writing them down – they act as reminders of how far you've come.

_____

_____

_____

_____

_____

_____

## REFRAME

If you take anything at all from this chapter, it should be this: you can heal at a pace that suits you, and you can ask for support from professionals and friends and family for as long as you need it. Don't expect too much of yourself.

## REDEFINE

Wherever you are in your post-partum period, what do you think you might need, moving forward? What do you want? How can this be facilitated over the first year of your child's life? Make a plan below. It doesn't have to be comprehensive or perfect – see it as a rough idea, an intention. It may be easier to achieve than you think!

_____

_____

_____

_____

_____

_____

_____

_____

_____

_____

_____

_____

# 31
# finding
# yourself again

**Who am I after childbirth?**

I'm in control of my identity and being a mum is a part, not the entirety of who I am.

Motherhood is probably the only job you will ever take on that will pull you in so many directions. In its early stages, it's normal to feel that you have been so consumed by the demands of your new role that you have lost yourself. It can take a while to find your feet and to figure out who you are, apart from your identity as a new mother. Shall we begin that journey together?

**Personality changes**

Did you know that having a baby can impact your personality? Yup, it's true. Some changes in temperament may be temporary, and are due to your birth experience, mental and physical health and/or hormonal fluctuations, but other changes are more permanent.

*It was the weirdest thing. I used to be so laid-back. My friends
would describe me as 'cool as a cucumber' and then, when I
became a mum, I was what I could only describe as highly strung.
Everything feels like a big deal. I thought maybe it was an early
post-partum thing, but actually, I'm starting to think it really is a
forever thing. I think I'll always be like this, and I would put it down
to the heavy sense of responsibility I feel as a mother. I'm trying to
get used to it. It's hard sometimes, but I'm making it work.*

*– Melissa, mother of two*

A changed personality isn't always a bad thing. You're still you, and
the core characteristics that make you who you are will remain. At the
same time, you are an evolving person whose personality will grow
and adapt to your new status. And some traits, despite feeling like
'negative' characteristics, might be appropriate for you right now.
For example, does being 'highly strung' mean that you are better
equipped to deal with the demands of parenthood? Does it mean you
are better organised? If it does, it might just be a positive thing for this
period of your life. As long as you are comfortable with yourself, see
the changes as positive, and/or necessary for your role as a mother,
and you are not harming yourself or others, you shouldn't worry.
Be proud of who you are and embrace the new, evolving you.

## Loss of freedom

Sometimes parenthood can feel like the most restricting, limiting time
in your life. Out goes the spontaneity – suddenly you have a baby or
child in tow, so you can't drop everything for a last-minute weekend
in the sun or a trip to a bar or cinema like you used to. And even when
you have good, reliable childcare or family who encourage you to take
a night off now and again (thanks, Grandma!), you aren't even sure if
you *want* to do the things you used to.

People who have not experienced this can find it confusing to hear
other mothers express a desire for a bit of 'freedom' from their child.
And how often have we heard phrases like 'If you wanted freedom
from your children, you should never have had them'? This type of 'all

or nothing' judgement is so unhelpful. Two or more things can be true at once: you love your child and are grateful to be a mum, but you also miss aspects of who you were before. And it's OK to express a need for freedom, too – all you're asking for is some time for yourself, and that's an important investment in your wellbeing.

Remember: you deserve space to rediscover who you are, and this rediscovery *is* achievable as a mother. Yes, your freedom might be limited now, but that doesn't mean it's unavailable. Note too that 'freedom' may look different now to what it did pre-baby, and that is fine.

## Loss of financial independence

This can be huge, as financial freedom is tied to a sense of actual freedom. Many mothers who worked before having children and had their own money are used to the sense of independence it brings. Maternity packages vary hugely depending on the company you work for. For some women, going on maternity leave means a big shift in earning and spending power. A sudden loss of financial independence can have a real impact on a woman's sense of identity and purpose.

> *I loved being a new mum, but worried constantly that I wouldn't be taken seriously by my work colleagues any more now that I had a child. I had quite a bit of disposable income after my regular bills were paid, and I miss being able to treat myself when I feel like it.*
>
> *– Samantha, mother of one*

I wish I could give you a quick fix for this one, but this is something you'll need to work through. If you have a partner, discuss with them how you'll share money, so you still have a sense of agency. Making a joint budget that includes a 'treats' account might give you a bit of wiggle room, so that whoever is taking parental leave can still buy the things they would like. If you're the one taking leave, and you know that you are likely to find the drop in income a challenge, start putting money aside as early in your pregnancy as possible – or even before you get pregnant, if that is feasible. That way, you'll have a bit of a cushion for yourself when you go on maternity leave and your pay drops.

Remember: the contents of your bank account do not define you.
Income can fluctuate no matter what stage of life you're in, and there
will be a time when you will be able to return to work (should you want
to) and feel that sense of independence again.

## Physical changes - what happened to my body?

Let's get real: not everyone enjoys being pregnant. The tiredness,
hormonal fluctuations and changes in appearance it causes are a
massive challenge for a significant number of women. And those who
enjoy being pregnant may still admit to struggling with their changing
bodies during and after pregnancy. Our identities are closely tied into
the way we look - and feel - in our bodies. We love our babies dearly,
yet we mourn for how we looked before they came along. There is
nothing wrong with wanting to look and feel good - and yes, over
time you can regain your fitness and muscle tone if that matters to
you. But no matter who you are and how much hot yoga and Pilates
you do, birth *will* change your body. Some women embrace this,
looking at their softer bellies, new curves, stretch marks and more
pendulous breasts as evidence of the great thing they have done - as
they should. It *is* amazing to have grown and birthed a human, and
then to have nurtured them through infanthood and beyond. Our
bodies - tall, short, plump, slim, curvy, dimpled, soft, toned, scarred or
smooth - *are* amazing. We aren't always encouraged to see them as
such, but they are.

We'll take a deep dive into body image in Chapter 32, but for now,
I want to encourage you with this: if you are struggling with the loss
of your pre-baby body and feeling like a failure if your body doesn't
look like the latest celebrity's, please remember that your body was
not meant to look like anyone else's - it was meant to look like the best
version of you. And that 'best version' will change depending on many
factors. Your feelings are normal and valid, however - so how might
you process them?

## Releasing the old you

The first step to finding your identity within motherhood is accepting the fact that your life will change, and the 'pre-baby you' will not be back. Sounds harsh, doesn't it? But it's true. For many people, fighting these changes is the biggest barrier to discovering their new identity. It can cause upset and resentment. Although these are normal feelings to feel, they need not dictate the course of your life. Nevertheless, it's OK to miss the 'old' you. Allow yourself to feel the way you feel and to process those emotions the way you feel is right. It's OK to cry, to share your feelings with your partner or trusted person, or with a debrief facilitator. It is also very important to remember that grieving a previous self or previous life does not make you ungrateful for what you have now; it doesn't make you unworthy of having a child/children, and it doesn't mean you'll never make peace with the new you. Show yourself time, compassion and patience. You'll find your way. You'll figure it out.

Remember, your need for an identity apart from your child does not equate to being a good or bad parent. We aren't supposed to lose ourselves in motherhood. You are a person apart from being a mother, and that person deserves good things, and time to breathe and recuperate. That person needs to care for themselves in order to care for those who depend on them. Your identity is ever evolving. There will be many more moments of self-realisation and adaptation – that's not just a motherhood thing, but a life thing. So go and find your new self, embrace her in all her glory and tell her she is amazing just as she is. *You are amazing.*

# debrief deep dive

## REFLECT

Do you feel like your personality has changed since you became a mother? In what ways? In your journal or in the space below, jot down the things that you are happy have changed and the bits that you aren't so happy about. Can you change those things? Do you want to change them? Don't censor yourself in this exercise. This is about being unapologetically you – whatever 'you' look and sound like right now.

_____

_____

_____

_____

_____

_____

## REFRAME

Allow these affirmations to remind you of the many wonderful facets of your identity, and add some of your own, if you wish:

- I am many things as well as being a mother.

- I take time to rediscover who I am and who I can become.

- Self-care is important and I make time for it.

## REDEFINE

If you could think of one thing that you would like to do for yourself, what would it be? You can make it as indulgent as you like. A facial? A mani-pedi or spa day? Cinema trip? A lie-in? Something else? Don't just think about it, write it down. Things always feel more tangible when they're written down, so let your imagination run free (pun intended!) and go for it! You can write in the space below, or in your journal, if you prefer.

_____

_____

_____

_____

_____

_____

_____

_____

_____

_____

_____

Now find a way to do your chosen activity. You may not be able to do it right now, tomorrow or even this week, but you can start thinking about how you're going to achieve it. Who will babysit your child? Do you need to budget or save for your chosen activity? Start thinking and planning – and most importantly, give yourself permission to do it, guilt-free.

# Finding each other again: parenting and your relationship

Your relationship with your partner goes through a profound adjustment when you become parents. I asked my good friend Catherine Topham Sly, relationship expert and professional counsellor at Insight & Connection, for some thoughts on how to manage this transition. As Catherine says:

*Before we become parents, most of us have romantic ideas about what parenthood will be like. Maybe you pictured you and your partner staring lovingly into each other's eyes while your baby slept contentedly nearby? I know I did. And then, 'WAHHH!' It doesn't quite play out like that, does it? You're sleep-deprived. Recovering from pregnancy and birth. Learning to feed. Adjusting to this whole new identity, lifestyle and level of responsibility. Trying to work out your roles. (How has one life changed so much more than the other?!) It's stressful. You talk less. Argue more. And sex? Ha!*

*And yet, everyone seems to be asking leading questions about how wonderful it all must be. Other new parents keep sharing photos with everyone smiling. You might wonder if you're doing something wrong.*

*You're not. It's totally normal to struggle with this transition. (And we're all better off when we talk about it more openly.)*

You and your partner have brought this wonderful little human into the world, and it can seem like a cruel trick to now have to work to reconnect with each other, right? But it is possible, and it's so worth the effort, especially when you understand how normal it is to feel like you need to readjust to life with each other now that your baby is here. I asked Catherine's advice on how to reconnect with your partner after childbirth.

'In a nutshell,' she says, 'keep talking. And keep touching.'

It seems so simple, doesn't it? Often the best ideas are. Catherine continues:

> Talk about how hard it all is. About how you miss your old life together. About how you're scared that things will never be the same again. About how you're not sure who you are any more. Talk about all the things you feel differently about, whether it's work, money, family, time, anything. Talk about your roles - who's doing what, and how you feel about it all. About how you want things to be, and how you can make it happen.
>
> And keep touching. Sometimes when we're with babies all day, and we're not that interested in sex, we stop touching altogether. But touch keeps us bonded. Get clear about the difference between touch that feels depleting, and touch that fills you up. Don't push your partner away - tell them what you need. Hold each other. You're going through a lot.

You may find you are able to have these conversations with your partner quite naturally, or you might need some help to get the conversation started. That's OK. You can use your birth reflection session as a starting point for a conversation, if you like, or refer back to Chapter 2 for ideas on how to open up if it's been a while since you've really talked.

'Before you were parents,' says Catherine, 'you probably connected most through the bigger moments, like days or nights out, and holidays. Parenthood pushes us to connect in the smaller moments.'

So what are some ways we can make the most of those smaller moments and build intimacy? Catherine offers the following tips:

- Pay attention when your partner speaks to you.

- Respond when they ask for your attention.

- Spend a little screen-free time together each day. (Even a few minutes can make a difference.) Show interest in the things they talk about.

- Open up to them about your worries, disappointments, moments of joy and excitement.

In Catherine's wise words, 'Becoming parents changes everything, including your relationship. That's totally normal. You can get to a place where you're more connected than ever, when you go on the journey together.'

# 32
# finding balance

**The 'perfect' mother, 'snapback culture' and other unrealistic expectations**

# I accept myself as perfectly imperfect.

One of the biggest barriers to adjusting to motherhood is the – frankly ridiculous – concept of the 'perfect' mother. The perfect mother will look different to different people, but you'd better believe she will be everything you think you're not, and she will flourish in every area you perceive you are failing in. The perfect mother is dedicated to her children in every way. She gets nothing but joy from her role, and appears to give everything to it. She's a stay-at-home mum who dedicates her days to a mix of arts and crafts, messy play and independent play, interspersed with nutritious snacks and meals, trips to the park and perfectly timed naps for her children (which they take without a fuss, and during which she tidies her already immaculate home). Or she is a career mum with the perfect childcare set-up, still able to run her household, spend time with her children and have regular date nights – plus incredible sex – with her buff, devoted partner... You get the picture!

If you're nodding in recognition, you know her. You've thought about her, envied her, and done everything in your power to be like her, but you feel like you never quite reach those levels of perfection, and do you know why? It's because the 'perfect mother' is essentially a unicorn – she's easy to imagine, but you'll never see a real one in the flesh.

## What's wrong with 'perfect'?

I get it – we all want to be great parents, but aspiring to be a 'perfect' mother is a sure-fire route to an unhappy life. This woman is an enigma, a fictional character, a figment of your imagination. She. Isn't. Real. It's easy to forget that, though, isn't it? You see her in your friends, in celebrities, on social media, in magazines. You even see her in your family members and in strangers you pass on the street. And every time you see her, she fills you with feelings of inadequacy and guilt. The jury's in on this one: 'perfect' is bad for your mental health.

The 'perfect mother' myth also favours the patriarchal view of women as created for childbearing and childrearing. If they dare to dream about an identity and role outside of this, they are considered irresponsible and selfish (whereas no one bats an eye at a father who pursues both a career and success outside the home). If both parents work, it's generally the woman who juggles her job, childcare and the majority of the housework. And the woman is more quickly considered a bad parent if she prioritises her career, even if she finds it (shock, horror!) fulfilling and/or her salary is essential to run the household.

The myth of the 'perfect' mother sets you up to fail with her unrealistic, unattainable goals. She highlights society's deep misunderstanding and/or complete disregard of what mothering actually entails. Motherhood is so many things. Yes, it involves sacrifice, selflessness and demands on your time and energy so that your children can thrive and feel loved, secure, safe and nurtured. But what that looks like in practice can be messy, chaotic and stressful. It can go from wonderful to woeful and back again in the space of a minute.

Here's my advice. Be content. Do the best you can. It will never be perfect, because no one is perfect. So kick the idea of the perfect mother to the kerb – I promise you don't need to be her. Each mother is different and should not have to bear the weight of anyone's expectations but their own. The best thing you can do for your sanity (and your children's) is to be content with being good enough. Our partners and children need to see us being human. They need to learn that it's OK to make mistakes and to get it wrong, to apologise, grow, and learn. They need us to be happy so that they can learn to be happy too.

## Snapback culture and body image

The unrealistic idea that you should be able to 'snap back' to your pre-pregnancy shape within weeks, if not days, of giving birth is closely tied to the 'perfect mother' myth. The mainstream media, social media and advertising companies celebrate women who are back in their pre-pregnancy jeans by six weeks post-partum, using words like 'glowing' and 'incredible' to describe them.

For some women, this can serve as motivation to get back to the body they want after having children. If seeing others doing it has motivated you to get fitter and regain a body you feel comfortable in, then I'm happy for you – but snapback culture can be dangerous for some. It wasn't too long ago that celebrities were publicly humiliated for 'holding on to baby weight', exacerbating the harmful narrative around snapback culture. Anything that promotes body shaming and comparison is grossly unfair and extremely damaging, especially to women who may already be struggling with self-esteem issues. Snapback culture doesn't recognise patience and progress, it doesn't see individuality and nuance, and it assumes that all women and birthing people have the same end goal. This is simply not true, and it is something you should remind yourself of continuously. If the pressure to fit back in your pre-pregnancy jeans is not helping you to make positive changes or feel good, then it is not serving you and you don't need it in your life.

It's fine to want to look and feel your best, but you don't need to rush, or punish your body in the process. It's not a race, and you don't get extra points for getting there the quickest. Whatever your goals, focus on your health and wellbeing, and use the tips opposite to help you prioritise what's important to you.

- **Know the reality.** It can take a woman's body up to two years to truly recover from pregnancy and childbirth. Go easy on yourself and have realistic expectations of your body.

- **Set manageable targets.** Know what is achievable for you, not just what your target is. Setting small, manageable goals will make any weight loss aim feel less daunting.

- **Don't compare.** Remember: things that you see on social media, on television and in magazines are only snapshots – you do not live the same life as these women, you haven't had the same birth, nor do you have the same body. So to compare is doing yourself an injustice. Focus on yourself and your own body and you'll be just fine!

- **Focus on feeling well.** Sometimes it's not so much about the weight loss; it's more about feeling well within yourself. This might mean simply getting your body moving. Motherhood can zap your energy and make you feel tired and sluggish. Getting out and moving your body will not only help with weight loss, if that is your aim, but will also help with your overall feelings of wellness and good health.

- **Keep an eye on your nutrition.** I spent the first three weeks post-partum eating Smarties. You know the big tubes that come out at Christmas? Yeah, those. I couldn't stomach anything else, and they were easy to eat and tasted good. Unfortunately, they also had a nutritional value of zero. When you've recently had a baby, eating a full meal can be challenging: there will be times where your food will be cold before you get to eat it, or you are only able to grab two quick mouthfuls before you are interrupted by a cry. Eventually, this can become the norm: grab what you can and keep moving. Whether or not you are breastfeeding (but especially if you are), a diet rich in nutrient-dense, fresh, unprocessed foods is best. If you are trying to lose weight, make sure you have healthy snacks and food choices to hand. If you are breastfeeding, don't restrict your calorie intake, but eat healthy foods such as oats or date protein balls, lots of fruits and vegetables, and foods rich in fibre and protein. These will release energy slowly throughout the day and fill you up so that you can avoid snacking on highly processed foods with low nutritional value.

## Don't be taken in by social media

Yes, social media can be a wonderful tool – I have benefited from it greatly. It's enabled me to connect with a wonderful community of mothers, soon-to-be mothers, not-quite mothers and grandmothers who are happy to share their stories and struggles with me and each other, creating an incredible sense of solidarity. But social media has a lot to answer for when it comes to promoting the myth of the 'perfect' mother and snapback culture. Each glossy image of a woman with a slim body and bright smile can make us veer between feeling inspired by other people's lives and creativity, and worried that we are not measuring up.

I try to post mindfully, as I don't want other mothers to feel less about themselves. But I know, as I blogged about my journey to motherhood, that I often found that capturing and sharing one 'perfect' moment in between many moments of chaos made me feel better and helped me remember the good parts of tough days. So I understand how strong the need to share when things are great feels. Everyone has the right to set boundaries for themselves and for their children. If you are finding that shiny images of 'perfect motherhood' are triggering you, making you feel bad or insecure, then you have the power to remove those sources of irritation from your social media. Mute, unfollow or block them. They will be none the wiser and you will probably feel much better. As they choose what to share, so you must choose what to watch. Use social media by all means, but don't let it use or control you.

# debrief deep dive

**REFLECT**

Have you bought into the myth of the perfect mother, perfect post-baby body or social media perfection? What societal stereotypes do you think might have influenced this? Have these myths served you positively or negatively? In what ways?

_____

_____

_____

_____

**REFRAME**

Consider writing out your own affirmations to use when you feel under pressure to be perfect, or to measure up to unrealistic expectations. Here are a few that have helped me:

- I will not give in to pressures that don't apply to me or my situation.

- I focus on my own health and wellbeing.

- I'm doing my best, and that's good enough.

**REDEFINE**

Mothering is hard. Showing up day in, day out, takes strength and resilience – perhaps more than you expected, and definitely more than you sometimes feel you have. And yet you keep showing up. You're already doing the hard thing. So take back control of your own narrative and ask yourself: 'is it time to ignore what society expects of me and to make the best choices for me?'

As you do this, show yourself kindness, love, validation and appreciation, because you are already the perfect mother for your child. You just need to believe it.

# 33
# parenting roles

**Parenting in a changing world**

# I parent according to my child's needs, not society's expectations.

Nurturers, carers, providers, protectors, managers, nourishers, guides, teachers, safety nets – parents (biological or otherwise) are all these things and more. The roles they play in their children's lives evolve as their children grow and their needs change. The question of which parent plays which role, when and why is also evolving – and so is the idea of what constitutes a family unit. The post-Second World War concept of the nuclear family (Father going out to work while Mother stays at home with the children and manages the household tasks) is not obsolete, but we have seen a significant reduction in the number of families living in this way. These changes came about at first because women entered the workplace, found they enjoyed working outside the home, and did not leave. And as living costs have risen, households in which both parents work are now the norm. There's also been a rise in single-parent households, same-sex parents, blended families and multi-generational households, further changing how the typical family unit in the UK looks. And as family set-ups have changed, so too have parental norms, as many parents push back against traditional expectations around their roles. When debriefing issues around parenting roles, I make no assumptions or judgements about anyone's family dynamic or the roles within it – each is as unique as the day is long.

## Debriefing parental expectations

I often hear about conflicts over the roles and expectations of one or both parents, especially in families where multiple generations may live under one roof. In other cases, parents may have experienced emotional harm due to outdated societal perceptions of how they should parent, or one parent might be struggling with an overwhelming mental load. Talking through, then taking ownership of, the roles that work for you is usually the first step towards resolving these conflicts, so I encourage parents to discuss their joint and individual responsibilities towards each other and their children. That helps them to think about the role they each play in their child's life and how they benefit the child, even if that role isn't considered 'traditional' by society. I also encourage them to look at their respective mental loads so that the main caregiver can feel supported to run the household and care for the children.

## The mental load

The mental load – or, in the words of Emma,[80] French cartoon artist and feminist author, the burden of 'always having to remember' – is that never-ending mental to-do list that keeps everything and everyone in the home organised and running smoothly. It's predominantly heaped onto the primary parent as the one who takes managerial responsibility for the running of the home. If that's you, you'll recognise it as the running mental list of things you have to remember to do – food shop, laundry, don't forget to include the clothes on the floor by the bed, buy more washing powder, take out mince for dinner, buy new school uniform, make fairy cakes to take in for school sale – at the same time as actually *doing* those and other essential tasks. It's like a combination of constant inner project management and endless mental plate-spinning. Even women whose partners are helpful and supportive can struggle with mental load. I know because I am one of them!

## The changing role of fathers

Single dads, divorced dads and dads in same-sex partnerships have changed the face of fatherhood, and one of the biggest societal changes in recent times has been the normalisation of fathers playing a more hands-on role in their children's lives. Nowadays, given the astronomical cost of childcare in the UK, many men have chosen to stay home to raise children, especially in two-parent families where their partner is the higher earner. And even in double-income heterosexual partnerships where they are the primary earner, many fathers still want to be emotionally present for their children. These men are taking on more responsibilities in the home, and recognise the need to share the load with their partners.

Despite these advances, the influence of the patriarchy is still strong. There are plenty of fathers who are happy with traditional gender norms and expectations, and happy to leave the lion's share of caring for a new baby to their partner. Many women choose to accept these traditional roles, while others battle against generational ideas from elders (both male and female), and their own inner voice, which tells them that their family should fit into nuclear and gender stereotypes. I know it isn't easy if your values and beliefs differ from those around you. Being aware of wider influences and how they enter your home and affect your dynamic, however, will help you quiet any voices that don't serve you – or at least, minimise them to a level that works for you and your family. Remember, how you and your partner decide to parent and the roles you take on is up to you. You don't need to justify yourselves to anyone else.

Many dads, of course, do a phenomenal job of supporting their partner and children, fully recognising their privilege in the patriarchal society that we live in and playing their part to combat and minimise the negative effects of harmful gender stereotypes. But even here, stereotypical assumptions persist. Have you ever had to bite your tongue when you heard the words, 'Oh, it's so lovely of him to babysit!' whenever a mother left their child at home *with their father?* It's not babysitting; it's looking after your own child! This frustrates fathers just as much as mothers, because most do not want to be referred to as 'babysitters' either. The vast majority want to play an active role in their children's lives and be seen as more than just a breadwinner.

## Being a single parent

When Covid-19 hit, my husband was in Spain and ended up being locked down there for three months, leaving me with an eighteen-month-old to look after. I was fortunate to have a very supportive family, and my mum and siblings were able to help me and ensure I didn't carry the mental and physical load alone. Nevertheless, the experience led me to take a closer look at, and reflect on, the challenges faced by single parents – not just through the pandemic but all the time.

Single-parent households account for approximately 1 in 4 UK families. That's around 1.8 million single parents across the UK.[81] Life as a single parent has many challenges, and the many single parents I spoke to were quick to point out to me that full-time sole responsibility for your child(ren) is *not* the same as having a partner working away! I may have been worried about him, my husband might have not been in the country, but I was not alone. I knew his physical absence was temporary and that he was coming back; this is a privilege that single-parent families don't have.

A high proportion (up to 90 per cent) of single-parent families is headed by women: this highlights the gender gap that we know exists. To think that the physical, mental and financial load will, in the majority of cases, fall on the mother – not as the primary, but as the *only* parent – is sobering. Financial hardships for lone parents were exacerbated by the pandemic, during which single-parent families were shown to be three times more likely to use a food bank than two-parent families, more likely to have accrued significant debt, and more likely to become unemployed, with an estimated 1 in 10 falling out of employment between 2020–21.[82]

The challenges facing single-parent families go back a lot further than the Covid-19 pandemic. The issue is systemic, with little attention being paid to the problems faced by lone parents, and government policies that do not prioritise them. If you are raising children alone, you'll play multiple roles in your child's life: in the middle of all that you do for your child, remember your responsibility to yourself. It's even more important that you access any support you need, to help you be at your best for your child(ren). That includes taking the advice throughout this book about self-care to heart. You might need to find creative ways to do this (see Chapter 36), but do it you must. Above all, remember that you are doing a phenomenal job and you are amazing.

## LGBTQ+ parents

Despite recent societal moves towards greater inclusivity and understanding of different family set-ups, those in the LGBTQ+ community still report being misunderstood, with their experiences under-recorded and under-represented. The heteronormative template for childbearing – a male-female couple – does not always reflect the diverse ways in which people with different gender identities and sexual orientations come to, and then navigate, parenthood.

Much of the research that has been carried out around LGBTQ+ people and parenthood stops at the pregnancy – acknowledging, for example, that lesbian couples is the fastest-growing group[83] using maternity services – and fails to explore the lived experience of these families. Like other marginalised communities, the LGBTQ+ community still faces societal discrimination, profiling and stereotyping. This applies during their pregnancies and births, and into the post-partum period. An example of this is *The NHS Long Term Plan* (2019),[84] which aims to offer support for fathers/partners of women who struggle with their mental health in the perinatal period, but fails to mention the diverse forms that families can take and the experiences of female non-birthing parents as *parents* rather than 'partners'.

Thankfully, many LGBTQ+ parents are speaking up against such inequalities and are creating useful resources to spotlight the unique challenges faced by their community as they navigate maternity and parenthood (see the Resources section).

# debrief deep dive

## REFLECT

What does your family set-up look like? Does it follow a 'traditional' model, or something different? Most importantly, does it work for you and your child(ren)? Is there anything you would change about it? Can you make those changes? If so, how could you do this? If not, can you find a workable compromise?

_____

_____

_____

_____

_____

## REFRAME

Just as the roles that were the norm several decades ago are different today, we can expect today's norms to change again as time moves on. The most important thing is that you and your partner/co-parent have a clear set of values that you live by that works for your family. Remind yourself of this using the following affirmations:

- Our family model works for us and our children are safe, happy, healthy and loved.

- I'm a traditional parent, and that's OK.

- I'm a non-traditional parent, and that's OK.

## REDEFINE

Remember, you are in charge of the roles you adopt as parents. What matters is that they work for you and your family, are not harmful, and enable you to parent well.

# 34
# parenting hazards

**Dealing with exhaustion, loneliness and burnout**

## Perfection is overrated – 'good enough' is good enough.

Let's be real: parenting is exhausting. As a newborn's sleep-wake cycle tend to last one to two hours, sometimes less, it's inevitable that tiredness and exhaustion feature as part of your life as a new parent. And as your baby gets older, they may still wake multiple times a night. You may have other children to care for and other responsibilities during the day, and so you may feel as though you are 'running on empty' most of the time.

> *I'm so tired all the time - more than ever in my life - and it doesn't feel like the type of tiredness that will go away with sleep. I'm talking bone-tired, zero energy, and I can't really see how that's going to change, even though I believe that at some point it will. My daughter is two now, though, and I'm still in the grips of exhaustion!*
>
> *– Louisa, mother of one*

I can relate to Louisa's experience – and you may also be experiencing something similar. Tiredness and exhaustion, left unchecked, can lead to burnout, and sometimes even depression. These can be hard to recover from, so if you are feeling too tired to care about yourself, and sleep isn't making you feel better, it's vital that you take this seriously. It's a sign that you might need some support.

## Are you exhausted?

Why are you so tired? The obvious reason for exhaustion is sleep deprivation, but stress can also wear you out or exacerbate any underlying feelings of fatigue. Common stressors include financial worries, relationship difficulties, parenting alone, having a birth injury or trauma, and caring for an ill child. If all is well in your life but you're still exhausted, I'd encourage you to consider the following factors:

- **Nutritional deficiencies.** Low iron and vitamin D levels can cause fatigue. You can visit your GP and ask for a blood test to check your iron and vitamin D levels – you may need to take supplements. If you live in the UK, you should be taking 10 micrograms of vitamin D daily during the winter regardless.[85] Check with your GP to ensure you are taking the correct dose.

- **Breastfeeding.** If you are breastfeeding, you are the only person who can feed your child unless you express milk (this is doable, but time-consuming). You'll be up during the night to feed your baby, and doing the day feeds too – and this will be tiring.

- **Loneliness.** Parenting can be isolating, and there is a correlation between loneliness and exhaustion. If you're at a different life stage to your friends and you are the only one who has a baby, if you parented through the pandemic, if you are a single parent, or if you're in a relationship but your partner is out at work all day while you are at home with your baby, you may feel lonely.

## Caring for yourself

We hear all the time about the importance of rest as an antidote to exhaustion. Adequate rest is a necessary form of self-care and an essential part of parenting, but in the middle of caring for their newborns, many parents fail to prioritise it. Instead, they power through tiredness to such a degree that some mothers will get to their child's eighteenth birthday before feeling that perhaps they have earned the right to rest! You might laugh, but I promise you – it's no joke. I do not want this to happen to you. We've touched on this before, but it's such an important part of wellness that it bears repeating. You need to make time for yourself. Don't fall into the trap of thinking it's selfish to explore your own needs. Exploring your needs does not need to be to the detriment of your child; in fact, it's to their benefit. When you are exhausted, it can be overwhelming to even think about what you might need, but at the very least, rest and fresh air would be a great place to start. Add on new needs once you have established a habit of resting and getting fresh air regularly.

### Rest

Rest isn't something to be earned; it isn't a reward. It's vital. Although 'running on empty' has been glorified by the fast-paced society we live in, it is simply not sustainable in the long run and can lead to all sorts of health problems.

Rest doesn't necessarily mean sleeping (although it might do to you). It means stopping for a bit. You could sit down with a book or magazine, sit in the garden with a drink, watch your favourite TV programme, meditate or ring a friend.

### Fresh air

When you have a little one, home can feel like the only safe space. You are comfortable there, you can feed there without worry, you know it's safe for your little one, you can be in pyjamas or loungewear all day – but do not underestimate how important it is to step out of the house and breathe in fresh air. It can do wonders for you and your little one. A change of scenery is a great way to give your mental and physical health a boost. It can help you feel less tired and shake off the fatigue that can come with motherhood. You don't have to go far: a stroll through the park, popping to the shops or even sitting in the garden is all you need, but give it a go. You might find you love it – and your baby probably will too.

If you struggle with feelings of loneliness, here are a few tips that may help.

- Connect – if you find this difficult to do in person, or you are unable to go out, the internet can be a great place to connect with other parents, and you may find this stops you feeling so isolated. Just be mindful of giving out personal information to people you don't know well – loneliness can make you more vulnerable to being taken advantage of, so be wise and stay safe online.

- Go to Chapter 36 and read about how to find your tribe and build your village. If ever there was a time you needed people around you, it's when you become a parent. You might have to step outside your comfort zone to do this, but you need your village!

- How about texting another parent and suggesting you go for a walk together? You don't have to commit to a lifelong friendship, but changing up your social circle and meeting other people will definitely help you not to feel so alone.

- Speak about how you are feeling. Tell your family or your partner. The more you speak about it, the freer you will feel, and you will create the mental space you need to make the changes you want.

- Lastly, you aren't alone. In many ways, feeling lonely is a normal part of life. You should reach out for support, however, if your feelings are getting stronger and worse. Speak to your GP or seek professional help.

**Parental burnout**

It was only when I became a parent that I understood how 'burnout' – a term I'd always associated with stressed-out execs and employees – could also apply to motherhood. Because, well, they're basically the same, aren't they? You are giving of yourself continuously, and you're stressed out, overworked and definitely underpaid. But, unlike a job, you can't walk out on your baby.

I didn't actually feel burnt out until my daughter was over one. In the first year of a baby's life, most parents are operating on autopilot. Particularly following a traumatic birth, all we're trying to do is get through each day, get our babies fed, get them washed, play with them and get them to sleep.

When Ihsan was about eighteen months old, I had a bit of a crash. And that's what burnout is like: a crash. Extreme exhaustion caused by high levels of stress around parenting is your rude welcome to parental burnout – you feel depleted, have nothing left to give, and even the simplest demand on your time feels crushing. You may feel low, irritable, tired (no, make that shattered), guilty, overwhelmed, trapped and resentful. To cope, you may under-eat, overeat, or rely on caffeine or other substances to keep you going. Literally everything feels like it's too much.

### *Causes of maternal burnout*

You won't be surprised to read that many of the things we have covered in the last few chapters – perfectionism, falling for the 'perfect mother' myth, feeling overwhelmed by your mental load, and more – are primary causes of burnout, along with prolonged parenting-related stress and inadequate rest.

### Dealing with burnout

Maternal burnout is real. It's not a sign of failure if you have it, and you're not a bad parent; it's just a sign that you have been doing too much and that needs to change – immediately. You need to stop, recognise that you can't do it all – especially without adequate rest, support and time to yourself – then you need to recalibrate.

### *How to do it*

Recalibrating will look different to everyone, but think of it this way: you have drained your energy reserves. They are empty. You now need to fill up your energy reserves. You do that by doing things that give you energy and bring you joy. Good nutrition, hydration and movement will all help, but you could also consider talking to a friend, having a good cry, listening to feel-good music, meditating for five minutes, asking a trusted person to watch your baby for half an hour so you can soak in a bubble bath – anything that makes you smile and feel like 'you' again. Each thing you think of, and actually do, is like a ticket to your personal 'good vibes only' club. And isn't that where we all want to be?

Other ways you can help yourself include all the things you have been learning about in these pages: setting boundaries, asking for help, prioritising self-care, talking to your partner or a friend about how you're feeling, and not comparing yourself to anyone else (especially the so-called 'perfect mother').

## How to deal with the mental load and perfectionism

We touched on mental load as it relates to parental roles in Chapter 33. Mental load need not always be negative; I think sometimes it can help you to feel more in control. But when it gets too heavy, you may need a few pointers on how to manage it.

- **Share it!** Sometimes it can feel like hard work asking for help, but in the long run you'll do nothing but benefit from some help. Write a list of all the things you are currently responsible for and see if you can reallocate any of these tasks to your partner, or supportive family and friends. If someone else can do it, let them!

- **Prioritise.** The thing that's taking up space in your mind, does it need to be done this very moment? If not, park it and deal with it when you have the mental capacity.

- **Find a way to switch off, to unwind.** It doesn't matter what you do, but find something that brings you joy, then indulge in it every now and again.

- **Relax.** The need to be doing and achieving can be exhausting, and you can only do it for so long before you burn out. Remember, even though it feels as though the household will grind to a halt if you do not do E-V-E-R-Y-T-H-I-N-G, the important things will get done – perhaps not in the way you would have done them, but they will get done and that's what matters.

**Getting help**

If your exhaustion feels debilitating, and you are too tired to think about doing anything (and sleep is not helping); if you're finding it difficult to cope with basic tasks; or if you're feeling hopeless or depressed; please speak to your GP, a birth debrief facilitator or a therapist. Most importantly, if you're having suicidal thoughts, seek help as soon as possible – organisations including Samaritans are available 24 hours a day, 365 days a year.

# debrief deep dive

**REFLECT**

It's hard to stop when you have so many demands on your time and energy, but you are allowed to be still. If you're feeling burnt out, it's a sign that you need to be kind to yourself, take the time to care for you, and remind yourself that you matter too. What energy-consuming thing were you about to do? Does it need to be done right now? What will happen if you don't do it? Probably, nothing earth-shattering.

Challenge yourself to rest, to sit down, have a cup of tea, to catch your breath and gather your thoughts – or let your mind wander and just 'be'. Journal what that would feel like for you.

_____

_____

_____

_____

_____

## REFRAME

Why not take five minutes right now? Take some deep breaths and say the following affirmations out loud:

- I listen to my body.

- I deserve some time to rest each day.

- I am worthy of love and support.

## REDEFINE

It's time to stop normalising exhaustion, whatever its cause. This is how you can do it:

- Make rest as important to you as breathing fresh air and staying hydrated. Yes, you may have to alter your sleep schedule to achieve this, especially in the early days, and you may have to step outside your comfort zone, and ask for help if you need it, but do it – it's worth it!

- Observe your children. Are you fulfilling their *actual* needs, rather than the things you think they need?

- If you haven't done so already, start believing that it's OK to be a 'good enough' parent. You don't have to be perfect. Likewise, your house can be 'clean enough'; it doesn't have to be immaculate.

- Keep setting boundaries around your time and energy so that you can be at your best for yourself and your child.

- Remember: being tired is a normal part of parenting, but burnout needn't be. You are always worthy of rest, so rest as often as you need to. And don't feel guilty about it.

# The maternity leave 'holiday' myth

The purpose of maternity leave is to allow new mothers to develop a relationship with their new baby and to heal from the physical and mental impact of bearing and birthing a baby. The fact that it is paid is a nod to the economy's reliance on women in the workplace. Increasingly, households today cannot be sustained on one income.

Paid maternity leave allowances vary across the world, ranging from nothing to a year or more. This speaks of the inequality that women face in the workplace and the lack of understanding of post-partum recovery.

When I was approaching the start of my maternity leave, someone said to me, 'I bet you're looking forward to some time off, hey?' Thinking about this now makes me chuckle. If I compare my three or four 12.5-hour shifts a week to 24/7 mothering, I can assure you that one certainly feels more like 'time off' than the other, and it isn't the mothering! Many of you reading this will relate, I'm sure. Before I had a child, I'd spend my annual leave going on a trip, staying in a hotel or Airbnb. These trips would feature long lie-ins, late-night dinners, indulgence, time, space, ease. We had so many choices: to do or not to do, to go or not to go, to see or not see… Mothering, by contrast, is a full-time job with no breaks, no holiday allowance, no financial bonus and no HR department to deal with any issues or concerns. There's also no option to go part-time, and no sick leave!

I love mothering my children. I'm grateful that I've been able to spend as much time with them as I have when they were very little – but it was not a holiday.

Supporting maternal wellbeing should include workplace support for parental leave so that mothers can enjoy their leave guilt-free. But in some quarters, maternity leave is still seen as an extended paid holiday. This leads to some women feeling like they can't confide in their work colleagues about any difficulties they may be facing, because they are already perceived as having a 'good deal' due to parental leave.

As a society, we need to improve our understanding of the post-partum period and why maternity leave is essential. Parental leave worldwide requires much further examination. In this day and age, all women should be entitled, by law, to an extended, paid period off work after having a baby, to rest, recuperate and recover. In the UK, the campaigning organisation Pregnant then Screwed is doing some amazing work in this area (see Resources).

# 35
# parenting again

**Trying for another child after a traumatic experience**

# I can grieve the past and look forward to the future; if I choose to, I can parent again.

The decision to grow your family is one that some of you will face with mixed emotions. For some, it's a no-brainer - you know you want more children at some point and are excited about the prospect of trying again. Or you may know that you just want one child. Some parents, despite wanting more children, are reluctant to expand their families, due to a trauma they suffered in an earlier pregnancy. For these parents, conversations around trying for another child can be fraught with anxiety.

Parents in this situation who see me for a birth debrief might want to process their previous birth so they can move forward, or they may already be expecting another child (or exploring the idea of expanding their family) and feeling fearful about how this new pregnancy will unfold. These fears are real. Processing previous birth experiences in these cases will always include a close examination of these fears, how to explore them safely, and how to create birth preferences that feel right and safe. If you are in this situation, what might this mean for you?

**Building a positive experience**

One of the first things to do is look at what a positive birth means for you, this time around. What may have mattered to you before might not matter this time, but different things might. For example, last time your priority might simply have been 'a healthy baby', but this time you might want to ensure that you feel part of each and every decision made, that your experience is centred, that you are supported to make informed choices so that, even if the birth doesn't necessarily go the way you planned, you can make peace with the outcome.

After a traumatic first birth, Pippa described herself as 'absolutely terrified' when she fell pregnant again, even though it was planned. Her fear for this pregnancy was 'a long, painful birth experience', so taking steps to avoid this became logical. For her, that meant an elective C-section, even though not everyone around her agreed.

> *My biggest hope was a peaceful, trauma-less birth, irrespective of mode. Others' greatest hope might be a successful vaginal birth. I learned there's no right or wrong 'greatest hope', but being honest about mine helped me so much. Being freed from others' expectations of what a 'good' or 'bad' birth was, and discovering my own instinct for what I wanted, meant I could finally make a decision based on that.*
>
> *Acknowledging that I mattered in the decision-making process was transformational. The birth debrief and birth option sessions I had went a huge way to affirming my own value. I [realised] it was also OK to make a decision for my own wellbeing. If my daughter becomes a mother one day, I want her to know that [motherhood] is not the point at which she ceases to matter.*
>
> *– Pippa*

For Pippa, knowing that her decision was what was best for her was all she needed to feel more relaxed and in control the second time around.

## Pregnancy and birth after loss*

Sadly, pregnancy loss happens every day, whether that is a miscarriage (meaning the loss of a pregnancy during the first 23 weeks) or a stillbirth (a loss after 24 weeks). Clinical descriptions of miscarriage can be difficult to accept for those grieving their loss. For example, calling a loss past twelve weeks' gestation 'a late miscarriage' can feel invalidating, as can describing a loss in the first trimester as an 'early miscarriage', when in either case, the woman concerned feels that she has lost a baby.

How people experience loss can only be dictated by them. There is support available for women who have suffered a loss due to miscarriage, stillbirth or ectopic pregnancy – please see the Resources.

## Dealing with others' reactions

Sometimes, one of the hardest things to deal with about a loss is how others react – and expect you to react. We are often ignorant about how to treat grieving people and how to speak about loss. Witnessing others' grief makes many people uncomfortable, and this can result in inappropriate reactions such as 'Well, it was early' or 'At least you know you can get pregnant!'

These types of responses, while well-intentioned, devalue the lived experience of the grieving person and don't acknowledge their feelings around their loss. As we have seen, loss is loss, and grief is an individual journey. No one has the right to place their own ideals and expectations on you. After a loss, give yourself the time and space to grieve and heal. A first step might be a birth debrief, but there are other organisations and groups who can offer additional support if you need it (see the Resources section).

Approximately 1 in 5 pregnancies will result in miscarriage[86], and 1 in 250 pregnancies ends in stillbirth.[87] A proportion of these women will go on to get pregnant again, and they will carry the grief of that loss through their pregnancy.

*I found out I was pregnant at the height of the pandemic. Despite the world feeling like it was falling apart, we were so happy in our little bubble, knowing our family were going to be expanding. Around nine weeks in, I experienced some bleeding. At first I thought it was just early pregnancy spotting (or at least that's what I convinced myself), but after two episodes, the second heavier than the first, I decided to call my local maternity unit. They advised me to come in, but due to the pandemic I had to go alone.*

*I went into the room for a scan as my husband sat in the car park waiting for me to call him. When they told me there was no heartbeat and that the baby was measuring around six weeks, my whole world felt like it was falling apart. I had had a missed miscarriage, and I was finding out alone.*

*I experienced so many emotions over the following weeks: anger, failure, guilt and shame. I felt I couldn't tell anyone as we hadn't announced our pregnancy, and I also feared trying again because I didn't feel I could go through it again.*

*In my subsequent pregnancy, I booked a debrief to go through all of the feelings and fears I had, and just being able to speak about it and have a better understanding put me more at ease. We welcomed our rainbow baby in the spring - and despite the experience of my miscarriage being something I will carry forever, we are overjoyed.*

*– Cynthia*

Hollie de Cruz[88] is a renowned birth educator and author of *Your Baby, Your Birth* and *Motherhood Your Way*. She is the founder of Here/Hear, an education platform for women through pregnancy, birth and motherhood. Hollie has worked with many women who've gone through the heartache of baby loss, and has personal experience of the journey herself. She highlights the feelings of conflict, disconnection, joy, sorrow, guilt and fear that accompany pregnancy after loss.

'Grieving the loss of a baby while growing a new life means that the overwhelming emotions of both are forced to sit next to one another, where maybe they haven't before,' Hollie explains. 'Despite growing resources and support, there is still so much taboo surrounding baby loss and pregnancy beyond that. Pair that with each experience being so completely unique, and we can be left not knowing how to process the way we feel or having anything to compare it to.'

## Joy and sorrow

Getting pregnant after a loss does not always mean joy. It doesn't mean 'moving on' or that you are 'getting over it'. Many people will have feelings of heightened anxiety and fear; they may not celebrate pregnancy milestones as they might have before. Feelings of grief will co-exist with feelings of apprehension and anticipation. This can be a complex road to navigate, and few people may understand your experience.

> *I feel so anxious in this pregnancy. When I had a stillbirth last spring, it threw my world into absolute darkness, and even though I am now pregnant again, the world is still not light. Every twinge or moment where the baby isn't moving is filled with dread, even though my rational mind knows that she is probably sleeping. The thing is, even when she is moving, I don't enjoy it. I can't allow myself to enjoy it. I'm so grateful to the midwives who let me go in and be seen whenever I want; I have been offered extra scans throughout this pregnancy. This has helped more than I can even articulate.*
>
> *– Alice, pregnant after loss due to stillbirth*

Alice's feelings are completely normal. If you are going through something similar, you will know what an anxious time this is and how much your anxiety can dampen your feelings of joy and excitement. Current UK protocols suggest that two consecutive miscarriages do not increase or indicate risk to a healthy subsequent pregnancy, so support only becomes routinely available after a woman has three miscarriages in a row. (This guidance is being updated at the time of writing, and new guidelines are expected soon.)

If you suffered a loss after 24 weeks of pregnancy, your care providers will be aware of this and will offer you extra support. Depending on the hospital trust you're with and the reason for the previous loss (if known), you will be offered more scans. If you are not happy with this, you can request more scans and appointments for reassurance. With support, you can allow yourself to feel the joy you deserve during your new pregnancy, alongside the grief you feel for your previous loss.

## Overcoming the fear

Here are some tips to help you to overcome the fear of a subsequent pregnancy, if this is something you are looking to explore. You can work through each one with a therapist or debrief facilitator, if you need extra support.

- Look at the things that upset you about your previous experience, and think about what could have made a difference.

- Speak to your partner about your fears, and listen to theirs.

- If you are already pregnant, speak to your community midwife about what is worrying you. Ask about how they can mitigate against the same or similar happening again.

- If necessary, work through your previous experience with a professional who specialises in birth trauma and birth-trauma recovery

- Practise mindfulness or take a hypnobirthing course to help you to relax.

- If you are suffering from mental health difficulties, speak to your community midwife or GP and seek the appropriate support.

- Change care provider if you feel that will make a difference.

- Ask those providing your care to ensure that you are kept fully informed about all your choices so that you can make informed decisions about your care throughout.

Above all, go easy on yourself. Show yourself the empathy that you would show to others if they were in the same position as you.

## Hypnobirthing as a healing tool

Hollie de Cruz recommends trying hypnobirthing if you are expecting again after trauma or loss:

> *When we think about hypnobirthing, we can draw associations with calm, joyous, stress-free, positive birth experiences that feel a far cry from what we're envisaging when navigating pregnancy after loss. Often, we become focused solely on having our baby here safely - sure that that is the only moment in which we may find peace again.*

This is understandable, but not necessarily conducive to the joyous pregnancy you deserve. Hypnobirthing can help you to reframe your experience to allow you to take back autonomy. Hypnobirthing isn't magic, though. Hollie says: 'It isn't about perfect births, or even positive ones.' It's about empowerment and learning tools to help 'restore some sense of confidence in your body and your baby' and 'nurture you in returning to your place as an active participant in this baby's birth'.

Hollie believes that hypnobirthing can have a profound impact on the way you feel as you navigate loss alongside the emergence of new life. Learning breathing techniques that help to short-circuit the body's stress and adrenal responses or learning massage techniques that deepen your sense of comfort and help you trust in your body again has benefited many birthing parents. Hollie concludes: 'Know that your experience is as unique to you as the love and loss that sit alongside each other deep in your heart. Every edge of this love forms who you are now, and who your babies are, too.'

If you are interested in learning more about hypnobirthing, I have included some further information about it in the Resources. You can also talk to your midwife or care provider about how you are feeling, find a doula who has experience working with bereaved parents, and/ or join local or online support groups where you can speak to your peers about their experiences.

# debrief deep dive

## REFLECT

If you are expecting again following a loss, all your feelings are valid. It's OK to feel however you feel, and nobody else has the right to comment negatively on your feelings.

It may help you to process your feelings if you write them down. Accept their presence, lean into them, and allow them to guide you.

_____

_____

_____

_____

_____

## REFRAME

Like me, Hollie is a great believer in positive affirmations as tools for healing the mind, body and emotions. She has included a few of her favourites below:

- I grieve for my losses and I welcome new life.

- I am on my own journey towards faith and acceptance. That journey doesn't have to look like anyone else's.

- I lean on the people who love me.

## REDEFINE

Remember: you deserve a positive experience, no matter what has happened in the past. If you're feeling strong enough, it can be helpful and comforting to seek out some positive stories of those who have navigated their own baby loss.

# 36
# find your tribe, build your village

**How to assemble a badass parental entourage**

# I will care for myself today by asking for help when I need it.

The saying 'it takes a village to raise a child' has become increasingly clichéd over time, yet it's relevant and true. Parenting is rewarding, but it's also a lot of hard work. I believe we need a community - a village - around us as we navigate parenthood. We were never meant to do this alone.

## Who is in your village?

Your village is simply the tribe of people who make up your personal support system - think of it as your parenting entourage! We all need a support network, even when we have a helpful, loving partner by our side - our partners will need help and a break too, even if they don't admit it. And no, I'm not talking about the personal assistants, nannies and bodyguards you see around celebrities, catering to their every whim. I'm going to show you how people like you can get the support you need to parent well – from other normal people – without needing a bulging bank account or a trust fund to do it. Healthcare professionals have some input here, of course, but I'm talking about friends, family members, colleagues, neighbours and fellow parents, whose support becomes more vital once the day-to-day support from healthcare workers begins to taper off. The 'village' is just as important for experienced parents too – perhaps even more so, as people tend to make less of a fuss with subsequent children, believing the parents to be seasoned pros who know what they're doing and who don't need help or support this time round. (Hint: They do!)

### Bola's story

The love, help and support my husband and I got from our church family when our baby was born was such a blessing. They set up a rota, and every evening a home-cooked meal was delivered to our door, piping hot and ready to serve, or to be put in the fridge to heat up the following day. Before our daughter arrived, our church had asked for a list of our favourite foods, and so there was nothing they brought over that we didn't like. My mum was with us as well, but she had her hands full with helping me with the baby while my stitches healed, and the meals included portions for her as well.

They were so considerate – we never felt we had to invite anyone in and play host for hours, although we did make tea for the odd visitor when we felt like it. But there was never any pressure to do so, and we felt so, so lucky to have that support and care. It saved us time, money and the effort of having to make decisions about what to eat and when. We could all just relax and enjoy bonding together as a family. It made the first few weeks of parenthood so much easier for us. Six years on, I still think about that gesture with gratitude. It's great now to be able to do the same for other new parents in our fellowship, and to tell my daughter how so many of the people she considers 'aunties' and 'uncles' in our small church did the same for us when she was born.

## Why you need a tribe

Historically, childbirth was a community affair. Women birthed at home, surrounded by elders and other women – people who were familiar to them, who knew them, and who could rally round and support them. These women would recognise if something was amiss postnatally, and if they didn't know what to do to fix or alleviate the issue, they would usually know someone in the community who did. New mothers didn't need to pluck up the courage to ask for assistance. Help and support was practical, emotional, spiritual, hands-on and there for both mother and baby.

In many other parts of the world, it is still the norm today to surround yourself with a community of older women, sisters and friends, or for family to come and stay for up to three months or more. Here in the West, however, the prevalence of hospital births has normalised a 'visiting-hours only' approach; the concept of 'village parenting' has gradually disappeared, with families living more separately than ever before. From the conversations I have had online and with clients, it seems that many people feel overwhelmed at the thought of letting others in, and can't think of anything worse than having family round after they have their children. And as new parents, it seems that we've gradually become less able to ask for the help we need, believing needing help to be a weakness. This way of thinking has become even more prevalent since the Covid-19 pandemic as we adjust to life post-lockdowns.

So why am I advocating finding your tribe of cheerleaders and helpers and building them into your village? Because I think this is so important, even if you fall into the 'keep out and leave us to it' category – in fact, *especially* if you fall into that category!

## Building your village

Your tribe – your village – is created by you, for you. It does not have to be overbearing or intrusive and it does not need to consist of close relatives or extended family. It doesn't have to include lifelong friends either – your village can include people of diverse ages and stages of their lives, and of any gender expression. It can consist of many people or a few. It can include online support and other resources and professional help, but these should preferably be secondary to your core village of trusted, wonderful humans who put you at ease and make you feel safe and cared for as you care for your growing family. No one needs to move into your home for weeks on end - though if that's something you would appreciate, then by all means factor that in. The most important thing is that your village exists, is easy to access when you need it, that you are centred and supported within it, that at least a few of its members are people you can see face to face, that you can lean on them, and they are there for you when you need them.

## Your tribe have your back

When my daughter was born, I had a tough time transitioning into motherhood. I wasn't coping very well, but it hadn't really dawned on me how poorly I was coping, as I was convinced that what I was feeling was a normal part of new motherhood. I was fortunate to have a large village around me filled with aunts and sisters, friends and family, forming a support network that I knew I could lean on - but as I said, I didn't know I needed help, so I didn't reach out to them.

One family friend came over to visit us three weeks after I had given birth. After observing me repeatedly asking my daughter to 'just be quiet for a moment' (because I found her crying so upsetting), my friend somehow sensed what I needed. Instead of focusing on my fretful baby, she asked about me. How was I doing? What was I finding challenging? What did I need? She let me know that I was doing great, and that a crying baby was not a negative reflection of my parenting ability. Essentially, she created a safe space for me to express myself without fear, and letting it all out lifted a huge weight off me. Before she left, this wise and wonderful woman gently asked my mum to keep an eye on me and reiterated that she was there for support if needed.

As the fog cleared and I found a parenting rhythm with my baby and was getting at least an hour's uninterrupted sleep at a time, my friend came over again and asked me how I was feeling. I could say truthfully that I was in a better place, and I'm so grateful to her for looking out for me during that time. She was the tribe member I didn't know I needed!

Your village can do things for you, like watch your baby or child(ren) while you go out for a walk or get some rest or 'you' time; provide cooked meals; clean your house; do your laundry; or run errands. They could come and make you a cup of tea, be a listening ear, and sound the alarm if they see you are really struggling and need more specialised support. Whoever they are, they are *your* personal post-partum tribe. Keep them close and lean on them – they are there to help you.

## But I don't have a tribe! Where do I start?

It's not too late to find or create a support network – even if you're several months (or years) post-partum. Here are some ideas.

- Join a parenting or neighbourhood group (online or in person). You may find some people there who you feel comfortable with.

- Reach out to other people in your life. Let them know if you have any needs that aren't being met, and ask them to help.

- Notice and accept offers of help when they arrive – it can be hard to say yes, but try it!

- Offer assistance to others – you may find they reciprocate, and a sense of community can be built faster than you think.

The key thing to remember is that your tribe members should be in addition to your partner, if you have one. This takes the pressure off both of you as you parent, and helps spread the load.

## Your tribe is fluid

Tribe members can come and go, and the size and composition of your support system will likely change as your needs change. You'll have your loyal tribe members, of course, but be flexible and open to asking new people for the support you need. Don't be discouraged if someone you thought would say 'yes' says 'no'. It doesn't necessarily mean that they aren't as nice as you thought they were; they may have other commitments and/or feel overwhelmed, too. They may be open to being asked again in the future, so do check this with them before you cross them off your list. Remember, a 'no' just means that this person might be better suited to a different task, or they aren't right for your tribe at this time, and that's OK – someone else will be.

# debrief deep dive

## REFLECT

Take a moment to reflect on who your village is. Who can you lean on? Who always gets you? Who has words of encouragement and wisdom for you? Who will bring food over for you, or do the washing-up while you rest? Who can you turn to in a time of need?

Grab a pen and your notebook, or use the lines here, and make a list. Don't worry about it being a long list. No one will see it but you, so it's OK if Auntie Carol doesn't make the cut! Remember, your village need not be big, and it can include whoever you like. The benefit of writing this down is that sometimes you don't see who is there for you until you stop and think about it.

## REFRAME

Reframe the act of asking for help as a radical act of strength and self-care. Instead of thinking 'I don't want to be a burden', 'I feel embarrassed to ask for help' or 'I should be able to manage on my own', try making the following declarations out loud:

- Asking for help is an act of strength. It will get easier each time I do it.

- I will care for myself today by asking for help if I need it.

- If one person says no, I will ask someone else.

## REDEFINE

What do you want your first few months post-partum to look like? What help might you need? I suggest you sit down and create a list. For example:

- I will need someone to collect us from the hospital.

- I will need someone to drop by for coffee and a chat one afternoon a week.

- I will need someone to go for a stroll round the park with me two mornings a week.

It's your list, so make it as detailed as you like. Once you have made your list, decide who in your village you could ask to fulfil each need, as I've done in the table on the opposite page.

| I need... | I will ask... |
|---|---|
| Someone to collect us from the hospital. | Uncle Michael has already offered! |
| Someone to drop by for coffee and a chat one afternoon a week. | Yasmine or Anisa (BFFs) |
| Someone to go for a stroll round the park with me two mornings a week. | Brenda (neighbour) |

Do this for each item on your list, then follow through and ask each person for the help you need. Consider asking as many people as you can in advance, and include one or two people who are happy to step in as back-up support in case your primary person becomes unavailable. That way they won't feel under pressure at being called on out of the blue, and you won't feel the embarrassment that can often come with having to ask for help at the last minute.

I hope you enjoy the process of building your tribe. As the late social activist bell hooks said, 'One of the most vital ways we sustain ourselves is by building communities ... places where we know we are not alone.'[89]

# conclusion

In December 2021, my beloved mum died. And three months later I gave birth to my second child, my son, Talha. Preparing carefully and consciously for Talha's birth, after a traumatic first birth and a profound bereavement, was a process of being deeply honest with myself. In the end it was a healing experience. I accepted what I could and couldn't have controlled in my first birth. I asserted my choices, overcame fear and regained a sense of agency. Talha was born into my arms, at home, as I had wanted. In truth, I experienced Talha's birth as a sort of rebirth of my own. It was an integration of what my mother had taught me about love, strength and resilience, and what I'd learned through mothering my daughter, Ihsan.

I was working on this book all through that time. And I hope it brings some of that strength to you, my reader. I want this book to enable you to actively engage with your own care as a pregnant, birthing and (forever!) postnatal person. I'd like it to give you agency over your own experience of motherhood. My message to you is this: YOU do your birthing, recovery, mothering. No one else can. Connect deeply to yourself, let go of societal expectations and be honest about what you want and need. Communicate that to the people you love around you, and trust them, and yourself. I wish you all the best.

# acknowledgements

To my mother, the most incredible woman I have ever known. She taught me not only how to mother, but also how to show up for myself in all the chaos of mothering. She's not here to read this, but her essence is on the pages.

To my sisters Tasnim, Salsabil and Zanjabil. Exemplary women of the highest calibre. Thank you for always anchoring me and keeping me humble, your smiles are affirming, your words uplifting and your strength inspiring.

To the two who made me a mother, Ihsan Sofia and Talha Yasin, you are my life's best work. Thank you for making my heart work harder and my brain work faster.

To my father, thank you for always encouraging my free thought and wayward behaviour. For teaching me the importance of self-belief and the value of going against the grain.

My husband, Umar, you are the best man I know despite the fact that you snooze your alarm 100 times and somehow don't hear the baby cry in the night. Thank you for your unwavering support, your trust and faith in me and for always being my loudest cheerleader.

To my brothers Hanif, Adil, Malik and Hammad. Thank you for being men for my own children to look up to. Wonderful brothers, fathers, uncles and friends.

To my sister-in-law, Nabila, thank you for always holding my hand, for being there when I welcomed Ihsan and advocating for me always. I consider you an honorary sister but really, the honour is mine.

To my whole family, what a support you have been, not only in this process but in shaping me and making me who I am today.

To my agent Silé, thank you for sliding into my DMs and championing my vision from start to finish, you really are something special.

To Vimbai, thank you for not letting me put my name to something that wasn't worthy of me. I appreciate it more than you know.

To one of my best friends, Hollie, you really are an inspiration, thank you for answering my calls and letting me say, 'last thing I'm gonna say' over and over. Thank you for your firm boundaries and for teaching me the importance of having them too.

To my childhood friends, Asisa, Fatiha, Fausia and Abdiya and especially my sister in law Sumiyya. You already know what you mean to me. I adore you all.

To my dearest brother-in-law, Abdal Hakim, thank you for always asking about this book, even when I thought everyone had forgotten, you never had, and I will never forget you.

To Jane Sturrock, thank you for believing in my book before I even knew what it was going to be and to Zoë Blanc for coming in and running it to the finish line.

To my community globally but specifically in Norwich and particularly to the women. You have all had a hand in raising and shaping me and I'm grateful for every single lesson, wisdom and kind word.

Lastly, to every single person that has debriefed their experience with me, this book is for you and because of you. I hold you in the highest regard, and will always be grateful for what you have done for me and allowed me to do for you.

# resources

**BIRTH DEBRIEFING: THE BASICS**

- Birthtalk – http://birthtalk.org

- The British Association for Counselling and Psychotherapy – https://www.bacp.co.uk

- The British Psychological Society – https://www.bps.org.uk

- CBT – https://www.nhs.uk/mental-health/talking-therapies-medicine-treatments/talking-therapies-and-counselling/cognitive-behavioural-therapy-cbt/overview

- EMDR – https://www.bacp.co.uk/about-therapy/types-of-therapy/eye-movement-desensitisation-and-reprocessing-emdr

- Information on the use of therapies in birth trauma – https://www.aims.org.uk/journal/item/cbt-emdr

- Naytal – https://naytal.uk

- Rewind Therapy – https://www.ptsduk.org/how-rewind-therapy-can-help-people-with-ptsd

- The Counselling Directory – https://www.counselling-directory.org.uk

- The Positive Birth Company – https://thepositivebirthcompany.co.uk

- van der Kolk, B. (2015) *The Body Keeps The Score*. London: Penguin.

## BIRTH TRAUMA AND PTSD

- The Birth Trauma Association – https://www.birthtraumaassociation.org.uk/
- Improving Access to Psychological Therapies: https://www.england.nhs.uk/mental-health/adults/iapt/
- Make Birth Better – https://www.makebirthbetter.org/
- PANDAS (PND Awareness & Support) – https://pandasfoundation.org.uk/

## SUPERPOWER #1: ASSERTIVENESS

- Dickson, A. (2022) *A Woman in Your Own Right: The Art of Assertive, Clear and Honest Communication*, London: Duckworth.
- Groskop, V. (2018) *How to Own the Room: Women and the Art of Brilliant Speaking*. London: Bantam Press.
- Healthline – https://www.healthline.com/
- Mind Tools – https://www.mindtools.com/
- Positive Psychology – https://positivepsychology.com/assertiveness-training/
- Sofer, O. J. (2018) *Say What You Mean: A Mindful Approach to Nonviolent Communication*. Boston: Shambhala Publications Inc.

## DON'T BREAK THE CHAIN!

- Abuela Doulas – https://abueladoulas.co.uk/
- Doula UK – https://doula.org.uk/

## BIRTHING WHILE BLACK

- Davis, A. (1981) *Women, Race & Class*. New York: Random House Inc.
- Igwe, S. (2022) *My Black Motherhood*. London: Jessica Kingsley Publishers, Ltd.
- Kendi, I. X. (2019) *How to Be an Antiracist*. London: Bodley Head.
- Lorde, A. (1984) *Sister Outsider*. New York: Crossing Press.
- Oluo, I. (2020) *So You Want To Talk About Race*. London: Basic Books.

## SPEAKING UP - SHOULD I COMPLAIN?

- AIMS – https://www.aims.org.uk/

- Birthrights – https://www.birthrights.org.uk/

## PERINEUMS, PATIENCE AND PERFECTION

- MASIC Foundation – https://masic.org.uk/

## OWNING YOUR FEEDING CHOICES

- La Leche League GB – https://www.laleche.org.uk/
- National Childbirth Trust breastfeeding support – https://www.nct.org.uk/baby-toddler/feeding/early-days/breastfeeding-support-nct

## WHEN BABY IS NOT BORN HEALTHY

- The NICU Mummy – Instagram: @the_nicu_mummy

## IS IT BABY BLUES - OR SOMETHING ELSE?

- Aiken, C. (2000) *Surviving Post-Natal Depression: At Home, No One Hears You Scream.* London: Jessica Kingsley Publishers.
- Kleiman, K. (1994) *This Isn't What I Expected: Overcoming Postpartum Depression.* Boston: Da Capo Press.
- Mental Health Foundation – https://www.mentalhealth.org.uk
- SilverCloud – https://www.silvercloudhealth.com/uk
- Tessa van der Vord, The Mental Health Midwife – Instagram: @mentalhealth_midwife

## GRIEF, REGRET AND REMORSE

- Baby Centre – https://www.babycentre.co.uk/
- Cruse Bereavement Support – https://www.cruse.org.uk/
- Help Guide – https://www.helpguide.org/
- Mind – https://www.mind.org.uk/
- National Childbirth Trust – https://www.nct.org.uk/
- Tommy's: Together, for every baby – https://www.tommys.org/

## IT'S OK NOT TO BE OK

- The Black, African and Asian Therapy Network –
https://www.baatn.org.uk/

## PARENTING ROLES

- The Agora Clinic – https://agoraclinic.co.uk/
- Family Lives – https://www.familylives.org.uk/
- Fertility Family – https://www.fertilityfamily.co.uk/
- Fertility Network UK – https://fertilitynetworkuk.org/
- FFLAG (a national voluntary organisation and charity dedicated
to supporting parents and families and their LGBT+ members) –
https://www.fflag.org.uk/
- Gingerbread: single parents, equal families –
https://www.gingerbread.org.uk/
- Jeffs, L. and Oakley, S. (2023) *The Queer Parent*. London: Pan
Macmillan.
- LGBT Health and Wellbeing – https://www.lgbthealth.org.uk/
- *The NHS Long Term Plan* 2019 – https://www.longtermplan.nhs.uk/
- The Queer Parenting Partnership – https://www.parentingqueer.
co.uk/
- Some Families podcast – https://podcasts.apple.com/gb/podcast/
some-families/id1499876261

## PARENTING HAZARDS

- Samaritans – https://www.samaritans.org/

## THE MATERNITY LEAVE 'HOLIDAY' MYTH

- Pregnant then Screwed – https://pregnantthenscrewed.com/

## PARENTING AGAIN

- Abigail's Footsteps: providing support for bereaved families –
https://www.abigailsfootsteps.co.uk/

- Ashworth, S. (2017) *The Calm Birth Method*. London: Hay House UK.
- Child Bereavement UK – https://www.childbereavementuk.org/
- Graves, K. (2021) *The Hypnobirthing Book – Childbirth with Confidence and Calm: The definitive guide to childbirth from the home of hypnobirthing*, London: Katharine Publishing.
- Here Hear – https://www.weareherehear.com/courses
- The Hypnobirthing Association – https://www.thehypnobirthingassociation.com/
- Lighthouses Therapy Services – https://www.lighthousestherapyservices.co.uk/
- Miscarriage Association – https://www.miscarriageassociation.org.uk/
- Nova Foundation – https://www.novafoundation.org.uk/
- The Positive Birth Company – https://thepositivebirthcompany.co.uk
- Teddy's Wish – https://www.teddyswish.org/
- The Little Birth Company – https://thelittlebirthcompany.co.uk/

If you would like to work with Illiyin directly please contact her via her website – https://mixingupmotherhood.com/ or Instagram – @mixing.up.motherhood

# endnotes

1   CBT (Cognitive Behavioural Therapy) is a talking therapy used to manage problems by changing the way you think and behave. It is commonly used to treat depression and anxiety.

2   The three-step rewind is a process that is used to gently work through traumatic or unwanted negative thoughts associated with pregnancy or birth.

3   EDMR (or Eye Movement Desensitisation and Reprocessing) is a psychotherapy treatment that was originally designed to alleviate the distress associated with traumatic memories. The aim is that treatment relieves stress, restructures negative beliefs and reduces psychological distress. (Shapiro, F. (1989) 'Efficacy of the eye movement desensitization procedure in the treatment of traumatic memories' *Journal of Traumatic Stress*, 2(2): pp. 199-223.)

4   For how to go about this, see https://www.birthrights.org.uk/factsheets/accessing-your-records/.

5   Though the service is only available privately for birth partners (unless they attend the NHS debrief with the mother), it is a worthwhile investment in their wellbeing. It enables them to feel heard, validates their perspective, and helps them to work through their own experience, which will differ from that of the person who has given birth.

6   Hyperemesis is a condition characterised by continuous vomiting throughout pregnancy (well past the normal 'morning sickness' experienced in the first trimester).

7   Sheen, K. & Slade, P. (2015) 'The efficacy of "debriefing" after childbirth: Is there a case for targeted intervention?' *Journal of Reproductive and Infant Psychology*, 33(3). https://doi.org/10.1080/02646838.2015.1009881.

8   https://www.birthingawarenesstraining.com/ive-debriefed-her-the-problem-with-debriefing/

9   But please don't let that deter you, as there are plenty of debrief facilitators and therapists out there who offer means-tested payment plans. You may have to search a little harder to find them, but it is a worthwhile investment of your time.

10  Post-partum haemorrhage (PPH) is heavy bleeding after birth, defined as losing 500ml (1 pint) or more of blood within the first 24 hours, or abnormal or heavy vaginal bleeding between 24 hours and 12 weeks. See https://www.rcog.org.uk/for-the-public/browse-all-patient-information-leaflets/heavy-bleeding-after-birth-postpartum-haemorrhage-patient-information-leaflet/

11  Pre-eclampsia is a serious condition in which a pregnant woman develops high blood pressure and protein in her urine (indicating possible kidney problems). See https://www.nhs.uk/conditions/pre-eclampsia/

12 Defensive practice is any medical procedure, decision or protocol that deviates from sound practice 'primarily to reduce one's risk of liability rather than to benefit the patient'. Sakala, C., Yang, T. and Corry, M. P. (2013) 'Maternity Care and Liability: Pressing Problems, Substantive Solutions' *Women's Health Issues*, 23(1). https://doi.org/10.1016/j.whi.2012.11.001.

13 When debriefing is carried out in an environment that is not safe for the participant, with a practitioner who is not trauma-informed, or who is defensive and lacks compassion, there is a risk of further trauma being incurred. Your facilitator should be able to recognise, and be understanding of, what felt traumatic for you, and should be sensitive to the things you find triggering.

14 https://mixingupmotherhood.com/

15 Your hospital will keep your notes for twenty-five years, and they are legally obliged to give these to you when requested. Obtaining a copy is simply a matter of contacting your hospital and requesting a copy.

16 https://www.makebirthbetter.org/what-we-do-1

17 https://www.nice.org.uk/guidance/CG156/chapter/Context

18 Qureshi, S.U., Pyne, J.M., Magruder, K.M. et al. (2009) 'The link between post-traumatic stress disorder and physical comorbidities: A systematic review' *Psychiatric Quarterly*, 80(2): pp. 87–97. https://doi.org/10.1007/s11126-009-9096-4

19 Ayers, S., Wright, D.B. & Thornton, A. (2018) 'Development of a Measure of Postpartum PTSD: The City Birth Trauma Scale' *Front Psychiatry*, https://doi.org/10.3389/fpsyt.2018.00409.

20 City Birth Trauma Scale © Ayers, Wright & Thornton, 2018. Frontiers in Psychiatry 9:409. Available at: https://cpb-eu-w2.wpmucdn.com/blogs.city.ac.uk/dist/1/2580/files/2020/08/City-BiTS-Version-2.0-2018-fillable-form.pdf

21 Alcorn, K.L., O'Donovan, A., Patrick, J.C., Creedy, D., & Devilly, G.J. (2010) 'A prospective longitudinal study of the prevalence of post-traumatic stress disorder resulting from childbirth events' *Psychological Medicine*, 40(11): pp. 1849-59. https://doi.org/10.1017/S0033291709992224.

22 Simpson, M. & Catling, C. (2016) 'Understanding psychological traumatic birth experiences: A literature review' *Women and Birth*, 29(3): pp. 203-7. https://doi.org/10.1016/j.wombi.2015.10.009

23 https://www.england.nhs.uk/mental-health/adults/iapt/

24 https://pandasfoundation.org.uk/what-is-pnd/birth-trauma/

25 https://www.psychologytoday.com/us/basics/assertiveness

26 Cloud, Dr and H. Townsend, Dr J. (2017) *Boundaries: When to Say Yes, How to Say No to Take Control of Your Life*. Grand Rapids, MI: Zondervan, p. 201.

27 Students of hypnobirthing will actively discourage sharing scary or negative birth stories, in fact, as they believe it affects the positive mindset needed for an empowered birth.

28 Parents or guardians normally give consent on behalf of minors in their care, but under-16s can consent to treatment under the Gillick competency rule, which allows minors who are deemed to be competent by medical staff (i.e. they understand the implications of what they are consenting to) to consent to their own treatment. See https://www.birthrights.org.uk/factsheets/consenting-to-treatment/#consentemergency

29  For more information on mental capacity, see https://www.birthrights.org.uk/factsheets/mental-capacity-and-maternity-care/

30  https://www.merriam-webster.com/dictionary/gaslighting

31  Fielding-Singh, P. & Dmowska, A. (2022) 'Obstetric gaslighting and the denial of mothers' realities' *Social Science & Medicine*, 301: 114938. https://doi.org/10.1016/j.socscimed.2022.114938

32  Sakala, C., Yang, T. and Corry, M. P. (2013) 'Maternity Care and Liability: Pressing Problems, Substantive Solutions.' *Women's Health Issues*, 23. https://doi.org/10.1016/j.whi.2012.11.001.

33  BMI was invented by mathematician Adolphe Quetelet in the nineteenth century. It is calculated by dividing a person's weight in kilograms (or pounds) by their height in metres (or feet) square. A result of 25 and above indicates that someone is overweight.

34  The Royal College of Obstetricians and Gynaecologists notes that while being overweight or obese during pregnancy does not rule out having a healthy baby, there is evidence to show that overweight women are at an increased risk of complications (for them and their baby), such as being more likely to have a baby weighing over 4kg (with associated potential for physical trauma during birth), gestational diabetes, pre-eclampsia, miscarriage or stillbirth. Your baby may also be more vulnerable to health complications.

35  There are questions surrounding the use of BMI as a measure of good health. It does not account for body fat percentage or distribution, and it does not account for the typically heavier muscle-to-fat ratios seen in people of colour, because it was created using only data collected from white Europeans.

36  If your low or increased weight is linked to an eating disorder, such as anorexia nervosa, binge eating disorder or bulimia, that is more serious and may require specialist help. Please don't be embarrassed to admit that you struggle with food. Reaching out for help is your first step towards wellness, and you can get therapeutic, behavioural and nutritional help. You deserve to be supported as you support the growth and development of your baby, so please don't try to deal with this on your own.

37  Usually Syntocinon, which is given by injection.

38  https://www.england.nhs.uk/wp-content/uploads/2017/12/implementing-better-births.pdf

39  Department of Health, Social Services and Public Safety (2010) *Midwifery 2020: Delivering expectations*. Available at: https://www.gov.uk/government/publications/midwifery-2020-delivering-expectations

40  Some midwives are also doulas. However, unless they are practising in their capacity as a midwife, they are unable to provide certain aspects of midwifery care.

41  https://www.npeu.ox.ac.uk/assets/downloads/mbrrace-uk/reports/maternal-report-2021/MBRRACE-UK_Maternal_Report_2021_-_Lay_Summary_v10.pdf

42  Ibid.

43  Ibid.

44  Royal College of Midwives (2022) 'RCM calls for end to migrant women maternity charging over safety fears.' Available at: https://bit.ly/3HbjytL

45  https://www.npeu.ox.ac.uk/assets/downloads/mbrrace-uk/reports/maternal-report-2021/MBRRACE-UK_Maternal_Report_2021_-_Lay_Summary_v10.pdf

46 The automatic, usually negative and often unfair assumptions we make about individuals without tangible evidence to support those judgements.

47 Reid, N. (2021) *The Good Ally: A guided anti-racism journey from bystander to changemaker.* London: HQ.

48 https://www.gov.uk/government/news/new-taskforce-to-level-up-maternity-care-and-tackle-disparities

49 White, D.G. (1999) *Ar'n't I a Woman?* New York: W. W. Norton & Company.

50 The harmful stereotype of the 'angry Black woman' made its way into mainstream media via the sullen character Sapphire from the 1950s US TV show *The Amos 'N' Andy Show.*

51 Ashley, W. (2014) 'The angry black woman: The impact of pejorative stereotypes on psychotherapy with black women' *Social Work in Public Health,* 29(1): pp. 27–34. https://doi.org/10.1080/19371918.2011.619449

52 Sue, D. W., Capodilupo, C. M., Torino, G. C., Bucceri, J. M., Holder, A. M. B., Nadal, K. L., & Esquilin, M. (2007) 'Racial microaggressions in everyday life: implications for clinical practice' *American Psychologist,* 62(4), 271–286. https://doi.org/10.1037/0003-066X.62.4.271.

53 Cooper, B. (2018) *Eloquent Rage: A Black Feminist Discovers Her Superpower.* New York: St Martin's Press.

54 https://www.geoffreykayemuseum.org.au/?s=legacy+of+j+marion+sims/

55 Washington, H. A. (2006) *Medical Apartheid: The Dark History of Medical Experimentation on Black Americans from Colonial Times to the Present.* New York: Doubleday.

56 Sini, R. (2017) 'Publisher apologises for "racist" text in medical book'. https://www.bbc.co.uk/news/blogs-trending-41692593

57 Chou, V. (2017) 'How Science and Genetics are Reshaping the Race Debate of the 21st Century'. https://sitn.hms.harvard.edu/flash/2017/science-genetics-reshaping-race-debate-21st-century/

58 Kapadia D., Zhang J., Salway S., et al (2022) 'Ethnic inequalities in healthcare: a rapid evidence review.' NHS Race & Health Observatory. https://www.nhsrho.org/wp-content/uploads/2022/02/RHO-Rapid-Review-Final-Report_v.7.pdf

59 https://www.birthrights.org.uk/factsheets/making-a-complaint/

60 https://www.england.nhs.uk/wp-content/uploads/2016/07/nhs-england-complaints-policy-amended.pdf; https://www.nhsinform.scot/care-support-and-rights/health-rights/feedback-and-complaints/feedback-complaints-and-your-rights

61 A surgical cut made by a healthcare professional between the vagina and the perineum during childbirth.

62 https://www.rcog.org.uk/for-the-public/perineal-tears-and-episiotomies-in-childbirth/perineal-tears-during-childbirth

63 https://www.clare-bourne.com

64 https://www.rcog.org.uk/for-the-public/perineal-tears-and-episiotomies-in-childbirth/

65 https://www.ox.ac.uk/news/2012-10-18-breastfeeding-could-save-nhs-millions-says-new-report?id=29567

66 https://www.rcpch.ac.uk/resources/breastfeeding-uk-position-statement

67 Many hospital trusts now train all their midwives according to the UNICEF infant feeding guidance, and the majority are either UNICEF accredited or in the process of becoming accredited. This means a move towards all midwives and breastfeeding

support workers being given the same training, so that they give women the same advice, not conflicting advice. This could make a huge difference to breastfeeding rates.

68 Black Breastfeeding Week (https://blackbreastfeedingweek.org/) started in the USA to 'raise awareness about the racial disparity in breastfeeding rates among African American women' (https://www.nct.org.uk/baby-toddler/feeding/early-days/breastfeeding-ever-black-and-white).

69 In the USA only 73.3 per cent of Black babies are ever breastfed, compared to 86.7 per cent of white babies, 90 per cent of Asian babies and 84.1 per cent of Hispanic babies. Black women have some of the highest rates of diabetes, asthma, breast cancer and obesity – all things breastfeeding can help to prevent. The reason this comparison is important is due to infant mortality rates in these groups: Black babies have a 10.8 per cent mortality rate, significantly higher than all other ethnic groups. (https://www.cdc.gov/mmwr/volumes/66/wr/mm6627a3.htm)

70 https://www.unicef.org.uk/babyfriendly/about/breastfeeding-in-the-uk

71 This is echoed by UNICEF's own guidance on breastfeeding and trauma: https://www.unicef.org.uk/babyfriendly/wp-content/uploads/sites/2/2021/12/Breastfeeding-and-Trauma-Dr-Kathy-Kendall-Tackett.pdf

72 Ibid.

73 https://www.nct.org.uk/life-parent/how-you-might-be-feeling/baby-blues-what-expect

74 Although some studies suggest that increasing your intake of omega-3 fatty acids – via supplements or limited portions of oily fish – during pregnancy can minimise your risk (https://americanpregnancy.org/healthy-pregnancy/first-year-of-life/preventing-the-baby-blues/).

75 https://www.nhs.uk/mental-health/conditions/post-natal-depression/overview/

76 Psychological shock should not be confused with post-partum shock (a serious physical condition that is caused by a reduced flow of blood to vital organs. It comes with physical symptoms such as confusion, chills, dizziness, and nausea or vomiting).

77 https://www.nct.org.uk/about-us/media/news/difficulties-baby-bonding-affect-third-uk-mums

78 Though if you find yourself relying on unhelpful behaviours as coping mechanisms (such as alcohol or substance abuse or disordered eating), please seek professional help.

79 https://mentalhealth-uk.org/black-asian-and-minority-ethnic-bame-mental-health/

80 Emma (2018) *The Mental Load: A Feminist Comic*. New York: Seven Stories Press.

81 https://www.gingerbread.org.uk/what-we-do/media-centre/single-parents-facts-figures/

82 https://gingerbread.enthuse.com/cf/singleparentsday2021

83 'Data from fertility clinics and the Office for National Statistics reveals that lesbian couples are the fastest-growing group in maternity services, with fertility treatment and live births increasing by 15–20 per cent in this group year on year' (Darwin, Z. & Greenfield, M. (2019) 'Mothers and others: The invisibility of LGBTQ people in reproductive and infant psychology' *Journal of Reproductive and Infant Psychology*, 37 (4): pp. 341-43. https://doi.org/10.1080/02646838.2019.1649919.

84 https://www.longtermplan.nhs.uk/wp-content/uploads/2019/08/nhs-long-term-plan-version-1.2.pdf

85 https://www.nhs.uk/conditions/vitamins-and-minerals/vitamin-d/

86 https://www.tommys.org/baby-loss-support/miscarriage-information-and-support/miscarriage-statistics#general

87 https://www.tommys.org/about-us/news-views/stillbirth-rise-england-and-wales-confirmed-ons

88 Hollie de Cruz can be found on Instagram at @hollie.decruz, or online at https://www.weareherehear.com/

89 hooks, bell (2014) *Yearning: Race, Gender, and Cultural Politics*. London: Routledge.